This work: "Agency: Moral Identity and Free Will", was originally published by Open Book Publishers and is being sold pursuant to a Creative Commons license permitting commercial use. All rights not granted by the work's license are retained by the author or authors.

Cover Image Credit/Copyright Attribution: IIIerlok_Xolms/Shutterstock

Agency

Moral Identity and Free Will

David Weissman

© 2020 David Weissman

This work is licensed under a Creative Commons Attribution 4.0 International license (CC BY 4.0). This license allows you to share, copy, distribute and transmit the work; to adapt the work and to make commercial use of the work providing attribution is made to the author (but not in any way that suggests that they endorse you or your use of the work).

Attribution should include the following information:

David Weissman, *Agency: Moral Identity and Free Will*. Cambridge, UK: Open Book Publishers, 2020. https://doi.org/10.11647/OBP.0197

Contents

Acknowledgments	ix
Introduction	1
Chapter One: Agency	11
1. Semantics	11
2. Two Points of Reference	11
3. Individuality	18
4. Purpose/Intention	19
5. Sensibility	23
6. Thought and Perception	26
7. Competence and Skill	30
8. Effort	31
9. Partners	31
10. Efficacy	32
11. Oversight	35
12. Frustration	38
13. Will	38
Chapter Two: Free Will	39
1. Introduction	39
2. Background	40
3. Freedom To and Freedom From	42
4. Ontology	44
5. Universal Determinism	45
6. Explanation/Prediction	47
7. Cause or Capacity	49
8. Leibniz or Laplace	50
9. "Things Are Not Up to Us."	54
10. Emergent Wholes, Their Properties and Powers	62
11. Character/Sensibility	65
12. Initiative	68
13. Productive Imagination	70

14. Consciousness	71
15. Choosing Freely	72
16. Last Thoughts	93

Chapter Three: Socialization — 95

1. Conflicted Aims	95
2. Idiosyncrasy	97
3. Talent	101
4. Interiority	102
5. Social Space	104
6. Normativity	106
7. Socialization	107
8. Collaboration, Cooperation, Command	110
9. Cities	112
10. Disequilibrium	115

Chapter Four: Autonomy — 119

1. Minerva	119
2. Semantics	120
3. Assertion	120
4. Self-Identification	122
5. Collaboration/Contention	123
6. Regulation	125
7. Oversight	126
8. In Itself, For Itself	128

Chapter Five: Moral Identity — 129

1. Three Perspectives: Agents	130
2. Three Perspectives: Nodes	141
3. Three Perspectives: The Whole	147

Afterword	177
Bibliography	179
Index	185

In memory of
Paul Weiss

Acknowledgments

Thanks to Alessandra Tosi and her team—Lucy Barnes, Anna Gatti, and Luca Baffa—for production values apparent in this finished book; to an anonymous reader for his persistent queries; and to Laura Rodriguez for marketing that's more than show. My wife, Kathy, mined the final proof for reams of my small errors. She was its final copy editor.

I'm grateful to all.

Introduction

Agency implies purpose, action, and autonomy. We are inventive, effective, and self-appraising. But there is an ambiguity. Does *agency* signify reality-testing in the near-world where the existence and character of other people and things are independent of our thinking? Or is agency the activity of a mind inspecting sensory data, ideas, and itself? These are alternative foundational claims: one material and existential; the other subjective and epistemological. Aristotle described agency in detail, but his formulation is obscured by the Cartesian tradition that elides thought with being. It supposes that we know reality when mind turns on itself, though agency is apparent to anyone taking a walk or calling a friend.

The difference between these views is suppressed rather than resolved when reality-testing is construed as the mere look of the data inspected: we only seem to be agents afoot in a world we haven't made. These are sample passages from Heidegger's *Being and Time*:

> [S]ciences have the manner of Being which this entity—man himself—possesses. This entity we denote by the term "*Dasein*."[1]
>
> Ontology and phenomenology are not two distinct philosophical disciplines among others. These terms characterize philosophy itself with regard to its object and its way of treating that object. Philosophy is universal phenomenological ontology, and takes its departure from the hermeneutic of Dasein, which, as an analytic of *existence*, has made fast the guiding-line for all philosophical inquiry at the point where it arises and to which it returns.[2]

Heidegger is rightly credited with bringing Hegel to ground— universals cashed out in particularity—yet his ontology is speculative in

---

[1] Martin Heidegger, *Being and Time*, trans. John Macquarrie and Edward Robinson (New York: Harper and Row, 1962), p. 32.
[2] *Ibid.*, p. 62.

© David Weissman, CC BY 4.0   https://doi.org/10.11647/OBP.0197.06

a traditional way. For Dasein is an intuiting ego: everything real because intelligible is located in the minds discerning it. This is phenomenology as it claims transcendental competence: minds discern reality's essential structure and details by inspecting experience and themselves.

Much of philosophy is comfortable with this bias and its deference to Plato's cave allegory: he alleged that minds can know the ordering principles of the cosmos because the quest for reality's Forms is intuition's trajectory.[3] Descartes inverted Plato's focus: distilling minds are self-discovering. Deflecting the skepticism of his first *Meditation*, Descartes discovered the theater where everything is set before our inspecting minds, all of it informed by mind's clear and distinct ideas. Nor is anything else thinkable. For what can we know or imagine when nothing is either conceivable or existent if not inspectable? *Esse est percipi* was Descartes' idea before Berkeley used the phrase. It embodies two claims: that evidence of existence is a necessary condition for existence, and that evidence isn't secured if a mind isn't aware of itself (thereby confirming its own existence) while inspecting things perceived. For "I am, I exist, that is certain. But how often? Just when I think,"[4] implying both awareness of something and mind's awareness of its own existence while inspecting that thing.

Put aside Descartes' gesture when he introduced a god as the *deus ex machina* justifying moral certainty that the external world is largely as it seems. For all states of affairs lying beyond the arc of consciousness earn Kant's designation as "negative noumena."[5] He reduced agency to the dimensions—the single souls—of Leibnizian monads;[6] he fortified the self-inspecting *cogito*, re-describing it as the agent responsible for schematizing experience in ways that satisfy the maker's values and interests. But this is odd: purpose succeeds because we're organized, stubborn, and clever, not because we create surrogate realities while staring at ourselves.

---

3   Plato, *Republic, Collected Dialogues*, eds. Edith Hamilton and Huntington (New York: Pantheon, 1961), 514a-517e, pp. 747–49.

4   René Descartes, *Meditations on First Philosophy*, in: *Discourse on the Method and Meditations on First Philosophy*, ed. David Weissman (New Haven: Yale University Press, 1996), p. 65.

5   Immanuel Kant, *Critique of Pure Reason*, trans. Norman Kemp Smith (New York: St. Martin's, 1965), p. 270.

6   G. W. V. Leibniz, *Monadology and Other Philosophical Essays*, trans. Paul Schrecker and Anne Martin Schrecker (Indianapolis: Bobbs-Merrill, 1965), paras. 1–19, pp. 148–51.

Why make these antique allusions? Because the subjectivist tradition is second nature to thinkers fearful that invoking agency's stance in the natural world would make them seem naive. Aristotle was confident that thinking, making, and doing engage human agents with other people and things. His assumptions—ontological realism, truth as correspondence, and a representational theory of perception—are known but discounted by skeptics who defend Cartesian subjectivism and Kantian idealism. Principal ideas of knowledge, perception, and agency fail to assimilate either his realism or the Darwinian implications of minds that evolve while accommodating their material circumstances.

Our subjectivist tradition construes us as passengers on a train: seeing the countryside through the windows of the observation car, we imagine saving the land while never leaving the train. What does it matter that philosophy distorts self-understanding by reducing agency to Cartesian self-reflection or Kantian world-making? Do we believe with Quine that "the quality of myth is relative," so reality has whatever character satisfies our "various interests and purposes"?[7] This is fanciful; it doesn't survive an accurate reading of agency, frustration, or error. These chapters face the other way: they mate Aristotle with Darwin, Peirce, and Freud. I assume that every living creature is situated in the material world, and that each has multiple effects on things or events that are otherwise independent of human agents and one another. Agency's profile emerges as we observe others and ourselves, then augment observation with inferences that identify the likely intra-psychic, material, and social causes for our actions and effects. We rebalance this schism—action or inspection—by controlling action with appraisal. Storms have effects they don't control. We alter our effects by revising our aims or their means.

Yet agency is elusive. This is true superficially because we often qualify subject terms with active verbs—"She tripped"—though it was a loose rug, nothing careless, that caused her fall. Donald Davidson made this point, though there are, he agreed, many actions rightly attributed to the agents causing them.[8] The more abiding obscurity is mental and material. Agency is too close and self-entangled for easy

---

[7] Willard Van Orman Quine, *From a Logical Point of View* (Cambridge: Harvard University Press, 1980), p. 19.

[8] Donald Davidson, "Agency," in *Essays on Actions and Events* (Oxford: Clarendon Press, 2002), pp. 43–62.

comprehension: too many of its effects aren't perceived, inferred, or foreseen. It once seemed that mystery dissolves because autonomy and free will are apparent; one could reliably say that mind is whatever self-inspection shows it to be. But nothing has changed more radically than this self-conception. Having analogized machine intelligence to human ways of thinking, we infer that consciousness and its qualifications are emergent effects of a body's nervous system. We fear that autonomy may fall to socialization and machine management: we sing any tune we please, though the tunes we know are usually familiar to our neighbors. For almost everything we do comes from an inventory accessible to all a society's members. Tastes change, choices alter, though changes are usually those we accept, not those we provoke. Autonomy is restricted to small initiatives—coffee or tea, white shirt or blue—in contexts requiring choices that individuals don't control.

Successful practice is evidence that our brains effectively process information about the ambient world and our responses to it, but there is no direct perception of brain's complexity and no comprehensive understanding of the gap between our powers of self-inspection and the neuro-mechanical processes of self-regulation. What's to be made of aims pursued steadily from provocation and desire through planning, initiative, frustration, and revision? Some thinkers tease subtlety out of introspective data; others reduce intention to the persistence of our behavior. Or, like Ryle, Wittgenstein, and Anscombe, they resort to a different sort of data. Ignoring the evidence of self-inspection, they parse the grammar of the words used when speaking of one's intentions. Yet different uses and different ways of construing them require verification. How is that achieved? We test alternate linguistic implications against experience and behavior, while supposing that choice and action are impelled by intentions and volitions known several ways: by self-inspection, by observing other people's behavior, and—in a preliminary way—by brain scans that trace their neural course. Grammar is suggestive, but never more than provocative because its rules lack the diversity and nuance of aims that are variously pursued and expressed. Nor is this surprising: anger and fear are persistent motivators; they are often disguised or suppressed, though never reduced to the grammar of *anger* or *fear*.

This essay embodies a tradition that runs from Jonathan Edwards and Ralph Waldo Emerson to C. S. Peirce, William James, and John Dewey.

Many agents—storms and trucks, for example—are impelled by other things; humans (and some other animals) are self-moving. Philosophy's American roots are dominated by ideas of agency, initiative, and self-control. Regulation wasn't urgent on the frontier, where people had few neighbors; it became an issue as America filled with immigrants. How would an open society constrain its citizens while liberating them from rigid practices and traditions? Seek opportunities, take risks, though effects may be consequential, so deliberate about aims and means. Purpose is often steady, but don't expect that it will always be present, like blinking lights, to inspecting minds. Is my trajectory fixed when driving in fog and rain? Wouldn't that detract from the care required to do it safely?

This tradition emphasizes autonomy, while acknowledging that freedom carries responsibility for controlling one's actions and appraising one's effects. Hard determinism objects that this self-critical response is illusory: it says that every current action is a moment in a trajectory initiated at time's origin, an arc we don't control. Chapter Two argues that hard determinism is false: many things we do are habitual; many habits have a lineage that includes DNA and its evolutionary survival in circumstances long superseded. Yet agents—material though we be—often address situations for which history has prepared no specific response.[9] Middle-aged, male, and childless, I hold the infant left with me while her mother runs an errand. The baby pauses, considers, then twists and screams; she isn't happy. I hold her tighter, then loosely; nothing works until I blow across her ear. The screaming stops; she relaxes in my arms. Where was this in my history? Where is hard determinism in any situation where an agent has choices but no established responses to circumstances that are novel or surprising? Evolution is deterministic: it explains the generation of speech and cooperation, though not their expression or effects in circumstances for which we have no preparation. For every situation invites free choice because uncertainty and initiative trump the causal tide: canny and skilled, we respond to situations for which there is no history.

Validating free will—choice when history isn't determining—is critical because moral responsibility requires it, and because having it

---

[9] An earlier version of Chapter Two was published as "Autonomy and Free Will," *Metaphilosophy* 49 (2018), pp. 609–45.

is a condition for moral identity. Rather than being programmed for action, I declare myself to others by appraising and regulating my effects on them. This isn't news: we don't convince others or ourselves that we avoid responsibility because we locate our choices within an ancient lineage. Arguments for or against free will won't change the fact that we do or don't have it; but they are consequential because of their real or potential effects on our attitudes. Hard determinism is demoralizing: don't imagine that any difference you make is one you've freely chosen, given that each of us is a vehicle for effects long ago determined. There must be compelling logic and evidence before we concede that our apparent control of judgment, choice, and behavior is an illusion.

These issues have a contentious history. My reading of Aristotle locates him within the pragmatic naturalist tradition because of his belief that mind is the activity of a body having a certain complexity, and because he invariably emphasized self-regulation and one's responsibility for action's effects.[10] Descartes is his contrary: mind is self-sufficient; it connects to body by way of the pineal gland, though ablating the gland wouldn't stop mind from making choices as it thinks, remembers, or imagines. Yet mind's choices wouldn't have effects beyond itself, given Descartes' reasons for doubting that there is an ambient world. Should we settle, as with Kant's "transcendental object,"[11] for an "as if" reality, one having no consequence beyond our inclination to assume it? Freedom to choose when thinking is, he said, all the freedom we have, but is that enough freedom to conduct the business of everyday life?

Subjectivism collapses because no one has identified these putative agents—Descartes' appraising *cogito* or Kant's schematizing ego—and because material systems are able to perform as dualism alleges they cannot. Consciousness and its qualitative data resist physiological explanation, though this obstacle is somewhat reduced by engineers who build systems acting in ways that would be described as conscious if performed by minds. Challenge passes to the Aristotelian side: what survives of choice when all its conditions are the capacities of material systems? What are autonomy, choice, and moral identity in the context of the body and brain? Answers seem apparent when observing people

---

10   Aristotle, *The Basic Works of Aristotle*, ed. Richard McKeon (New York: Random House, 1941), 431a1–435a10, pp. 593–602.
11   Kant, *Critique of Pure Reason*, p. 137.

who go about their ordinary tasks: weighing likely outcomes, they estimate costs and benefits before deciding what to do. Some agents identify with a role having specific tasks and duties; they perform as the role prescribes. Others innovate. Either may interrupt standard or experimental practice because of regretted effects; we plausibly say that both could have chosen to act differently. Determinists agree that self-inspection seems to confirm these powers, but nature, they say, is a closed book. We aren't autonomous, and don't have free will; history is the unspooling of causes and effects whose trajectory was decided at the start; whenever, whatever its character. Is this judgment supported by empirical and logical evidence or is it an *a priori* dogma? These chapters are an appraisal: I conclude that hard determinism is multiply flawed with very little supporting argument or evidence.

Why does it matter that this version of the determinist argument is false? Because there are critics so skeptical of libertarian excesses that they gloat when saying that freedom is a delusion. Their posture squares comfortably with discoveries of several kinds: that mind is a physical system performing in fundamental ways as computers do; and that thought, perception, and memory are material processes. Yet biology doesn't confirm that every contemporary choice is the current expression of a trajectory started eons ago. Someone believing that reasons make no difference when making hard choices would throw up his hands or use a Ouija board when deciding: let history choose. For reasons that seem to justify a choice have a cosmetic but no causal effect if all was determined at the beginning of time. I propose an alternative that eschews both unconditioned freedom and the determinism which explains that every event—past or future—was decided by natural laws and the conditions prevailing at time's inception. *Soft determinism* is the hypothesis that every event has causes sufficient to determine its character and existence, many that are past but some that express the interests or values of agents responding to current circumstances. For it often happens that actions are provoked by situations having no antecedent in an agent's history. Laplace assumed that causal energy is continuously transformed when sustained in accord with laws that have operated since the beginning of time. He would have us explain an agent's response by citing those laws and original conditions. I argue that this explanation is incomplete: it ignores the myriad times when causes are insufficient to provoke an effect until completed by the responses of agents engaged by provocative situations.

Are there considerations—evidence and arguments—that defeat hard determinism? My solution has four elements:

i. Agreeing that every property and event has causes sufficient to determine its existence and character, it affirms that choices underdetermined by their antecedents alter the trajectories of causal histories. This happens when choice or action ensues because one or more features in a current situation provoke an unprogrammed response.

ii. We have this power because of three factors: *a.* Agents in one causal lineage often address new or surprising situations having constituents in lineages independent of their own. Having no fixed reaction (or overriding a fixed response), agents experiment; they test and revise their actions until effects satisfy their needs. *b.* Emergence has sufficient causal conditions (life emerges from assembled molecules and cells), but its effects are liberating. No longer restricted to the powers of their lower-order constituents (organs, cells, and molecules), agents have a repertoire of powers and skills that redirect the causal trajectories of both themselves and the things with which they interact. Or the causal tide is interrupted when inherited responses are inhibited. *c.* Will is two things: life-force, and a power that energizes and enacts particular aims. Both emerge when evolution produces living things shielded from their environments by permeable surfaces (cell walls, for example) that resist intrusions while supplying access to nutrients and partners. Every such agent is an evolutionary experiment: how will it adapt to circumstances when its external buffer enables the development of capacities for using circumstances to its advantage? Millenia pass as these functions evolve, and others emerge. In humans, emergent powers include deliberation, judgment, will, and choice. Is a situation new or surprising? Free will is the activation of powers that evolution has enabled: powers for reality-testing, coping, and restraint. Creatures less endowed, react; we consider our options. The full history of will's causal lineage goes back very far: all emergents do. Its activation as free will is the effect of current situations: responses are inhibited until circumstances are appraised, options are considered, choices are made: I see and like it, but don't buy it.

Calling will "free" doesn't imply that the act is unconditioned; it signifies that willing is free from external constraints, when its sufficient conditions are local to the psychic space where decisions are made. An observing god might predict will's evolution with near or perfect accuracy; its guesses about agents' responses to particular states of affairs—addressing situations for which there are no prepared responses—would be no better than likely.

iii. Agency is an essential topic in the thinking of pragmatists for whom thoughtful action is the key to understanding our relations to one another and our circumstances. Yet pragmatism too often reduces to the urgencies of practical life or the values and planning that make action effective. We emphasize actions in the public world; we neglect interiority, though one is altered by a book, a play, or the horror of an accident. Active in the near-world of things and opportunities, active in relations to one another, we too often ignore the resonance of taste, skill, and deliberation. Their cultivation is decisive for aesthetic and moral judgment. Autonomy is incomplete if sensibility is unformed.

iv. Equilibrium implies a vague but useful measure of agency's principal aims. Signifying moral, aesthetic, and emotional balance in the relations of agents to those they engage and within agents themselves, it expresses a psychic and moral ideal: in control of ourselves, we are also responsible for our effects on other people and things. Many factors explain the want of balance, but philosophic ideas—hard determinism, for example—are a symptom: why learn to modulate our responses if all was settled long ago? We reduce the severity of this effect by dispelling several persuasions. They include the bellicose reading of Nietzsche's persuasion that power and action are our *raison d'être*; Descartes' belief that intellect is self-sufficient; the Hegelian, Heideggerian aversion to privacy, and Plato's disdain for emotion. We repair these excesses by binding the extremes. Women were once excused from being publicly effective, men from educating sensibility. Equilibrium implies the convergence of these contraries. Like health, it signifies a condition to which we aspire, one whose absence may explain both our displacements (money, status, and possessions) and our addictions (alcohol and dope). Agency is these two things: control of one's circumstances; cultivation, appraisal, and control of oneself.

Free will is conceptually enabling: it clarifies the requirements for socialization, autonomy, and moral identity. Yet autonomy is problematic: a factional or atomized society is perpetually barren and thwarted. Its individuals can't organize for common or complementary aims; they lack the milieu required if art or ideas are to sensitize taste and talents. This essay construes socialization as the process of folding autonomous agents into the fabric of meanings, roles, and rules responsible for order, productivity, and mutual understanding. The conditions for free will—self-sufficiency, resistance to intrusions, and inhibition—make us singular, but vulnerable because inaccessible or unintelligible to others. We risk being unable to sustain ourselves because unable to acquire habits and sensibilities that would make us interesting or useful to other people. Separate but equal is a political problem; separate but accessible and mutually responsive is a psychological and moral virtue.

Moral identity is the achievement of socialized autonomies. We participate in an earthly version of Kant's kingdom of ends while facing two ways: enjoying our separate talents, tastes, and opportunities, we are also responsible for duties to other people, and to the systems—families, friendships, businesses, and states—in which we participate. Autonomy is crystallized discipline; it makes us resourceful and reliable. The chapters that follow elaborate these themes by addressing agency's constitutive variables: free will, socialization, autonomy, and moral identity. They argue that action is constrained by circumstances, rules, roles, and affinities, but free within those limits. The degree of one's freedom varies: slaves have little or none; the wealthy residents of Paris or New York have a lot. But everyone has projects, beliefs, and inclinations. Agency implies autonomy; but autonomy wants power, opportunity, partners, and a voice.

Chapter One

Agency

1. Semantics

There are words for mind's activities—*judgment* and *choice*, for example—but no word that implies their integration. Possible candidates—*character* or *sensibility*—have the wrong emphases. *Agency* is vague, but useful: it signifies purpose, cause, and appraisal in agents who control circumstances and themselves to some degree. Fire and wind are also controlling, but their actions lack intention, inhibition, and credit or blame. *Agency* implies those qualifiers.

2. Two Points of Reference

Agency has two principal elaborations. One locates agents in the material world while describing their interactions and effects. Aristotle, C. S. Peirce, and John Dewey are its principal exponents. An Aristotelian or pragmatist pastry chef is capable of thinking, doing, and making. He or she imagines the cake to be made, then assembles and bakes the ingredients. The other view is Cartesian: it proposes that *esse est percipi*: nothing is real, knowable, or thinkable if it isn't inspectable when set before conscious minds. Thinking, on this Cartesian model, is at once an act of doing and making: dreaming and perceiving create content that is relentlessly scrutinized for clarity and distinctness; thinking is self-discovery and self-appraisal. Two figures express these competing views. The first represents Descartes' emphasis on the autonomy of minds structured by their interiority.

© David Weissman, CC BY 4.0   https://doi.org/10.11647/OBP.0197.01

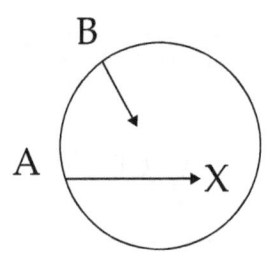

A = Awareness   X = The content of awareness   B = Self-awareness

Figure 1: A solitary mind, with awareness, content, and self-awareness.

Figure 1 represents an autonomous mind turned on itself. *X* signifies perceptual or ideational content for first-order awareness, *A*. *B* is second-order self-awareness. Descartes supposed that *A* and *B* are mutually conditioning. Lower-order awareness enables second-order awareness by supplying its content (*A* and *X*). Nor is being perceived incidental to the existence of *A* and *X*, for Descartes, anticipating Berkeley, argued that nothing exists if there neither is nor can be confirming evidence of its existence: *X* exists only if it is or can be perceived or conceived by *A*; *A* exists only if it is or can be perceived by *B*. Self-awareness, too, is subject to this condition. It is self-confirming because reflexive: *B* is aware of itself while aware of *A* and *X*.

Descartes' first *Meditation* implies the distinction between knowledge claims (necessarily true because the possibility of error is eliminated) and opinion (less than knowledge because fallible). Necessity is guaranteed if claims are true logically (because tautological), or because the matters known stand directly before inspecting minds. *A* (awareness of content) and *B* (self-awareness) satisfy this second condition: *B* reflects on *A* and *X* when they are accessible to *B* without error or distortion because *A* and *B* are the acts of a mind that inspects itself while inspecting whatever content qualifies it. There is no gap between awareness and its object, no place for error because the object of awareness is a qualification of the mind itself.

Figure 1 is pertinent to remarks about agency because it represents a mind whose actions are said to be perpetually accessible—visible—to the mind itself, and because inspecting minds are said to have no reliable access to the ambient world. The figure provokes questions for which Descartes supplied inconclusive answers: *i*. Is perceptual content merely imagined, or is some part of it acquired from extra-mental sources? Is God its source or is the material world perceived and engaged? *ii*. Is

B the mere observer of first-order receptivity or is it responsible for using rules or ideas to differentiate and organize the data *A* receives? *iii*. What does mind know of itself: is all of it exposed to self-perception or inference, or is part of it unconscious and inaccessible? (These issues are finessed, not solved, when Descartes invokes "moral certainty" in the sixth *Meditation*.)[1]

Descartes supplied Kant with an answer to the first of the questions above when his fourth *Meditation* made these two claims: that will is the power to give or withhold assent, and that assent is always to be withheld until ideas are clear and distinct.[2]

There are, however, two criteria for clarity and distinctness in Descartes: ideas are clear and distinct if their negations are contradictions, or if they appear with clarity and distinctness (as the *cogito* is said to do) before the mind's eye. This second condition is much looser than the first, for minds may generate clear and distinct images in either of two ways. Imagination may set them before the mind as in dreams, though dreams may be as paradoxical as Escher drawings. Or thought's content—its representations—are suspected of inaccuracy. It was Kant who introduced a looser truth-condition prominent when elaborating the monadic character and powers of the transcendental ego (his version of the *cogito*):

> I have been reproached for following a similar procedure, namely, for defining the power of desire as the *power of being the cause, through one's presentation, of the actuality of the object of those presentations*. The criticism was that, after all, mere wishes are desires too, and yet we all know that they alone do not enable us to produce their object. That, however, proves nothing more than that some of man's desires involve him in self-contradiction.[3]

What does this imply about imagination's innumerable fantasies? Are they all true merely because of the vivacity with which they strike the mind? Which are false if all are clear and distinct?

Figure 2 is a response to Kant and his idealist successors when they argue that imagination supplies all the content of experience.

---

[1] René Descartes, *Meditations on First Philosophy*, in: *Discourse on the Method and Meditations on First Philosophy*, ed. David Weissman (New Haven: Yale University Press, 1996), pp. 100–08.

[2] *Ibid.*, pp. 85–90.

[3] Immanuel Kant, *Critique of Judgment*, trans. Werner S. Pluhar (Indianapolis: Hackett Publishing, 1987), n.18, pp. 16–17.

It represents a mind constructing a stable map of the ambient world while responding to successive interactions with other people or things. This is a representation of the materialist-realist ontology common to Aristotle and Peirce:

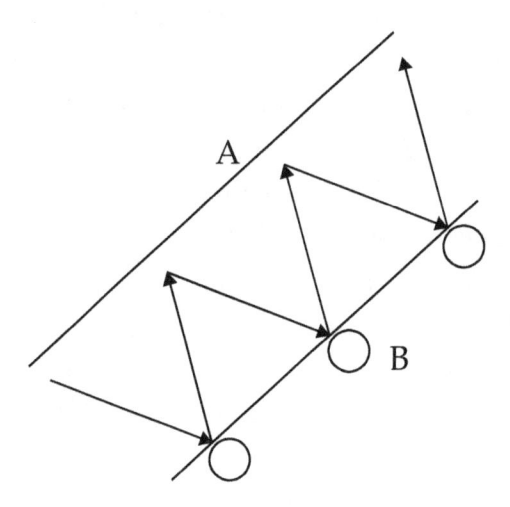

A = Reality   B = Mind's changing representations of reality
○ = Mind integrating new information into its model of reality
↘ = Information   ↗ = Expectation

Figure 2: A mind that integrates sensory data while testing its hypotheses and plans in the near-world.

Action is stifled without information of the ambient world and the beliefs it justifies. Having information requires direct perception of the states of affairs relevant if a need or desire is to be satisfied, including words exchanged by cooperating agents. Perceiving smoke, inferring fire, we deduce that fire would be visible, were the hypothesis true. Looking for the evidence (Peirce's version of induction), we confirm, fail to confirm, or falsify the inference (it's steam, not smoke).[4]

Perception is often construed as passive when compared to active thought, but this assumption fails to register the conditions for perceptual constancy: including the scanning which confirms that new data are sufficient to sustain a current perception or different enough to force its revision. Accordingly, memory and imagination are as critical to the content and stability of perceptual experience as Kant supposed.

---

4   C. S. Peirce, *Collected Papers of Charles Sanders Peirce*, vols. I–VI, eds. Charles Hartshorne and Paul Weiss (Cambridge: Harvard University Press, 1934–35), V, paras. 418–34, pp. 278–89.

Though sensory data are the effects of mind's interactions with things perceived, not, as he implied, the products of imagination, posits of thought's conceptualizations, or the effects of a source unknown.

Both accounts acknowledge that mind interprets perceptual data: hypotheses speculate about the character of or conditions for states of affairs represented by sensory data; or the data are construed in ways appropriate to its meaning-bestowing stories (they invoke the gods who created us). Both styles acknowledge that interpretations require appraisal because all are susceptible to error. But these alternatives supply contrasting profiles of agency's context: thought and imagination create scenarios construed as our circumstances; or perception supplies the information required if we're to engage other people and things effectively.

Ideas of truth vary accordingly. Truth is coherence if experience-creating minds are the only reality. Imagined data, thoughts, or sentences relate only to one another, because there are no extra-mental states of affairs they satisfy (or none accessible). This is world-making in the style of Kant's argument that experience is created, sustained, and justified by the maker's interests and values: science is better than nursery rhymes, but only because of its scale, detail, and the range of its applications. Coherence is, however, a feeble standard, because stories of all sorts—scientific, religious, or patriotic—are unfalsifiable, unless contradictory.

Distance from Kantian world-making is the strength of its Aristotelian-Peircean competitor. There are three measures: *i.* Mind doesn't have to generate all its perceptual content if sensory data are the effects of things perceived. For reality is causal, not merely a sequence of data organized by habits or rules. Experience is one of its effects *ii.* Mind has less to do: experience isn't stabilized by mind alone, if some things perceived as stable—streets and houses—are stable in themselves. *iii.* Theories and plans cohere with one another and the ambient world if corrected when tested because, we infer, reality is coherent.

The plausibility of the subjectivist model rises or falls with the idea that truth is coherence. This is principally a Kantian, not a Cartesian, defense. Subjectivism is ambiguous in Descartes: emphasizing the *cogito*, he was all the while a Platonist for whom perceptual data owe their identity to the ideas used to differentiate and organize them.

Innate ideas, like the Forms, are not pliable under the pressure of one's values and aims; percepts stabilized by one's clear and distinct ideas should themselves be stable. Kant was more sensitive to the relativity of conceptual systems, hence to the variability of data whose character and organization they schematize. Quine, too, was permissive:

> From among the various conceptual schemes best suited to these various pursuits, one—the phenomenalistic—claims epistemological priority. Viewed from within the phenomenalistic conceptual scheme, the ontologies of physical objects and mathematical objects are myths. The quality of myth, however, is relative; relative, in this case, to the epistemological point of view. This point of view is one among various, corresponding to one among our various interests and purposes.[5]

Intelligibility requires coherence, but the standards for coherence vary between logical rigor—necessity—and the weaker standards of fantasy. Thought's resistance to incoherence or contradiction is a function of the syntax and semantics of individual sentences, but also of the thinker's aims, values, and context. That estimate is complex because it depends on both the words used to differentiate and organize data, and their interpretation by the schematizing agent. Can one speak to gods or the dead? That question is a solecism on some interpretations, though not on all.

The coherence theory is vulnerable in four principal ways: *i.* Contradictions are barred because incoherent. *ii.* There is no standard for the coherence of narratives that don't qualify as logical deductions. Metaphor, allusion, changes of topic or direction: every detour is acceptable in conversation until we lose track of the flow. *iii.* Coherence fails as a test of truth because it fails to identify and discredit coherent fantasies. How many novels, poems, ads, or religious parables are coherent but false? *iv.* Coherent narratives are resisted when the partisans of significance-bestowing beliefs or practices confront one another. Why not convert to a different religion or abandon a local team for one native to a town I've never visited? Because each persuasion demands unqualified loyalty to a cohesive tribal identity. Where consistency is a formal value, these commitments are substantive values. Their parts cohere, if only superficially, because of

---

[5] Willard Van Orman Quine, *From a Logical Point of View* (Cambridge: Harvard University Press, 1980), p. 19.

an amalgamating tradition. But why call beliefs or traditions true? Isn't loyalty a sufficient virtue?

Descartes and Kant were troubled by the disconnect—the gap—between the content of experience and its extra-mental referents. But is that a bridge too far, or only the sometimes troubled distance from expectation to encounter? Saying what you like is possible; doing what you like is not when action, resistance, and error are ineliminable features of experience. Truth as coherence doesn't test that distance when its stories are unfalsifiable fantasies. But it is sometimes a logical test of alleged truths: so, the Pythagorean theorem is tested and proven by a deduction, though what it proves is the truth by correspondence of the proof's conclusion: that the square on the hypotenuse is equal to the squares on the sides.

Coherence becomes free-standing—not evidence for truth as correspondence—in circumstances where empirical evidence for correspondence is lacking: speculation about nature's cosmological origins is an example. Not wanting to curtail this impulse, we encourage hypotheses that exceed our ability to confirm the states of affairs imagined. We could withdraw, conceding that our guesses aren't verifiable. But then we obscure the transition from a concern for truth to delight in coherent, still testable speculation. There is pleasure in fantasy, but also the challenge to cosmologists and physicists who breach successive barriers by discovering evidence once presumed inaccessible. Religious communities have a different emphasis: they urge beliefs and practices that turn everyday pursuits into meaningful rituals. More than nourishing, meals with prayer are a dedication. This, too, is coherent, though no evidence—not habit or passion—converts practices into truths.

Autonomy and will can go either way: agency expresses itself when practical inquiries locate us within the ambient world, but also when imagination contrives stories that infuse our lives with significance. These stories inform our practices and define our tribal loyalties. Why prefer truth to meaning, when the two are as different categorically as numbers and rain? There may be no decisive reason, absent soccer riots or religious wars. Truth and appraisal are critical values in practical life, but sobriety is a minority taste when weighed against the longing for significance.

3. Individuality

Individuality in thought and skill is apparent; it doesn't reduce us to ciphers wearing generic identities—men or women, young or old—until marketers or political candidates address us: present your goods or your program in attractive ways and we'll buy or vote as you prefer. Why affirm a different individualism, one appealing to distinctive intellects, sensibilities, aims, loyalties, or scruples? Because the emphasis on generic identities is an assault on judgment and difference. Ablating private voices has several costs. We lose the dignity that comes with responsible autonomy; democratic political life suffers when private voices can't organize to protect their interests or pursue an ideal. When is the general will realized? (It wills the good for all.[6]) Every time people going different places in separate cars turn onto highways where all observe traffic laws that minimize their risks.

Descartes'—"I am, I exist"—is everyone's emblematic point of reference.[7] But who am I, what might I be? We resist invasive socialization by defending our private spaces: hear his advice—"doubt...deny... refuse."[8] Everyone resists occasionally, because we have different aims and share a persistent desire for self-expression. Wanting to declare ourselves, we stare down others by doubting their authority. This is every adolescent voice: "You can't tell me what to do." Participation in social goods is most consensual, least forced, when others tolerate our choices. But that isn't everyone's fortune: many desires and most talents are suppressed or undiscovered. We find work that pays our bills, not vocations sensitive to our abilities. Individuality flourishes when intellect and sensibility are moved by provocative tasks: steering a boat or playing the viola. Though time-serving—work that atrophies one's skills—is more familiar than work that's useful. Money, status, perks: these are simulacra of well-being; getting them is the price for conceding one's autonomy to roles that are intellectually and emotionally underwhelming. Who, apart from artists possessed of intimidating originality or people able to pay any bill, can resist the mix of social threats and inducements?

---

[6] Jean-Jacques Rousseau, *The Social Contract and Other Later Political Writings* (Cambridge: Cambridge University Press, 1997), p. 60.
[7] Descartes, *Meditations*, p. 64.
[8] *Ibid.*, p. 66.

The steady practice required of musicians is a discipline too severe for most people, though talking to adults steeped in their musical lives is revelatory. Most like what they do; they're annoyed by ancillary details but nourished by playing well with people of complementary skills. One of Nietzsche's remarks speaks to their intensity:

> To become what one is, one must not have the slightest notion of what one is...The whole surface of consciousness—consciousness is a surface—must be kept clear of all great imperatives...Meanwhile the organizing 'idea' that is destined to rule keeps growing deep down—it begins to command; slowly it leads us back from side roads and wrong roads; it prepares single qualities and fitnesses that will one day prove to be indispensable as a means towards the whole—one by one, it trains all subservient capacities before giving any hint of the dominant task, 'goal', 'aim', or 'meaning'.[9]

The education evoked here requires learning of a sort that isn't taught. What are the points of reference if "consciousness...must be kept clear of all great imperatives"? How shall we understand the "rule [that] keeps growing deep down...before giving any hint of [its] dominant task, 'goal', 'aim', or 'meaning'"? This is purpose beyond the aim of any school, purpose as the keel of autonomous lives. There may be several ways to learn it, though adversity of two sorts is instrumental. One is alienation: socialization loses its force if children excluded at home or school find other sustaining themes, friends, tasks, or values. The course is harder for those who lack even that much support: people alone, people insulted, those who swallow every reverse while coming back for more. This is resistance that "keeps growing deep down," resilience that drives individuals in ways and directions for which socialization has no answers.

4. Purpose/Intention

Every living thing acts to preserve and satisfy itself: *purpose* and *intention* signify its trajectories. The words are interchangeable in many contexts, or they express complementary states of mind. Either may signify an aim; the other its steady pursuit.

---

[9] Friedrich Nietzsche, *On the Genealogy of Morals* and *Ecce Homo*, trans. Walter Kaufmann (New York: Random House, 1969), p. 254.

It's often supposed that will is episodic: a pressure turned on or off. But purpose—our efficient, formal, and final cause—is steady, not sporadic. Specific aims for work or pleasure are subordinate to a persistent challenge: make life viable for others and oneself. Recall Kant's emphasis on imagination and his claim that time is the form of internal intuition: we integrate memories of things past the better to anticipate those to come. This was also Nietzsche's emphasis when writing of the *will to power*, an animal force impelling agents into the future as they adapt to evolving circumstances. People who simplify their duties sometimes imagine a time when there are no more, but that doesn't happen. We are forward sequencing machines who join fragments of the past and present while advancing into the future. Like sharks who never sleep, we're poised for action because self-concerned, responsible to others, and aroused already.

Discussions of intention are fraught because of the verificationist concern that intrapsychic states are inaccessible to observers. Aristotle seems naïve: writing allusively of faculties and capacities when he couldn't pin down their intrapsychic basis, intention and free will seemed evident to him. Subsequent naturalists have proceeded accordingly: they too have expected that these conditions would be disclosed when life is explained as the complex expression of its material constituents. Physiologists and engineers have gone a long way toward confirming Locke's speculation that God could have enabled matter to think.[10] But consciousness and its qualitative contents are elusive. It was once considered unthinkable that matter could live; we await an equivalent explanation for awareness and its content. Having it would reduce the mystery of human life without eliminating anything we find significant in ourselves.

Descartes did careful physiological experiments and made drawings of nerve tracks running from perceptual inputs to muscular responses. He imagined constructing a mechanical fox and speculated that all mental activity might be physical. Yet his arguments in the second *Meditation* and the dictum ending it—that nothing is better known to mind than the mind itself—convinced generations of thinkers that all mental life is set before our inspecting minds. It is often assumed,

---

10 John Locke, *An Essay Concerning Human Understanding*, Volume Two (New York: Dover, 1959), p. 193.

without qualification, that purpose/intention falls squarely within the range of activities whose occurrence is confirmed unequivocally by inspection. Experimentalists such as Wundt[11] and Brentano[12] worked within the Cartesian model by testing subjects' responses to varying stimuli, though others mistrusted those results because the internal states of their subjects weren't accurately calibrated. Henry Maudsley[13] dismissed spiritualistic accounts of mind while describing mental pathologies as evidence of degenerate physical states. He anticipated eliminationist views of intrapsychic activity, a position espoused currently by thinkers who suppose that mental activity is only neural, and that the obscurity of consciousness disqualifies it as an authoritative basis for understanding cognition or intention.

Behavior has always been a basis for inferences about mental activity: I know that you speak a language we share by hearing you speak it. Yet behaviorism hadn't received its status as a totalizing explanation for mental activity until Watson formulated his program in the 1920s. See what people do, alone or when responding to other people or things; base all your conclusions about mental activity on publicly observable evidence. Don't infer unverifiably that observables reveal operations which are themselves unobservable. Regard mind as a black box from which ensuing behaviors are intelligible without regard to activities unknown to observers. Behaviorism of this sort is less extreme than eliminationism. It isn't denied that people have minds: it's rather that activities within them are both indiscernible and incidental to the fact that behavior is effective or socially appropriate.

Purpose with a plan, control of resources and oneself, are hallmarks of agency, hence the disorientation provoked when Ryle and Wittgenstein deplored the idea that intention is an internal psychic state. Ryle's *Concept of Mind*, 1949, acknowledged that language gives credence to Cartesian dualism: talk about judgments, enjoyments, or intentions implies the existence of "a ghost in the machine."[14] Yet, this imagined

---

[11] See Wilhelm Wundt, *Principles of Physiological Psychology*, Volume 1 (Emeryville: Franklin Classics, 2018).

[12] See Franz Brentano, *Psychology from an Empirical Standpoint* (New York: Routledge, 2014).

[13] See Henry Maudsley, *Body and Mind: An Inquiry Into Their Connection and Mutual Influence, Specially in Reference to Mental Disorders* (London: HardPress, 2018).

[14] Gilbert Ryle, *The Concept of Mind* (New York: Barnes & Noble, 1949), p. 15.

agent is merely a projection of the words invoking it: having learned to use words signifying people and things, we use them analogously to entify mental activities. Ryle would have us respond by reconstruing the ontological commitments of our speech: inhibit the commitment to bogus posits; *judgment*, rather than an activity inaccessible to observers, is reparsed as an achievement word, a claim we confirm by seeing how the word is used. Do I avoid gambling with someone else's money? Credit me with sound judgment. This is Ryle's anticipation of Wittgenstein's claim that linguistic analysis is to be used therapeutically: the fly escapes the fly-bottle.[15]

Elizabeth Anscombe applied these lessons in her *Intention*: ignore intrapsychic inclinations or purposes, whether long-term or current. Regard intentions as processes; concentrate on acts in progress. We show our intention to dress every morning by dressing; the aim of crossing a street is manifest when crossing it. Anscombe's argument proceeds, in the style of Wittgenstein's *Philosophical Investigations*, with a torrent of linguistic subtleties and an occasional dictum. Distinguishing overt behavior from allegedly intrapsychic activities, she remarks that those occurring intrapsychically would have to be "known without observation," though "there is no such thing as a cause known without observation"[16]:

> And 'what causes' [intrapsychic phenomena] is perhaps then thought of as an event that brings the effect about—though how it does—i.e. whether it should be thought of as a kind of pushing in another medium, or in some other way—is of course completely obscure.[17]

> And in describing intentional actions as such, it will be a mistake to look for the description of what occurs—such as the movement of muscles or molecules—and then think of intention as something, perhaps, very complicated, which qualifies this. The only events to consider are intentional actions themselves, and to call an action intentional is to say it is intentional under some description [of behavior] that we give (or could give of it).[18]

---

15 Ludwig Wittgenstein, *Philosophical Investigations*. trans. G. E. M. Anscombe (New York: Macmillan, 1953), para. 309, p. 103.
16 G. E. M. Anscombe, *Intention* (Ithaca: Cornell University Press, 1957), p. 15.
17 *Ibid.*, p. 18.
18 *Ibid.*, p. 29.

Intention still only occurs in present action. That is, there is still no such thing as the further intention with which a man does what he does; and no such thing as intention for the future.[19]

So intention is never a performance in the mind, though in some matters a performance in the mind which is seriously meant may make a difference to the correct account of the man's action—e.g. in embracing someone. But the matters in question are necessarily ones in which outward acts are 'significant' in some way.[20]

Anscombe's behaviorism is Wittgenstein's: don't ask for a word's meaning—mind's way of construing the word—ask for its use in public forums.

Why is their behaviorism preferable to the idea that intrapsychic intentions—some voluntary, others habitual—direct motor activity? Why exclude the inner realm from our accounts of practical rationality while continuing to use words such as *purpose* and *intention*? Because ordinary language exhibits the texture of experience, the forms of life that make experience intelligible. Get rid of the metaphysical posits evoked by concepts such as intentions lurking "behind" rational actions; extirpate all references to the "inner life"—your personal intentions included—then observe that process verbs crystallize your ideas of mind: they express everything purposive and appropriate in muscular activity; nothing else need be said or inferred. But does that purge the mystery of other people's aims? A companion orders lunch, leaving me to infer her intentions: is she a vegetarian? I have a plausible answer when lunch arrives, but how much easier if I had asked her preference. Or am I barred from asking, because her mind is a "mysterious realm"? Could she have answered? She seems resolute; is she a mystery to herself?

5. Sensibility

Sensibility is inclination and resonance: wanting fresh air, breathing in and out, one feels the surge of it. We acknowledge behavior without pretending that interiority is a black box, nothing within it intelligible to the inhabiting agent. In music and literature, friendship, pleasure and pain, we're never uncertain that they have multiple effects. Yet

---

19   *Ibid.*, p. 31.
20   *Ibid.*, p. 49.

methodologists—worried about public standards of verification—shun the inner space because of its alleged obscurity. Their anxiety seems perverse to people immersed in emotional conversations or those stymied by a crossword puzzle.

Consider a subway system where trains shuttle passengers between stations linked by tunnels. The human nervous system is an analogue. Assembled neurons channel signals that originate as sensory data or self-generated impulses. The system's outputs—speech or motion—affect other things, but here too some activity is focused by the system's internal sensors, by pleasure or pain. Some subways have stations designed by architects or artists, though many riders are content if their stations are serviceable but drab. People, too, are careless; sensibility is a private domain, however public and accessible its expressions. It isn't cultivated because we are overworked or distracted by popular entertainments; or because cultivation is thought to be an indulgence. Why consider it vain? Because one's private life should be simple, dedicated to tasks fixed by duties to others; because there is something dangerous about people overly devoted to their private lives; or because their conceit is offensive. These are a volley of reasons for suppressing inclinations that distinguish us. But why inhibit a power that enhances our lives as often as pain afflicts them? Why not educate sensibility to distinguish and appraise some fraction of the nuances to which it's susceptible?

America has several excuses for its impatience with sensibility's cultivation. The first is our immigrant history: people unintelligible to their neighbors suppress their cultural differences to seem mutually innocuous. A second is the frontier: people living there had little time for pleasures or skills incidental to labor or defense. Third is our aversion to tastes that are aristocratic or effete; we prefer vigor and plain speaking. Fourth are distractions—popular music, sport, or film—that testify to our democratic tastes. A fifth excuse is more recent: technology provides instant access to goods that are otherwise inaccessible without talent and resources (a piano): there's no need to learn singing or an instrument if music is available online. These reasons steep for generations until one loses sight of the reality they obscure. Where skill and sensibility are allied, the lack of one reduces acuity in the other. Unexploited talent isn't used or enjoyed. Where "nothing is better known than the mind itself," introspection is shallow access to a resource we're slow to cultivate. Yet interiority isn't invisible: emotion and its provocations—people, sports, music, and nature—are familiar. Its active powers—resonance and artistry—are also well known but often ignored or belittled.

Resonance is always private, though its provocations may be shared. Excitement is mutual when spending time with a friend or celebrating victory in a stadium crowded with a team's fans. But difference is pervasive and easily confirmed: see people waiting for attention in a hospital emergency ward, each face wreathed in a different pain. The nursing staff has no issue with the essential privacy of experience and no inclination to override it by identifying a common organic cause. Yet there is this difference between two kinds of experiential content. Some, like pains, are distinctively private; socialized responses may converge on an imagined limit, but we can't learn to feel them the same ways. Others are socializable, given exposure and education: immerse yourself in a culture and notice that you come to enjoy music, dance, food, and sociality as its members do. Participation creates neural and experiential changes, until sensibilities converge on similar responses. How does one know the experiences are similar? Partly by seeing others as they respond—with pleasure or fear—to situations in which one participates; partly by talking of the experience, or reading what others make of it. Yet finding a vocabulary appropriate to a domain of activity or expression (music or dance) exceeds most people, critics included. They approve or dispute what they've seen or heard, but no one seeing only what they write can measure a critic's responses against the events provoking them.

Aristotle would have understood that a piano isn't melodic unless tuned and voiced. He would have agreed that sensibility is formed by the training and practical experience that create internal order. This process can't be perpetually conscious without distracting from current tasks: one doesn't relate appropriately to others by calculating one's every response or pausing to dwell on every feeling. Yet something is missing if one acquires mechanical facility but no consequential interiority. Pianists are perfected by practice and habit, but synthesizers aren't (yet) great pianists. The day may come when engineers write software that seems to express a machine's interiority, its discerning ear and taste. We who hear them will falsely suppose that their music communicates intellect and feeling in sound. But half the ancient dyad will remain. Playing for others will join the complementary sensibilities of artist and audience; the machine will feel nothing; auditors hearing the same music will resonate alone. Credit the engineers for a sensibility missing in their machines.

6. Thought and Perception

Where purpose drives initiatives responding to need, thought and perception supply content and direction.

6i. Aims and means: Aims typically express one's inclinations or duties; their means follow suit. But there are alternative aims, and reasons for challenging those preferred. Means too are variable, so they too are open to dispute. Justification penetrates wherever choice goes.

6ii. Hypotheses: What's to be done; how and with whom? Each question provokes a hypothesis, a speculation estimating where I am, what I need do, and the resources or help required to do it. These are the successive moments of orientation in Figure 2: the agent perceives a state of affairs and considers how to respond.

Framing hypotheses is the art of imagining relationships—Earth to the Sun—while inferring the empirical differences their reality would make. Where many relationships are conceivable, this second condition is decisive: we can't choose among the competitors, affirming the truth of one or another, without perceptual or logical evidence of its truth. The frustration of no evidence or insufficient evidence distinguishes many scientific hypotheses from those of practical life: expecting this key to open that door, we know when it does or does not.

Where are we; where do we want to go? Plans bridging the distance between aims and circumstances have two parts: one maps the relevant terrain; the other specifies the sequence of steps to one's objective. Both are hypotheses tested by searching for, then engaging the postulated states of affairs. Practices are standardized ways of addressing other people or things, but these too are hypotheses and tacit plans. Each is compromised when action misfires because altered circumstances have made them inappropriate.

6iii. Interpretation: There are many occasions when information about one's circumstances determines one's choices: looking for the door, one turns when seeing it. Yet states of affairs are not the only factors deciding one's choices: we acquire access to some contexts—jobs, for example—by acknowledging their rules and accepting their roles. Other situations require an interpretation that infuses a context or activity with meaning; its "world" is the web of meanings and values projected onto material things. Interpretation supersedes hypothesis when meaning—significance—is the determinant; buildings are more than structures if they're used as churches or homes. Uniforms or titles express one's status; religious symbols intimate that material things are imbued with divinity.

Hypotheses are true or false; meanings are neither. Affirming a story requires one's commitment to its narrative, not evidence of its truth. For "world" is equivocal: it signifies the totality of actual states of affairs, and also the domain of one's interpretation. Stories foster loyalty by locating us in relationships whose other participants, whether people or powers, give us identity, purpose, and value. This compares to truths that make no personal claim: we acknowledge them without feeling their significance. Hence the persuasions that truth is bloodless, and that loyalty is superior to truth because passion is better than indifference.

6iv. Imagination: Artistry provokes intellectual and emotional resonance by way of things artists make, a power founded in imagination and an array of mechanical skills. The perceiver's task is relatively simple: construe a work perceptually, intellectually, or emotionally; discern its form, see its coherence; enjoy its notes, or words, or shape. Compare the working artist: he or she is focused and intense, but not always happy. Having an idea and a passion for expressing it, artists are oddly displaced. Other tasks are forgiving: strike out this time, do better the next time at bat. That flexibility is missing when a directing idea is sensitive to every note or brush stroke.

The agent who paints or writes makes him- or herself the vehicle for choices that seem to come from another place. Descartes' remark—that nothing is better known to the mind than the mind itself[21]—is flawed. The painter-writer seems directed by an automatic pilot; the inventive

---

21 Descartes, *Meditations*, p. 70.

part directs action while out of sight; the conscious part follows along. Remember Plato's account of poets in the *Apology*: interpreters understood their poems better than their authors.[22] That rings true when one considers artists who make no dramatic show of their work: having an idea, deploying it in a favored medium, he or she works steadily without discerning the source of evolving ideas. Why this division? One speculates that associations are provoked and organized by generic heuristics as they apply to specific ideas in a process too ample and quick for the detail, scale, and speed of awareness. Work slows or stops if one tries to inspect it.

Do artists enjoy their work as much as people viewing or hearing it? Perceivers often have catholic tastes; they enjoy things of several kinds, usually work done by others. Artists are perfectionists when regarding their own efforts, but passive or grumpy when viewing that of others; many can't perceive or consider another's work without revising it in ways appropriate to themselves. How could we bridge the gap between the passive recipient and active artist? People buy fast cars despite speed limits: sitting in traffic jams is pleasure enough if the motor purrs and one sees burls in the walnut dashboard. But this is attenuated satisfaction: someone else makes the car; we distinguish ourselves by buying it. Autonomy looks the other way: it wants authenticity while uncertain about the means for achieving it.

Sensibility resembles a nerve: the excitation impelled by both postures—artist or perceiver—provokes a desire for more arousal. Both intensify the feeling that sensibility is the sustaining causes of one's vitality. But these are different powers. People watch its tournaments but never play tennis; cultivating taste creates connoisseurs and critics without creating artists. Why have both? Isn't singularity a perpetual warning against the unintelligibility of doing things on one's own; don't stand apart because most social benefits require that one collaborate with others? Or is art's authenticity an aberration we stifle, but share? Why not let everyone learn skills for transforming materials in ways directed by imagination while controlled by skill. It doesn't matter how dramatic the product or how successful the art; the activity itself is critical because nothing less enhances the sense of autonomy when something made or done satisfies one's judgment that it's well done.

---

22 Plato, *Apology*, 22c, p. 8.

This demand is a challenge when mastery seems unnecessary to those awash in things made ready-to-please: buy what you can't do or make. Yet passivity is costly if we lose self-esteem because of it. Bake or knit, fix cars or teeth: the endeavor is less important than the activity because agency wants the satisfaction of self-expression. It has many possible outlets; let talent and opportunity determine which they shall be.

This dilemma is a tension in our lives as agents: learn the conventional techniques or go your own way. Nearly everyone enjoys the advantages of socialization; a few have uncompromised lives as artists. Many others find spaces and tasks in which to express themselves, but most workers are over-worked, under-paid, and too little educated to liberate themselves. What could we do to relieve their frustration? Acknowledge it: identify some of their talents as children, then maximize opportunities for their training and expression. This week's graduation ceremony at New York's School of American Ballet included a program of dances featuring the graduates. The program described several prize winners and their exceptional trajectories: from early childhood to SAB. One can't imagine a society that does as much for all its children. Lives are a mystery to the living, because there are so few spaces for education and self-discovery. One's service to craft is impelling because of what it creates and the people affected. But there is a correlative demand on those of us who will always be anonymous: make sense of yourself; educate a talent, then feel your strength when it's released.

6v. Transcendence: Thought exceeds itself when directing our engagements with other people or things in ways that acknowledge their distinctive properties or interests. Doing this many times a day, we transcend ourselves by accommodating them. But *transcendence* is used more often as an aesthetic, moral, or religious command: discover the sublime in music or art; become the moral exemplar who serves the poor or a community of fellow believers; exceed your finitude by addressing your god. This is transcendence as our final cause. Being-in-the-truth, we achieve perfection when thought or sensibility fulfills itself in one or another of these significance-bestowing modes. But this account is hyperbolic; a fact perceived when stretching it doesn't cover the majority of human careers: butcher, accountant, or salesman. Rejecting truth's elision with meaning leaves the imperative's other expressions intact: cultivate thought and sensibility without mistaking metaphor for reality.

6vi. Disputed priorities: Mill's *On Liberty* cites three regions of liberty: consciousness and conscience; tastes and pursuits; and the freedom to unite for any purpose not involving harm to others.[23] Mill supposed that inclinations should be ascetic: tastes would incline to those discerned by intellect. But thought loses this authority in the consumer culture where advertising and other people tell us what to want. Sensibility, as Mill construed it, would be shaped by possibilities intellect discovers and refines; yet thought as we understand it is instrumental to the satisfaction of tastes acquired without thought: the punishing job required to pay for an elegant car. Agency is always qualified by socialization, but autonomy is reduced if thought can't discipline its inclinations.

7. Competence and Skill

Agency is more than motion. Activities are diversified by one's aims, materials, and techniques. Every skill (reading or rowing) is conditioned by the dispositions acquired when training shapes capacity.

Reductionists suppose that dispositions (capacities, skills) raise no ontological questions—they needn't be construed as the properties of agents—because all they imply is expressed by counterfactuals affirming what an agent would do in circumstances of a kind: wheels would turn, the car would move if ignition was sparked, the brake released, and the accelerator pressed. But isn't the disposition founded in the proper relations of the car's parts? Isn't the truth of the counterfactual conditional on this matter of fact; and isn't it true that the dispositions of human agents depend equally on the preparation and functional interdependence of bodily parts? Learners of every sort—athletes, musicians, and paratroopers—practice to embody skills appropriate to their tasks. Or should we suppose that the student who labors for days and years to master a skill comes to embody nothing at all, though it's truly said that he or she is now capable of doing what he or she couldn't previously do?

---

23 John Stuart Mill, *On Liberty* (Indianapolis: Hackett, 1978), pp. 11–12.

Agency presupposes this degree of ontological realism: no amount of linguistic legerdemain relieves the agent of having to embody the capacities or skills qualifying him or her for the task at issue. But this isn't mysterious. Knives cut because of their fine blades, not because a true counterfactual rightly cites what they can do while ignoring their material conditions.[24]

8. Effort

Many actions seem effortless because they're facilitated by habits or circumstances, though agency is experienced as bodily effort when activity and responsibility induce strains that are muscular, moral, or mental. Effort is ignored at moments of conceptual clarity, aesthetic delight, or facile speech, but not when working long hours, or concentrating on matters that resist us. Fatigue is reduced by habit, planning, or luck; it isn't eliminated because agency is the activity of bodies depleted by the work they do.

9. Partners

A few elementary things are done alone, though most activities we value and many we take for granted require collaborators: citizens, friends, spouse, or teammates. Finding partners is easier when an aim is shared. But there is also another condition: we need partners whose skills are appropriate to an aim. There is no team without players adept at its positions; no full orchestra without horns and winds.

People who satisfy these conditions may fail as partners because they have interest and skill while unable to subordinate personal desires to the reciprocity required by the demands of partnership. A city bus driver needs to accommodate his passengers when they want to exit: a driver who repeatedly ignores their signals would do better driving a truck. This is socialization, as it qualifies autonomy, a topic reserved to Chapter Three.

---

24 David Weissman, "Dispositions as Geometrical-Structural Properties," *Review of Metaphysics* 32:2 (1978), 275–97.

10. Efficacy

There is prudence in the expectation that we shall be tomorrow as we are today: organized life breaks down if people can't reliably anticipate what their roles require. Ethical practice is taught with all the seriousness of professional discipline: do what we expect, do what you say you'll do. Competence is aspiration and skill, the enabling condition for efficacy and duty. It tolerates changes of pace, direction, and means, but resists turmoil when circumstances change abruptly.

Efficacy has several measures: is an aim achieved with resources used efficiently, in reasonable time, at little or low cost to partners or others? How well has the agent performed: were his or her skills fully exploited? Is clumsiness explained by the lack of rehearsal or planning, by lapses of attention, or for want of coordination among the partners? Wanting stability because having it is often a mark of safety and because it makes planning easier, we acquire habits that adapt us to our circumstances. This is our version of the least energy principle: deliberation is unnecessary if we're habituated to situations where nothing has changed. But needs, resources, and aims vary from person to person, and within the histories of individuals. There are, therefore, these contending impulses: a viable accommodation is our steady purpose, but aims or means are revised because of indecision or if we're thwarted by circumstances. We experiment when flexibility seems cheaper than the wholesale revamping of established objectives; only the failure of every variation convinces us that an aim is too costly or unachievable.

Agents are *i.* controlled; *ii.* they are causes affecting other things, and, by way of feedback loops, themselves.

10i. Control: Human agency for Aristotle, Peirce, and Dewey is the activity of people having a degree of control over their actions and effects in the public world. A rolling stone affects things in its path, while having no control of itself. A gymnast does both: he maintains his balance by controlling the rings from which he hangs. Social control is often construed as the expression of an authority's power over its people; but it is also, more hopefully, the collaborative power of a society's members as they organize to achieve its aims.

Personal control looks backward and forward: the past is a reservoir of education and acquired ability. Practice enables a skill's refinement: throwing a ball is clumsy until it's done several times. But self-control is more than muscle control: we have aims, partners, scruples, and resources. These are variables one manages within a social space articulated by layered permissions and constraints; free speech, but no slander. Social control is often disguised: one has access to only those goods and services that are profitably sold. Control is significant if it enables or proscribes ideas, vocations, or partnerships one favors. Hence this simpler calculation: where is the locus of initiative? Does every agent have the means and authority to make choices appropriate to his or her aims, age (five, fifteen, or fifty), and circumstances? Why so young? Because autonomy is learned, and because practice begins early.

10ii. Cause: Agents are causes.

10iia. Four causes: Aristotle recognized four causes: material, efficient, formal, and final:[25] matter is the stuff altered in ways foreshadowed by the plan directed by an aim. He supposed that material cause is passive to qualification, though each of the causes is active when joined in agents who engage other people and things: cooks are the material agents who use recipes when baking cakes. Each of agency's active modes—thinking, doing, or making—implicates all the causes, though examples emphasize one or more: drawing is different from thinking; designing requires both.

Aristotle's emphasis on temperance implies two causes—positive and negative feedback—that aren't separately acknowledged, though agency is ineffective without them. Positive feedback is inciting: friends seek one another's company because each provokes the others in mutually pleasing ways; a runaway stock market cools when negative feedback makes buyers prudent. Oversight may go either way: persuaded that projects are more expensive than they're worth, we inhibit actions they require; delighted by an intensifying friendship, we pursue it. Both versions embody the other four causes: information is the formal cause that provokes or inhibits actions that achieve or avert wanted or unwanted effects.

---

25   Aristotle, *Basic Works of Aristotle*, ed. Richard McKeon (New York: Random House, 1941), 1013a24–1013b3, pp. 752–53.

10iib. Nodal causation: Agency is badly served when colliding billiard balls—impact and scatter—are the standard points of reference for understanding causal relations. Motion's mechanics are the same but perspective is different when causation is regarded as *nodal*: agents preside over the domains of their effects. Trees are nodal: from foliage to roots, each nurtures and defends things living or inert within the body of the tree or the shade it casts. An ensemble of trees—a wood or forest—is an ecosystem in which each tree affects others while sovereign in its space. Human societies are more like forests than we imply when reducing their members to single agents or homogenized classes: workers or management, buyers or sellers.

There is also this emergent effect when a node affects other things within the range of its influence: the circle of things affected is transformed into the moral space for which the node is responsible. Most such effects are ignored because they're trivial and unintended, but some relationships—those binding doctors to their patients or teachers to their students—are consequential. A classroom is one moral space; Greek dramatists understood that a play's audience is another. Each participant thinks and feels in ways that qualify as moral because the activity instructs thought and sentiments while integrating the participants. But a mob, too, is a moral space. Some have a leader who presides over individuals regulated by the messages and feelings he passes among them.

10iic. Self-regulation: Agents regulate themselves out of regard for their effects. Responsibility points two ways when agency is the point of reference: to one's actions, and to one's moral posture. Most actions in everyday life—opening and closing doors—leave us morally unaffected; but ignore all that is morally inconsequential to consider the posture of agents whose choices and actions are sensitive to their effects. Children are taught to consider their impact on other people and things; they learn as early as four or five that unforced actions redound to an agent's moral identity. We suspect moral preening in people who are perpetually mindful of moral lapses in others or themselves, but this is one of the benefits of character: habits control actions that reliably express an agent's values. Tradition, vocation, desire, and social context determine the network and intensity of one's duties. Individuals choose relationships and opportunities suitable to the depth of their tolerance for duty.

Yet we're liable for effects that aren't seen because urgency or excitement deters us from looking, or because they're unforeseeable. There are defenses: we maximize effects appropriate to a current aim while minimizing those considered harmful. We're conservative because that makes us mutually predictable and productive, and because familiarity with one another and our tasks facilitates control of the near future. We look for collaborators who share our values and aims, because effects are less secure if partners have values or priorities different from one's own.

11. Oversight

Imagine a dancer as she sees her posture in the mirror behind the barre: observing a drooping hand or elbow, she corrects it. Most of us don't have immediate feedback; we depend for information on observers or the people or things we affect. Information is often fragmentary; we're rushed, and don't consider it. Yet agency is less clumsy, more precisely calibrated to intentions if we regulate ourselves while overseeing what we do.

The criteria used to appraise one's effects vary with the practice and domain at issue: bakers aren't assessed in the same terms as dentists. Are there moral or aesthetic criteria that apply across domains? This is one of the harder questions, because of cultural and social diversity: we don't agree about the standards appropriate to elementary tasks and relationships, let alone those more complex or consequential: never murder, except in war. Aesthetic tastes vary radically but aesthetic criteria—harmony, rhythm, coherence, and surprise—are more easily universalized because discerned in work that is otherwise strange: in the calligraphy, for example, of languages we don't read.

Agents are self-appraising because self-correction and -control are conditions for successfully completing many tasks, and because one appraises work completed: is it good, or good enough? Many things are done thoughtlessly; they're effective, and don't need scrutiny. But sometimes, we take stock: was I effective; what part of the task would have been better accomplished had I been more skilled, or if I had understood it better? What were my effects on partners or bystanders? The Cartesian perspective is ineliminable, however severe the pressure for social conformity: what did I do; how well did I do it?

No one is fastidious in everything done, though some actions express one's sense of mastery; doing them poorly reduces self-esteem. But there is no accord about the tasks or values appropriate to this sense of pride. One may idealize truth, reliability, cooperation, and care, but not everyone does. Why are we casual about qualities sometimes regarded as essential to moral and communal health? Because we're skeptical about these ideals: societies survive when some members are careless about every such virtue. No matter that the machine isn't performing as it could, or that using it this way is destructive: a bicycle with a flat tire is still a bicycle; one can ride on the rim.

Why hold oneself to a different standard if life is satisfactory without it? There is no higher reason, merely a regret similar to one's feelings for flowers that bud but don't bloom. Is there, nevertheless, an obligation to fulfill oneself, a duty that no one can enforce if a person doesn't care to make himself responsible for the self-discipline appropriate to his talents, duties, and circumstances? This is the urging to which people often submit. Accepting the discipline of others may seem cowardly or feeble until one considers what such people do: they're learners of all sorts; dancers, pianists, writers, cooks, or parents. There are vocations here for everyone. Each can find a niche in which to drive him- or herself to a vertiginous standard. What of the many people whose self-persuasion doesn't require this exertion? There is often nothing to do; let them be, except as they suppress motivation in others.

There are also two uncertainties, each generated by socialization. *i.* Are the standards of self-appraisal distinctively my own, or does oversight express the interests or attitudes of groups in which I participate? Do I appraise myself in their terms, or my own? Agency is under tension from these two poles: one an agent's perception of the least conditions for success; the other, the group's tolerance for a norm that may have an orientation or standard different from its own. People dissatisfied with public standards or those of a team or business make themselves unpopular until their work establishes norms that others espouse. Aristotle was reassuring: aim for the mean. Nietzsche condemned his tolerance; "herd morality" was his diagnosis. *ii.* Whose agent am I? What remains of individual purpose when collaboration limits idiosyncrasy and imagination? That is the effect when a team member is obliged to choose the standards with which he's appraised: should he be judged in their terms or his own?

Efficacy intimates success: work was done; an aim was achieved. But agency without achievement is confounding. Oversight exposes numerous reasons for failure: obstacles multiplied; costs mounted; the objective was vague; the plan was fragmentary; partners were unreliable; resources were inadequate; the agent lacked persistence or skill. Each of these faults may be chronic; four are noteworthy:

11i. Unrealistic aims: Pole-vaulting thirty feet is plausible on the Moon, but not on Earth. Some obstacles are reduced with practice and circumstances, but others can't be breached because of natural limits or missing resources. How do we know that objectives exceed us, given the example of Plato or Roger Bannister? Do we challenge ourselves until defeated, or rethink our aims? Ego ideals are often fragile because excessive; charity amidst frustration is a generous instinct.

11ii. Contrary aims or values: Wanting marriage while refusing every offer is puzzling: is every suitor wanting, or are you confused? Contrary desires are self-subverting; anyone stymied by them does better to suspend hope or activity while considering his or her attitudes.

11iii. Short- versus long-term aims: We often judge efficacy by considering short-term effects, though many things—children, marriages, careers—are better appraised recurrently. This is more complicated than the wisdom of Aristotle's remark that late success feels better than slow decline or a flameout after early achievements. For some aims or actions—tonight's movie or dinner at a new restaurant—are judged for their immediate effects. Education or a career are better appraised with hindsight.

11iv. Change: Every aim and plan is vulnerable to the evolution of one's circumstances. Partners, resources, context, one's skills and stability: each is a contingency beyond an agent's control. That most are stable much of the time explains our success. But how do we protect ourselves from the risk that every situation or resource may change without warning? Repetition makes us careless; we ignore the question because we're lulled into neglect, or because we believe that persistence overcomes most obstacles. There is also prudence: we insure ourselves with fail-safe plans or facilities: alternate roads, other people to call, fire departments, or hospitals.

12. Frustration

Much that we do is life-enhancing; though we're diminished by bad choices, crude plans, inadequate resources, poor collaboration, or circumstances that oppose us. Or we fail because agents beset by conflicted aims, feelings, or values can't organize themselves for their tasks. Consider just the last of these flaws. Aristotle's term for it was *akrasia*.[26] We translate his Greek as *weakness of the will*, though this condition occurs when resolve is sabotaged by a conflict of attitudes. One side is powered by values or interests expressed by rational ideas or aims; the other favors values or interests driven by one's passions. Unable to resolve the conflict, action is paralyzed, or the issue is decided, at cost to one side or the other, when agents act impulsively.

Why can't we avert intrapsychic conflicts? Because interests are opposed or because we believe them opposed. We're sometimes paralyzed by offsetting anxieties: I should see a doctor but dislike blood tests. Action stops until fear of a cascading aliment exceeds fear of the test. We acknowledge half of Hume's dictum: reason is often slave to the passions. This is agency hobbled by the complexity of our nature: we deliberate, choose, and plan; but agency stumbles when we're overcome by anguish or regret.

13. Will

Purpose without will is intention without the power to do things intended. But we're not always sabotaged by ambivalence. Isn't that sufficient evidence of will? It isn't because of an unresolved debate. Is will a power that initiates action or redirects the course of actions afoot? Or is there an inertial force—a causal tide—that moves blindly through us from the beginning of time? Because, if so, autonomy, free choice, and responsibility are deceptions: all we do was determined by causes initiated in the remote past. This is the belief that we, like other creatures, are hard-wired; we respond to stimuli, but our actions are determined by the lineage of causes acting on and within us: we don't choose. Chapter Two affirms an alternative: it considers reasons for saying that we have free will. The causal tide is diverted, if only a little, by our choices and actions.

---

26 Aristotle, *Nicomachean Ethics*, 1147a10–1152a35, pp. 1041–52.

Chapter Two

Free Will

Are we the vehicles of energies and trajectories past, or agents who redirect the causal tide for reasons of our own? Hard determinists suppose that efficacy expresses nature's original stock of motion and energy, nothing added. Volition's power to divert the tide is an illusion, if this is so. Autonomy is a conceit: humans, no less than windstorms, are ephemeral moments in causal histories established long ago. What part of this is true?

1. Introduction

Vision has eyes, sound has ears; will seems disembodied. Referring volition to mind was once a way of grounding it, though nowadays, when consciousness is suspect, that ascription is inconclusive. We redeem it by construing will as an expression of hierarchically organized brains. Dewey's description of the reflex arc, in 1896, is our point of reference: will is inhibition or release in agents poised to satisfy interests or desires.[1]

Thinkers who contest free will embed us in causal chains that invoke the universal determinism of Laplace's demon. They agree that we seem to choose among alternatives, but, they say, the experience of choice is illusory: everything happening today was predictable from the beginning of time, given original conditions and the laws of nature. This is contestable: Jack and Jill were mutually unknown until friendship and marriage superseded their indifference. Marriage inhibited choices

---

[1] John Dewey, "The Reflex Arc Concept in Psychology," *Psychological Review* 3 (1896), 357–70.

that each was accustomed to making, though it promoted some that neither had considered before. Their relationship was emergent; duties created by its reciprocities blocked those parts of causal history enabled by their separate lives. Was their bond predictable? There was no sign of it in their separate causal histories; marriage was unforeseen until they discovered one another. Yet eclipses of the sun are fully determined; why assume that this coupling was not? Because its inception was a blind date arranged by a randomized lottery. Compatibility evolved by fits and starts when each partner adapted to the other's hopes and expectations. Marriage was an intrusion that redirected causal histories for reasons current and situational, not historic. Responses to novel or surprising situations often redirect the causal tide from within it.

2. Background

Autonomy is self-regulation. Much that we do is habitual, though many actions—rising for work, walking faster to get there—are willed. Choice is a hallmark of autonomy, so it matters that will's freedom is challenged. Are we free when responding voluntarily to circumstances? Or is will never free because our mechanical nature makes us subordinate to a history of sufficient causes?

There is, so far, no explanation for the emergence of mind's conscious qualities and actions—color, pain, thought, and choice—but life, too, was once a mystery; perhaps inquiry will also expose the exhaustively material conditions for conscious phenomena. Other aspects of our materiality are already understood. Like machines, we're programmed by society or DNA. Autonomy enables us to satisfy rules at a pace of our own; it doesn't establish that we do anything freely. The law-governed processes moving through us started eons ago; hard determinists say that we carry their messages while unable to initiate our own. The more we understand, the less free we seem to be.

An opposed tradition supposes that will, like all mental activity, falls to Descartes' remark that nothing is better known to mind than mind itself.[2] Mental structure and activity are, he thought, comprehensively

---

2   René Descartes, *Meditations on First Philosophy*, in: *Discourse on the Method and Meditations on First Philosophy*, ed. David Weissman (New Haven: Yale University Press, 1996), p. 70.

inspectable, no part hidden or obscure. Philosophy canonized this perspective; self-knowledge required finding oneself in the mind's eye. Or so it seemed. Skepticism about self-awareness and self-control is unrelenting when both are regarded as evolutionary afterthoughts. Freedom, virtue, and responsibility are conceits if all we do is fixed by our bodies and causal histories. Imagine a future conversation between householders and their robots: "This isn't a dispute between humans and machines but, rather, plain speaking from one machine to another. You do a few things well; but, for the most part, not so well as us." Which side is speaking? Do we think better of ourselves if neither side comes away fearing that the other has won the argument?

Our knowledge of will and autonomy is grounded in conscious reflection, because this is our first source of information about everything. Yet volition is problematic; is it directly perceived or merely inferred from action and its effects? We lack Descartes' conviction: there may be no mental activity that is accurately and exhaustively known to introspection. Consciousness is the filter through which mental activities are discerned, not the theater in which they are directly perceived. Nor do we safely infer that their character when conscious accurately represents them when preconscious: there may be little or no isomorphism between the two. Integrating our points of access—inspection and inference—will be problematic, until we have a detailed account of the neural conditions for conscious experience.

I understand autonomy on analogy to a horse and rider moving at speed across a plain. The horse—our bodies—does most of the work; mind adds purpose and direction. The rider whispers in the horse's ear; he doesn't know why this works, but often it does. Like the rider, we credit ourselves with voluntary self-control; we deliberate before acting, then choose the option that seems best suited to our interests and circumstances. Human will is an internal power for affecting nerves and muscles when provoked by desire or deliberation. Will is explained by the altered levels of dopamine that affect brain sites where neural or muscular activity is initiated or suppressed.[3] Animals display purpose when moving as appetite or safety requires; their self-control is variable to a degree, though largely instinctual. Will in them may

---

3   Jay Schulkin, *Effort: A Behavioral Neuroscience Perspective on the Will* (Mahwah: Psychology Press, 2006), pp. 56–61.

be an elaboration of tropisms familiar in plants responding to light or water. People lacking will would resemble anemones in ocean currents, though we humans, more like sharks, are always moving or ready to move: memory and imagination are active when muscles are loose.

Skeptics concede that we seem to have free will, and that moral and intellectual autonomy require it. But there are two kinds of autonomy: one is inflexible, the other adaptive. Light bulbs have the first: being mechanically self-sufficient, each works—given energy—because of its design. Living things are autonomous in the other way: we anticipate and adjust our behavior to altered circumstances. This difference would once have seemed rigid; it isn't anymore. Mechanical control mimics human self-control when feedback is self-correcting (self-driving cars that learn to observe lane markings; machines that improve their skill at chess or Go by surveying games they've played and lost). Feedback is deterministic if free will has no opportunity to interrupt a causal loop. Hence the reduced stature implied when hard determinism supposes that human self-control is only a version of the control embodied in sophisticated machines. Are we responsible for our judgments, intentions, and behavior; are we self-reproving? Could we resist a fad or oppose a mob? The rhetoric of self-regulation implies this authority. Do we have it?

Our margin of freedom is uncertain because of two ambiguities. One obscures the difference between freedom to and freedom from, the power to act or will in pursuit of one's aims versus exemption from control. The other is universal determinism, the idea that no act or choice is free because each has sufficient causal conditions that stretch forever backwards. Is there no relief from history; was everything decided at nature's inception?

3. Freedom To and Freedom From

Freedom from signifies that one isn't controlled by forces or agents that include impulses, attitudes, other people, or things. *Freedom to* is the opportunity, power, and right to choose and pursue one's aims. These phrases express the Enlightenment's political nerve. Its aim was physical, intellectual, and moral autonomy; discover yourself by eliminating arbitrary controls on your actions and identity. Liberation required doing or believing as good judgment prescribes; reason would be its discipline. Yet this opposition—freedom or restraint—is misconstrued if we assume that freedom to will and act presupposes exemption from the materiality of one's body and context. That idea implies Kantian spontaneity: choice or action initiated from a position outside space and time. The alternative is categorical: one is never free to do something when free from everything else. Here are six illustrations:

3i. "You're free to choose," we say, though choices or plans are limited by aims, values, needs, resources, or likely effects. Circumstances are confining: there is no way to do as one chooses irrespective of them.

3ii. "Having the skill and resources required, I'll do it (bake a cake, fly the plane)." This is situated freedom, the autonomy that comes with having appropriate means when choosing to act. "You're free to go if you like" is cruel when addressed to people having no way to go because disabled or imprisoned.

3iii. "You're free to disappoint us (your family, friends, or partners)." This formula, intimating a neglected duty or broken law, invokes a limit one may be unwilling or unable to breach. Statutes (traffic laws) protect us or facilitate practices that would be chaotic without them. Duties locate us within core systems we've formed or inherited. Freedom to abandon those roles lapses at the point where families or friendships are sabotaged.

3iv. "You've considered all the reasons for and against acting. Now do one or the other." Good reasons are causes or permissions; having a lawful desire and resources, one acts. This, too, is situated autonomy, though now the tipping point has shifted. Before, it was resources; do it if you have them. Now, when resources are assumed, preferences are established by deliberation. We're not free to do what good sense tells us not to do, though passion sometimes overrides good sense with effects we approve.

3v. "Stop what you're doing." This implies an inhibiting power, will as circuit-breaker. We don't always see the costs of our choices; better stop before they accumulate. This, too, is evidence that we are not free from circumstances, reasons, or likely effects.

3vi. "You're free to blink or remember." It may be alleged that these are actions of the only sorts unconstrained by anything but the power to do them, though here, too, an ability (a capacity justifying the use of *can*) is their material condition. Freedom from every condition—in the way of Sartre[4] or Descartes in the early *Meditations*—would entail our inability to do anything.

Will's freedom is situated, never exempt from material, prudential, moral, or legal constraints. Is it free within those limits, and, if so, to what degree?[5]

4. Ontology

Some determinists say that every effect has ancient causes, all lawfully determined to produce it. This is event causation; it works mechanically by transferring energy or averting its transfer. Agent causation (not considered here) is ascribed to human agency by writers who doubt that human intentions can be understood in the terms of mechanical relations.[6] Event causation is the power and process responsible for the global drift of material change. Is human autonomy the temporary shield that delays our subjection to the causal tide, or is talk of freedom a conceit?

Hard determinism emphasizes that every event has causes sufficient to produce it, and that every process and event is constrained by natural laws. It demoralizes libertarians of every stripe. Though its conclusion is only dogmatic when no inventory of laws, lineages, processes, and current conditions supports its claim that every effect was incubated in nature's original conditions. Where, for example, were the myriad emergent systems—living things, families, friendships, and cities— stabilized by the causal reciprocities of their parts? Determinists explain that these effects were predictable, given the natural laws controlling their generation. Yet contemporary philosophic opinion is distinguished

---

4 Jean-Paul Sartre, *Being and Nothingness*, trans. Hazel Barnes (New York: Citadel, 1956), pp. 409–534.
5 See Robert Kane, *A Contemporary Introduction to Free Will* (New York: Oxford University Press, 2005), for a review of most contemporary views.
6 See, for example, Christian List, *Why Free Will is Real* (Cambridge: Harvard University Press, 2019); and David Weissman, "Christian List, *Why Free Will is Real*," *Metaphilosophy* 50 (2019), 743–47.

by a difference that makes no difference. Humeans aver that causality is constant conjunction and that laws are regularities.[7] Or laws are described as the higher-order sentences of axiomatized theories,[8] though data confirming their validity—the regularities reported—are said to supply the whole meaning of their content. Nature is a grab bag of possibilities without essential internal constraints, if laws responsible for generating regularities reduce to the phenomena observed.

We require a different ontology, one sensitive to natural order and normativity, if what we say of causality is correct to nature while tolerant of autonomy and free will. Aristotle is a useful guide. He argued that natural normativity is secured by laws existing *in rebus*.[9] Those are laws of motion, and (an idea foreign to Aristotle) rules of assembly implicit in the geometry and topology of spacetime. Laws of this kind are exhibited in the regularities of the periodic table and patterns for the assembly of natural kinds. Is universal determinism viable when modified to acknowledge that nature's constraints are located within it? Here are some reasons for believing that we should distinguish two of its versions.

5. Universal Determinism

Determinism comes in two versions: hard and soft. The soft affirms that we humans live within the natural world as self-stabilizing modules. Having innate powers or those acquired by engaging other people or things—learning to walk and talk—we've become agents of change, *causa sui*, affecting other things and ourselves. Much that we are was caused by conditions we didn't control; yet now we choose what to do, decline it, or stop doing it. *Causa sui* has theological sources, though it applies in our time to machines engineered to manage themselves. Discipline has that effect in us,[10] but with this difference: having learned to read, we choose our books.

---

[7] David Hume, *A Treatise of Human Nature*, ed. L. A. Selby-Bigge (Oxford: Clarendon, 1978), pp. 155–58.

[8] Ernest Nagel, *The Structure of Science* (New York: Harcourt, Brace, and World, 1961), pp. 33–37.

[9] Aristotle, *Metaphysics*, 1001b-1002a14, p. 729.

[10] C. S. Peirce, *Collected Papers of Charles Sanders Peirce, Volumes I–VI*, eds. Charles Hartshorne and Paul Weiss (Cambridge: Harvard University Press, 1934–35), V, paras. 5.440–5.442, pp. 294–96.

Soft determinism agrees that every event has causes sufficient to produce it. So, choice, too, is fully determined, with the qualification that principal causes decisive for volition are internal to the chooser. Every event satisfies natural laws (laws of motion and laws controlling the assembly of atoms, molecules, and neurons), though nature tolerates alternate choices without interposing a specific law for each. Or should we suppose that people entering a supermarket engage a tangle of laws—a different one for every product sold—until each shopper is entrapped by a law obliging him or her to buy the item it favors?

The efficient causation and holism of this formulation would offend Hume. He reduced reality to the force and vivacity of percepts before identifying causality with the constant contiguities of "impressions."[11] But why suppose that practical life is the artful manipulation of percepts when that makes no sense of productive activity: dentistry or dance, for example? Hume's theory ignores this implication because he believed that *esse est percipi* expresses a truth that bars penetration into the ambient world. I assume that causality is energy exchange or inhibition, and that energy's transmission is inferred, though we have no percepts of energy itself. The successes of practical life are a paradox, physics has a kinetic but no dynamic interest, if energy is only an "inference ticket."[12]

Assume that causal efficacy—efficient causation—is congenial to soft determinism, then consider that hard determinism resists the autonomy enabled by this other version. Hard determinism avers that nothing can deviate from trajectories fixed at the beginning of time; every change is the current moment in a lineage having a lengthy past and perhaps an infinite future, however diverse or complex its origins. We believe that attitudes (values) and reasons fix choices calculated to satisfy interests or needs, that autonomous bodies and neural complexity enable the speed, flexibility, and efficiency of our responses. But this is naïve: personal development and idiosyncrasy are the effects of causes we didn't and couldn't control. Peter Van Inwagen put it simply:

> If determinism is true, then our acts are the consequences of the laws of nature and events in the remote past. But it is not up to us what went on before we were born; and neither is it up to us what the laws of nature

---

[11] Hume, *A Treatise of Human Nature*, p. 1.
[12] Gilbert Ryle, *The Concept of Mind* (New York: Barnes & Noble, 1949), pp. 121–27.

are. Therefore the consequences of these things (including our own acts) are not up to us.[13]

Notice how much of human agency is diminished if this remark is true. Everything thought, willed, felt, or done was caused long ago; all of it satisfies natural laws, and none of it is "up to us."

Comprehensive determinism is unarguable if one agrees that nothing comes from nothing. For if something exists, if only oneself, then there must have been a cause or set of causes sufficient to create it, and so on to infinity for every previous state of affairs. Soft determinism concedes this point; it, too, locates us within comprehensive causal networks. Why prefer it to hard determinism? Because it identifies breaches and barriers in the causal tide, and because the softer version emphasizes autonomy's role in the emergence of selfhood, hence the implication that each of us is the cause of his or her responses to other people and things. Hard determinism has no regard for habits and ideas formed in the interplay of memory, talent, and imagination. It ignores ingenuity: having to innovate in situations that are nowhere anticipated in one's causal history. Some constraints are historical, but others—tight shoes—are current. Hard determinism wants to be comprehensive: sets of conditions, from history to the present, are sufficient to produce effects that are foreseeable in a lawful world. Soft determinists emphasize contingency, risk, and the asymmetry of explanation and prediction. Where agents are the critical variable, *freedom* is shorthand for their shifting priorities in circumstances that are, themselves, unstable. Hard determinism is lopsided: there is too much emphasis on history; no recognition of opportunities unanticipated by the causal stream, or those enabled when emergent properties or functions block old histories. Though situations are often baffling in some respect, so initiative and experiment are required before we can respond effectively to them.

6. Explanation/Prediction

What is explanation's relation to prediction: are the causes specified by an explanation sufficient to predict all the properties of their effects?

---

13 Peter Van Inwagen, *An Essay on Free Will* (Oxford: Oxford University Press, 1983), p. 16.

This collateral issue clarifies the difference between these two versions of determinism.

Both determinisms, hard and soft, agree that every effect is explained if we can cite causes sufficient to determine its existence and character, given natural laws. They disagree about prediction. Hard determinists suppose that everything was decided, hence predictable, at the beginning of time; our inability to make accurate prediction is the effect of having imperfect information about nature's laws and original conditions. Having that information would enable us to predict, in principle, what an agent will do. Though these determinists identify only a few of the conditions for any event; most are buried or disguised in its history. Soft determinism is equally confounded by the density of historical antecedents, but it has the advantage of emphasizing the current choices and actions of existing agents. It can't predict what they will do, because volition is often an event's determining condition, and because the variability of an agent's responses to evolving circumstances makes choice uncertain.

Here is an example favorable to hard determinists. Adopt construction rules for assembling triangles: attach the endpoints of three line-segments of any length to one another so that the three angles formed are equal to one hundred eighty degrees in a flat space. Suppose that this rule, with original conditions, is sufficient to explain the generation of every geometrical property or relation in the domain of flat-space triangles. Now generalize to spacetime, and ask this question: do geometry's construction rules (construed as natural laws determining the assembly of phenomena in spacetime) decide the character of all reality, as general relativity implies? It would be true, if so, that motion and a geometrized spacetime (as originally configured) have determined the existence and character of everything existing since the beginning of time. Hard determinism would be vindicated. A geometrizing god would know all that is, has been, or will be. But consider: Neptune moves as the sun determines, but could the god have predicted Beethoven or Stravinsky? Would its failure be evidence that complexity obscured its view, or an effect of the style each composer developed when responding to the musical culture of his time? Why say that such things are unpredictable? Because altered circumstances may provoke an agent whose aim or understanding is disrupted: "Sorry. I thought you were the mailman." These are reactions caused in the moment, not those prepared over eons of time.

Hard determinists suppose that having perfect information would enable them to make predictions that are certain to be correct. Why? Because inferences less rigorous would have conclusions that are only probable because contingent. But do we have evidence that antecedent conditions and construction rules—natural laws—were necessary and sufficient to determine the existence and character of all that is? No: many phenomena—some determined at the last moment, others better established—are unexplained. We're puzzled by a sudden power failure, but also by transitions that created life and mind from carbon and proteins. Could it have happened that their organization or processes were altered by an event or condition independent of anything in their history, hence a situation—an electrical storm, heat, or pressure—to which life or mind was the unpredicted response?

Predictions' failures can be reformulated as a question about laws, rather than causes: can we predict values for dependent variables signifying effects, if there are values for their conditions? That seems unproblematic because of correlations that facilitate prediction by linking causes to perceived effects: genes to red hair. Yet correlations are not the generative laws required to warrant inferences from effects to their determining causes. (Those are inferences available to an omniscient god; it knows what color hair will be by seeing how genes control metabolic processes.) We know very few such laws as things rise through the trajectory from molecules to cells, bodies, and beyond. Hard determinists aren't deterred because their postulate is an ambitious philosophic idea. They gamble that science will confirm the symmetry of explanation and prediction by discovering conditions sufficient to determine the existence and character of all phenomena from the beginning of time: there will be reliable inferences from carefully specified effects to the lineage of their sufficient causes. Deliberation and choice are conceits if this proves true, though confirming evidence is scarce because complexity obscures the intermediate processes responsible for those effects.

7. Cause or Capacity

Hard determinism might claim an easy success with an argument no one known to me has proposed. Consider that the material possibility for every current property or state of affairs was anticipated in the capacities of nature's original conditions: they could combine or transform in ways that would eventuate in life and mind. Incapacity at our origins would have entailed the non-existence in our time of properties and powers everywhere apparent. Does this entail that current states of affairs trace a straight and determined though obscure and complex trajectory from those original conditions?

That inference exploits an ambiguity in the relation of cause and capacity: namely, the mistaken idea that capacities are self-actuating energies that impel the changes perceived as causal. But that is a *non sequitur*. Knives have sharp edges enabling them to cut, dig, or spread paint. Capacities for all these effects are static until an agent supplies energy and motion while using the knife to do one or another. For capacities enable effects without themselves being their efficient causes. Specific changes in nature's original conditions—probably capacitated for alternate evolutions—likely occurred when contingencies of assembly, pressure, or flow produced stirrings—causes—that eventuated as nature evolved. Hard determinism bets on the combination of causes and capacities, not on the idea that nature is the evolutionary effect of an original set of self-actuating capacities. The capacities anticipated various outcomes; causes explain the subset we have.

8. Leibniz or Laplace

No reference to ancient times is required if the whole resembles a jigsaw puzzle, every piece shaped to mesh directly with neighbors and mediately with the rest. Autonomy would be altogether suppressed were it true, as Leibniz claimed, that nature is pervaded by internal relations: everything calibrated to everything else.[14] This could be construed in either of two ways. Things were, at one time, so packed together that all were marked in ways that abide since their separation as distinct causal lines. How many of nature's features are marked in this way—all, many, or a few—if this is so? Or nature remains a dynamic whole: everything is perpetually affected, directly or mediately, by every other. This second alternative is a version of universal internal relations. It, too, allows of alternate readings. One closer to Leibniz

---

14 G. W. V. Leibniz, *Monadology and Other Philosophical Essays*, trans. Paul Schrecker and Anne Martin Schrecker (Indianapolis: Bobbs-Merrill, 1965), para. 39, p. 154.

would short-circuit the emphasis on origins, causes, and laws because time and converging causal streams would be incidental to the global—holistic—entanglement of a complex idea. God sees its simplicity, as we do not. The other would explain entanglement as the effect of global causal relations such that every thing is both cause and effect of every other, whether directly or indirectly. (We are affected indirectly by galaxies that expired before the formation of our galaxy.) Things considered discrete should be reconstrued, were this true, as phases or portions of the complex whole. So, things and their perceivers would be reconceived as complexes of mutually determining qualities: the hand as seen. Much would be unknown to people having a limited view of the whole, though situations yet to occur would resonate already in those current: the future, as much as the past or present, would be settled by universal reciprocal determination.

Is either of these ontologies—the colliding streams of hard determinism or a global system of internal relations—likely to be true? Credit both ideas with the assumption that nature experienced explosive inflation after beginning as a small, dense, and dynamic plenum where every point was affected directly or indirectly by every other. But they diverge: hard determinism supposes that nature evolved, differentiating itself into separate causal streams that cross or collide. Every current entity or state of affairs has, on this telling, a dense history of converging causal lineages: parents, grandparents, and great-grandparents. It may be true that all humans share a single great-grandmother, yet we have different grandparents, and blood lines that separated eons ago. The Leibnizian story reads this history differently: we assume naively that the relation of a percept to its cause is unproblematically causal, though the Leibnizian account avers that *causal* and *convergent* are the wrong words for describing it. Attention and perspective falsely project separations, then things, causes, and causal streams into the weave of qualitative differences. These ideas play out in different ways when used to interpret simple examples: is it Laplacian or Leibnizian when Jack and Jill meet? Laplace would construe their meeting as the converging of mutually independent causal lines. Leibniz would have said that the lines were never independent: Jack and Jill needn't discover one another (though mutual awareness dawns), because they are already linked.

Now consider what difference these views make in the context of disputes about free will. Imagine an able but distracted driver as he moves safely through traffic, until a moose bounds onto the road in front of him. Too late to brake, he swerves and misses it. Spinning the wheel required the volition commanded by nerves and muscles; its proximate condition was the flexible response acquired by years of driving. Was there also a longer causal history, perhaps one originating before the Punic Wars? Maybe, but why speculate unverifiably when nothing in history is relevant to the details of his situation? The sufficient cause was a current perception that disrupted the driver's evolving gestalt. His response, a complex of will and action too fast for deliberation, was provoked by the disruption. His causal history prepared him for driving and even for responding to emergencies, but that experience wasn't sufficient in itself to cause the saving swerve. Its cause is well-described as existential: the driver didn't swerve because impelled by his history, he swerved to avoid the moose.

There are two other ways to interpret this situation, both inimical to free will. One is congenial to Leibniz; another favors hard determinism. The interpretation is Leibnizian when the relation of the driver's percept to the moose is wrongly construed as causal. We mistakenly speak of a causal relationship—the moose percept caused by seeing the moose—when there is only the eternal but contingent coupling of a percept and its referent. Ideas cohere in God's mind, though none is a free-standing thing, and no correlate is cause of another. God is the only substance; he thinks all his ideas at once, and he is their only cause. This persuasion is raffish but odd. Holism and entanglement seem entailed by the idea that the cosmos began as a superheated plasma before fracturing into myriad shards, each having a character somewhat independent of others. Yet every number in most telephone directories is independent of the rest: each could be changed without altering others. This degree of independence is characteristic throughout nature: causal lines often cross or join to create autonomous strands, but many strands never cross. God may know the essential coherence of the Leibnizian world, no detail falsely abstracted from the whole, but we do not.

Is hard determinism more compelling? It isn't, because of a strangely Leibnizian impulse within it. Does the look of a bounding moose appear to the driver because he is linked to the moose within the holist weave?

Does each confront the other at the moment when their entanglement has ripened, or because their independent causal lines have converged? There is urgency to the dialectic because the Leibnizian solution entails a tighter determinism: there is no margin for indeterminism if every qualification is perpetually determined by its place within a plenum where the existence and character of everything is a function of all the rest. For suppose that the moose runs in front of his car while the driver's independent causal lineage generates the impression of a moth, not a moose. The causal streams don't converge, with this effect: the driver discounts the perceptual evidence and doesn't swerve. Does he hit the moose? He does not, because swerving is the contemporary effect of seeing the moose, a situation in which histories converge, not an effect immanent in either causal line.

Why is hard determinism a closet version of Leibnizian internal relations? Because hard determinism needs the Leibnizian thesis to avert having to concede that swerving has only this encounter, not history, to explain it. Seeing the moose is incidental if seeming to see a moth or mouse would have had the same effect: he swerves in each of these situations. See these determinists as they exploit Leibniz's internal relations without endorsing his theism: let every choice and action be explained by the global holism, the global determinism created by nature's cohesive (holistic) evolution from its original conditions.

These implications are closer to home if we imagine a conversation between two strangers, one asking directions, the other imagining simple answers. Hard determinists hear the first question—"Where am I"?—as an effect generated by the speaker's causal lineage. But what of the second speaker's response: "Corner of State and Madison, Chicago." Is that an effect of his causal history, or is it the effect of that history coupled to this alien because unanticipated request coming from an unrelated lineage? We have these three interpretations: *i*. The Leibnizian isn't surprised by the query or its response because, he believes, everything is implicated in everything else. *ii*. The hard determinist is embarrassed: he can't explain why independent causal histories are aligned such that the response to every question is an appropriate answer. You ask for salt, and I pass it. Is there a pre-established harmony, so that independent causal lines never formed: everything was and is connected to everything else? *iii*. Or is it true that the two speakers do stand within lineages that were independent until this moment, when a speaker freely responds to another's surprising question with an appropriate answer? He speaks from within his lineage (he knows where he is), though his response is provoked by a question having no precedent within his history.

Is everything decided, as Leibniz and Laplace tell us, by internal relations or long ago by natural laws and original conditions? We often devote considerable time and energy to making things happen, but we could trouble less if reality is designed to harmonize questions with answers, needs with resources. But aren't there disappointments, and worse? Yes, but they can be ignored at moments when reality has been organized, from its inception, to reward us. No wonder people speculate that a benign Leibnizian deity oversees us. But look away: efficacy also has this other explanation. The bread I buy is the one I ordered. The driver swerves because his vision is reliable: seeing the moose, he averts an accident.

9. "Things Are Not Up to Us."

What are the implications of Van Inwagen's skeptical précis? What is autonomy—self-regulation, self-direction—when everything has causes affecting all it is and does? Is there freedom to choose one's direction when choice seems foreclosed by the myriad causes shaping antecedents, hence oneself? Autonomy is never more than notional, if this is so. Nor is the experience of volition more than a conscious tic if choices and actions are determined by ancestral causal conditions. Hard determinism is nevertheless faulty because its version of history—cosmic or human—is simplistic. Consider its principal claims: *i.* Locating humans within long causal chains entails that personal choices are predetermined. For every current affair is the most recent in a possibly infinite succession of events. This is the causal tide, the array of histories generated, sustained, or amended by successive efficient causes. *ii.* There is nothing arbitrary or speculative in this thesis because causal trajectories satisfy or embody deterministic natural laws. Nothing happens by chance; every outcome is foreshadowed. All would be foreseen by an omniscient god. Here are some responses:

9i. The causal tide: Hard determinism avers that every current change is the last in a history that extends from time immemorial (the time of the Big Bang or before) to the present: a garrulous crow is the current event in a lineage that may have no beginning or end. There are myriad histories, each integrated within the tapestry of cosmic time. But nature's content has two principal constituents. One is implied by energy's conservation: none is lost or created. The other, its complement, is the sequence of forms—the qualitative effects—produced when matters are altered or transformed by their interaction. You bake cakes, I brew coffee: two fractions of the total energy cache. Energy isn't exchanged without interacting causes, but the qualities of causes and effects are contingencies relative to the stable pool of energy.

Imagine that energy is stripped of qualities, exposing energy raw: no longer apples or pears, just the energy they embody. This distinction is consequential, though it implies an ambiguity: how loosely are these two—energy and its expressions—connected? Should we affirm that energy is the material reality while its expressions are dreamlike phenomena, perhaps fantasies of a kind projected onto the ambient world as we think about or imagine it? That would be a retelling of Plato's cave allegory: people imagining stable entities or processes as they strain to make sense of shadows on the cave walls.[15] Only the presumed reality—energy, rather than Forms—would be different. This implication is unintended because it reduces nature to a disembodied surd or, as in Plato's metaphor, a story confirmed merely by repeating it. The alternative avers that energy's relation to its expressions is that of identity. The expressions are protean, their measures are diverse, though energy retains its essential character as nature's way of creating stability or effecting change. Accordingly, every energy exchange—every causal relationship—bundles and transfers energy in a specific qualitative form: knives cut as spoons do not.

Distinguishing the finite energy pool from qualitative effects is tantalizing because it suggests a possible response to hard determinists. The energy pool remains intact—it courses through every change—though qualities have no effect on subsequent events if they are extinguished before later effects have occurred, or if emergent phenomena have powers and effects that displace their antecedents. This distinction—energy versus its contingent expressions—is ignored when

---

15 Plato, *Republic, Collected Dialogues*, eds. Edith Hamilton and Huntington Cairns (New York: Pantheon, 1961), 514a-517e, pp. 747–50.

determinism supposes that nature is a continuous surge from its origin. Is the tide sometimes interrupted—its effects superseded—by jumps in the qualitative record? Are there barriers that shield later events from the qualities or dispositions of some antecedents?

There are four points to consider: *ia*. the alleged weave of quality-preserving causes versus qualitative breaks in the causal chain; *ib*. ambiguities in the idea of a causal tide; *ic*. the relative independence of causal strands; and *id*. causal history versus the priority of current situations. A fifth point—emergence—requires a separate, subsequent entry.

9ia. Is nature a continuous weave of quality-preserving causes? Every qualitative change is energized by our world's stable pool of energy: energy is often conserved as a specific quality or complex: dinosaurs reproduced their kind for eons. This result satisfies hard determinism, though it doesn't follow that every qualitative change is conserved to affect its successors or that there is qualitative continuity in lines of natural succession. Punctuated equilibrium is the thesis that evolution makes jumps. Genetic sports enable new functions and behavior because of altered bodily structures: flight or speech, for example.

There are sufficient conditions (molecular and environmental) for the altered structures, hence sufficient conditions for the altered behavior, though the grunts of a preceding generation are not a sufficient condition for whatever is articulate in the speech of its successors.

9ib. Ambiguities in the idea of a causal tide: There is ambiguity when the alleged flow of causes and effects is thought to imply that every change presupposes the collaboration of all its antecedents, though antecedents are partitioned: an effect is caused by some but not by most others. The metaphor is also ambiguous in these other ways. It obscures the different weights of causes that are proximate or remote, necessary or sufficient. It ignores discontinuities, causes that perish because they are unsustainable in themselves or unsustainable because of inimical circumstances (depleted resources or competitors). Some events can't have a direct effect on successors because exterminations, wars, or depressions preclude later effects by annulling them, or because they are too remote to affect the light cones of others. Most things, events, or forces come and go with no permanent grip on reality, though some (gravity and DNA) are enduring causes of subsequent effects. Birds are less secure: they derive from dinosaurs, though dodos have no heirs.

Nature's historian resembles a knitter reconstructing a garment chewed by moths: find and tie the severed strands. Nature, too, is more ragged than we imply when invoking the idea of its continuous weave. We acknowledge the half-truth but defend against its exaggeration: yes, to energy flow and conservation; no, to the steady continuity of qualitative change.

9ic. Mutually independent causal strands: It is essential to my argument for free will that causal strands are, for the most part, mutually independent. The unfamiliarity of people meeting for the first time exemplifies situations in which previous history leaves both parties unprepared for their encounter, hence unable to make informed choices about what to say or do. The possibility of having no information about one's prospective circumstances may be challenged on the slender basis that the independence—hence unfamiliarity—of situations-to-come is implausible when every causal lineage embodies myriad cross-stitches. Could we know (remember or anticipate) more than we think we do? Or does history create a weave so dense that trying to recover buried strands would defeat the most scrupulous search for evidence, much of it indecipherable or destroyed? Every human is a remote cousin, yet one often meets people with whom one shares no identifiable ancestor.

9id. Causal history versus the priority of current situations: Where muscle control activates or inhibits movement, raising and turning a hand seems an unproblematic example of free will. Hard determinists prefer this other surmise: every event is the successor to ancient causes. But is that so? Consider my gesture: I'm imitating someone who's teaching me the hand signals used as insults by members of his tribe. I've learned the gesture because of a chance meeting at a local bar, not because this effect has sufficient conditions in my causal history. Here, as often, a new or surprising situation provokes a response enabled by emergent powers: thought, perception, memory, or imagination is challenged in a way having no antecedent in one's experience.

Hard determinism implies that history is the unspooling of original causes as they shape subsequent history. Unforeseen complexities create surprises, but their essential ingredients and conditions (energy and the laws of motion) were there from the start. This part of their surmise is plausible and likely true, though it misses two things: *idi*. the difference between efficient and formal cause; and *idii*, responses to situations that are unanticipated by the agents' causal histories (Jack and Jill).

9idi. Efficient and formal causes: Suppose history is the transformation of primordial factors—energy and spacetime—present at the hypothesized start when geometry and topology prescribed limits to nature's evolution. Efficient causes exhibit the energy driving qualitative change and changes of motion. Particles were formed by imbalances—a formal cause—in the original energic broth. Later, stabilized particles emerged as organized ensembles within regions of greater size: molecules and weather, for example. Every formal cause frames its circumstances; each is a complex, a configuration that establishes limits on actions or changes appropriate or possible within it.

History preserves the record of efficient causes in the respect that their portion of energy is conserved. Formal causes are less secure because they include configurations or assemblies that are often ephemeral: people standing in line or waiting for a bus. A presiding god would see both factors: energy and its configurations. Energy's flow would seem lawful, perhaps necessary in a parochial sense because native to this possible world (not necessary universally, because energy may behave differently in other possible worlds). The god would also observe formal causes: some are inconsequential; others constrain the formation of atoms or molecules, or the behavior of people working together. Much else would be less assured: there might be no discernible design, for example, in the evolution of public enthusiasms or city clutter.

Formal cause is critical to situations where choice flourishes (for reasons considered below) because situations having the same constituents are distinguished by the formal causes that organize them. So, teams use the same players in different configurations; they organize a defense for one opponent using a different configuration to defend against another. Now consider an opposing offense: imagine it's surprised by the other's defense, until it sees and acts on opportunities neither had anticipated. This is the reality of teams testing one another in the early stages of a game, if each lines up in ways the other hadn't anticipated.

9idii. Unanticipated *situations*: Situations are structured ensembles: formal causes organize their quantitative and qualitative features. Most come and go while leaving no trace, because of having no efficacy or stability as wholes: a basket of laundry, dishes in the sink. Solutions are familiar; habits, rules, or practices direct our responses. But some occasions are baffling; with no useful memory or habit to prepare us, we improvise or react. Imagine walking on a remote mountain trail during a storm. Rain intensifies; I run for cover as lightning crackles above. Yes, I've been caught in the rain before, though never out here where birds cower and light flashes all around. There will be habits on which to rely if something like this happens again, but now—and for every novel situation—history is suggestive but not determining.

Hard determinists might speculate that situations are disguised by their apparent novelty, though recognized all the while: we don't recall having encountered them before, though we know what to do because they're familiar. Or the agent is truly unprepared, though his or her preparation is irrelevant because fate (converging causal streams) have determined the outcome. Placid as a Venus's flytrap, situations seem inert until we excite predetermined effects by engaging them. But is it plausible that circumstances, so blandly passive to inspection, impel responses we can't inhibit? Imagine entering a building where buzzers are the point of entry for the many apartments. How do I decide which to press? The buzzers are indifferent; ring any one, the choice is mine. Having no information appropriate to an informed choice, I close my eyes, reach forward, and press the buzzer closest to hand. What happens next: whom do I meet; what shall I do? Could an omniscient god advise me?

Hard determinists tell a reassuring story: a car moving at reasonable speed in a straight line—a time slice in one lineage—is struck by a meteorite from another. The convergence of these histories seems accidental, though their intersection was prefigured. Does it follow that every situation develops as trajectories collide? All choices have conditions sufficient to determine them, but choice's determinants include values, aims, and information about a situation's qualitative features, more rarely information about the lineage of its conditioning antecedents. Jack and Jill's marriage has emergent effects that neither anticipates. Often befuddled, they navigate current situations because of converging values and aims, not because of ancient solutions.

9ii. Natural laws: Hard determinism appeals to "natural laws," though law's status is moot. Very little in modern or contemporary philosophy challenges the belief that natural normativity is a myth exposed and dispatched by Hume's phenomenalist analysis of causation,[16] and his remark that *is* doesn't entail *ought*.[17] Theorists who reduce causality to regularity deplore the naiveté of thinkers still provoked by observing that the offspring of mice are mice, not rabbits. Humeans suppose that the regularity of this sequence is the whole content of the law explaining it, though regularity is the fact needing explanation, not the norm explaining it. That reason is DNA, a cause both formal and efficient.

Sympathetic to the Aristotelian idea that natural laws exist in things they control and to Descartes' surmise that the normativity of kinds (qualitative differences Aristotle described as *substantial forms*[18]) is founded in the geometry of space,[19] I suggest that there are natural laws of two sorts. Those controlling the evolution of causal processes are generative laws that limit energy exchange: fires caused by striking matches. Laws of the other sort establish the geometrical configurations available to causal processes; principles of least energy (shortest paths) are presumably founded in their trajectories. Spacetime is the elemental substance transformed when laws of the two sorts converge as geometrized laws of motion. So, one construction rule creates circles by bending lines; another produces triangles by joining line segments. Materiality complicates these recipes as genes direct the assembly of proteins.

This is a strongly necessitarian view of natural laws. Does it justify the hard determinist claim that all causes pertinent to today's choices have ancestries going back to the beginning of time? Does it validate Laplace's formula?

> We may regard the present state of the universe as the effect of its past and the cause of its future. An intellect which at a certain moment would know all forces that set nature in motion, and all positions of all items of which nature is composed, if this intellect were also vast enough to submit these data to analysis, it would embrace in a single formula the

---

16 Hume, *A Treatise of Human Nature*, pp. 12–13.
17 Ibid., p. 469.
18 Aristotle, *Metaphysics*, 1041a7–1041b32, pp. 810–11.
19 See René Descartes, *The Geometry of René Descartes*, trans. David Eugene Smith and Marcia L. Latham (New York: Dover, 1954).

movements of the greatest bodies of the universe and those of the tiniest atom; for such an intellect nothing would be uncertain and the future just like the past would be present before its eyes.[20]

No natural change could stray from the specific determinations permitted by law; everything that is was predictable from the start, given the lawful evolution of original conditions. Where each of a tree's limbs bend or twist in particular ways, there is a law that can, in principle, explain its formation.

Put aside doubts about the strict determinism of natural laws. Notice instead that this formulation ignores an apparent qualification: the configuration of this tree's limbs differs from that of trees nearby, though all are subject to the same laws. This is true of nature more generally: small sets of laws—whether generative or formal—apply across all of nature's myriad domains and differences; any variation that satisfies them is tolerated. Explicating universal determinism by citing natural laws is, therefore, less decisive than it seems. Supplement them by citing the original conditions (Laplace's "all positions of all items") whose evolution was and is controlled by laws.

Yet determinism, however well founded, is itself the enabler of deviations in nature's evolution. They occur because of capacities that first evolved with the emergence of living things. Those were organisms whose cell walls created protected interior spaces. Filtering nutrients and information while defending them from intruders, these spaces enabled simple organisms to inhibit responses while surveying their circumstances. Prioritizing their interests, they evolved mechanisms for satisfying their interests in safety, food, or sex. Hard determinism was breached, because those primitive choices expressed an agent's appraisal of its situation: which needs were more likely to be satisfied, given its circumstances? That appraisals and choices were primitive is assumed; yet they evolved as defenses were fortified and flexible responses were refined. This was practical freedom in its earliest expressions. Why believe that this inference is correct? Because such creatures survived to reproduce and evolve; because fossils confirm their evolution; and because the brains in our bony skulls are principal

---

20 Pierre Simon Laplace, *An Essay on Probabilities*, trans. F. W. Truscott and F. L. Emory (New York: Dover, 1951), p. 4.

evidence that the surmise is true. This is determinism as it generated inhibition, deliberation, and choice.

Hard determinism presents itself as impregnable: every event is powered by energies embodied by its antecedents. Each is a moment in a continuous swathe, a tapestry of histories multiply cross-stitched, all constrained in every detail by natural laws. Yet we hesitate, because an observing god would acknowledge ruptured stabilities, expired causal strands, and this evolutionary sport.

10. Emergent Wholes, Their Properties and Powers

Hard determinism ignores emergents and their causal roles. A triangle's properties emerge when its line segments are connected. Systems emerge—molecules from atoms, teams from their players—when reciprocal causal relations bind their parts. This is a representation of emergence as it starts with elementary particles and rises to complex systems:

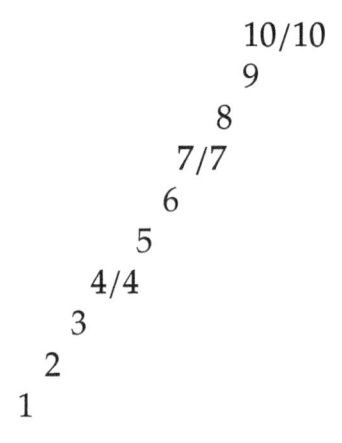

```
                        10/10
                         9
                        8
                       7/7
                      6
                     5
                    4/4
                   3
                  2
                 1
```

Figure 3: The emergence of complexity, with stability at 4, 7, and 10.

Suppose each number of this series signifies phenomena of increasing complexity: 1=particles; 2=atoms; 3=molecules; 4=cells; 5=tissues; 6=organs; 7=animal (human) bodies; 8=families; 9=villages or tribes; 10=cities or states. The trajectory stabilizes at points 4, 7, and 10 because they signify entities able to obtain and stock energy sufficient to maintain themselves. Everything short of these points falls back to the next lower stable order for want of that capacity.

Laws having application at the early orders may be strongly deterministic because spacetime geometry constrains bonding and the formation of atoms and molecules. This may still be true at level 4, though regularities at levels 7 and 10 are disrupted by the diversity and complexity of things whose formation they regulate: social development is variable; communities have distinct histories, forms, and resources. They evolve in different ways. But *variable* doesn't mean *indeterminate*: triangles formed by joining three line segments, like tunes created by joining five notes, are determinate. Every such structure has a decided character because the properties and relations of its constituents are determinate. Subsequent changes or elaborations may evolve in various ways, but each of them will also be determinate. An orchestra joins many musicians in an ensemble capable of playing many sorts of music, though all produce music of determinate tones and rhythms by playing in determinate ways. Every brain is a system of many neurons, each having a specific character and function while linked in specific ways to others. Brains are adaptable and responsive to evolving circumstances; they are sometimes underdetermined because uneducated or unmotivated, but they are never undetermined. What they will do is nevertheless determinable because reasons and collateral—mutually independent—causes decide what their subsequent determinations (the modifications of previous determinations) shall be. Free will is enabled by the structural features of some living things, as argued below; it doesn't supervene as a bloom lacking conditions sufficient to produce or explain it.

Emergence is critical to free will in two respects: *i.* Living things are monadic; their walled interiors are spaces that buffer intrusions; *ii.* Abilities that evolve within these spaces are strategies for successful responses to internal and external challenges. These are powers for deliberation, judgment, and choice, hence for reasons that function as causes. They vindicate the idea that free will is a biological adaptation, not a mysterious power that alters the causal tide from a position external to it.

10i. Living things are monadic: Living things are complex systems having an inside devoted to life-sustaining processes, and an outside that buffers relations to other things. The outside is a barrier to intrusions and an entrée to information about the entity's circumstances. The inside is a protected space where agents deliberate and choose when they've acquired faculties and strategies for coping with external challenges and opportunities: what to do, when to flee.

10ii. Reasons as causes: We often deviate from a lineage of antecedent causes when deliberation affords reasons for choice and action. These are two things: the emergent power for interrupting—redirecting—the stream of causes, and one's reasons for intervening. Reasons are justifiers: given circumstances and values, they warrant choice and action appropriate to an aim. Justifiers are odd because they needn't cite actual states of affairs. I may keep my closets tidy because the ghosts living there don't like disorder. Though too casual a regard for truth isn't sustainable: sympathy and imagination embellish the margins, but truth—reality testing—is the control that makes choice viable. Justification requires it; we align ourselves with things as they are, or as we imagine they are. Reasons may be commanding because meaningful (my god requires it); because they express interests or needs (we're cold); or because they require that one inhibit choice and action out of concern for others. Many reasons are traditional, but some are contemporary and situational: take an umbrella, it's raining.

10iii. Free will reconstrued: Will is a biological adaptation to external circumstances, a power acquired under the protection of the internal spaces created when monadic living things emerged. The will to live is an impelling drive rooted in life itself, a steady backdrop to the choice of particular aims: coffee or tea, walk or ride. Why call willing *free,* falsely implying that it's unconditioned? Because will is exempt, to a degree, within these spaces from determination by other things, considerations, or processes in or outside them. This doesn't imply a shortage of conditions—including reasons—sufficient to provoke it.

Kant supposed that free will sets action's trajectory from outside the tide of material conditions,[21] but there is an alternative: choice and action redirect the tide without escaping it. We deliberate within the tide, hesitating but never leaving it. Preventing a rout saves lives or careers: we don't step out of history when changing its direction.

---

21 Immanuel Kant, *Groundwork of the Metaphysics of Morals*, trans. Mary Gregor (Cambridge: Cambridge University Press, 1997), p. 52.

11. Character/Sensibility

Character, sensibility, and *personality* name different aspects of the structure giving autonomy its force and coherence. Character is a set of stabilizing habits and attitudes. Sensibility is resonance. Personality, style and mien, is the shallower term of this triad; I ignore it.

Character is agency's keel: it comprises instincts, inclinations, and aims. All are educated in the style of one's society, while embodied as reciprocally regulating habits; liking noise, I don't exceed the tolerance of neighbors who don't like it as much. Sensibility begins as innate irritability before acquiring form as a responsive weave of information, tastes, and sentiments. It looks two ways: we learn from others; but incorporate their effects as an array of distinguishing tastes, desires, and vulnerabilities. Hard determinists evoke the energic tide as if every next change has no resources for ignoring or opposing its antecedents. But sensibility blocks inputs opposed by one's aims or tastes: fashionistas sometimes resist new styles.

Add situations and consider this obstacle to hard determinism. Sensibilities address situations by way of *gestalts*. These are a sensibility's windows into the ambient world; like eyeglasses that enable sight, gestalts direct our search for features pertinent to our intentions and attitudes. All are holistic; each has a fore- and background that projects the thinker's aims or anxieties onto the map of his or her circumstances. Each is a formal cause: an interpretation, hypothesis, or plan. Configuration dominates the thinking of architects, painters, and photographers; scientists and novelists hypothesize or interpret. Plans prepare us for practical life; framing a situation, they direct our interventions by sequencing actions and expected responses in ways relevant to our aims. Frustration measures the discrepancy between the values or objectives expressed by a gestalt and the effects accruing as it provokes an action; equilibrium is established when action's effects satisfy the interests prefigured, or when a new gestalt, better adapted to circumstances, displaces the one before.

Orientation is usually steady; gestalts are conserved when aims and circumstances are stable. But mind would be regularly disoriented if action were forever encumbered by gestalts superseded by altered circumstances, understandings, or desires. That doesn't happen, because gestalts are regularly revised or replaced. This is consequential for the determinist argument because it implies that evidence for bits of one's past is lost. Why? Because the gestalt is an orientation, a form; one may remember some or all its constituent details, but not the way they're integrated: not the gestalt. Its effect on choice and action, however significant, may terminate without intrapsychic evidence of its role: I don't recall how I saw things, or why. Hard determinists may reply that every gestalt has effects on psychic memory that abide, buried but real. But this is a surmise: sometimes true and verifiable, it is often unverified and unverifiable. Something comparable happens on large scales when stars or debris sucked into black holes escape as radiation: information about the material ingested is not (it seems) recoverable from escaping energy. The cycle from birth to death has an equivalent effect: dust to dust when most of the middle is lost.

Does the brain refresh itself during sleep, purging the previous day's business? Not always: people are often dominated by the same concerns for days or more. Effective accommodation to changing conditions is, however, essential to well-being: we may edit or replace outdated gestalts every few moments when action requires that we clear outdated information or expectations from thought or perception. For we're often surprised by evolving situations. Needing to adapt, wanting to secure ourselves while controlling them, we adjust our ways of perceiving the near-world. That purge rebukes hard determinism: the past cannot determine all we do because we eliminate some part of our information about it when confronting altered circumstances.[22]

Imagine causal strands linked by partners newly acquainted. Is their convergence anchored in the remote past, rather than a recent chance encounter? Hard determinism fails this test for three reasons pertinent to sensibility:

11i. Hard determinism alleges that everything current is the latter-day effect of natural laws as they regulate the transformation of original conditions. But is that so? Jack and Jill met at a boxing match where she was one of the fighters, and he was an usher. They stayed in touch after

---

22 Shuntaro Izawa et al., "REM sleep–active MCH neurons are involved in forgetting hippocampus-dependent memories," *Science* 365:6459 (2019), 1308–13, https://www.doi.org/10.1126/science.aax9238

learning that both raise bats. This is too many accidents for any of nature's laws. What explains their affinity? Sensibility, not law. Relationships are situational; they're sustained by reciprocity, passion, and the negative feedback that quashes arguments, not by laws and original conditions.

11ii. Sensibility is often a barrier to the effects of its antecedent formations. Consider the athlete traded from one team to another. His old team values ingenuity—players take chances—the new one emphasizes teamwork. He navigates the difference by suppressing what he learned from his former team while acquiring the discipline of the new one. Teams, jobs, or marriages: sensibilities respond to altered circumstances.

11iii. Novel situations provoke ingenuity. A news story, several years ago, described a man who saved his life when pinned under a rock by cutting off his arm. No historical narrative explains his courage; what law determined it?

Hard determinism founders when a novel situation is coupled to a sensibility of moderate complexity: there will be effects, relevant laws will be satisfied, but four contingencies make the character of those effects uncertain: *i.* The occasional instability of a sensibility's values makes decision unstable: am I sure that I like this? *ii.* The shifting pressures of competing inclinations (chocolate or a diet pill) makes aims inconsistent and planning ineffective: I thought I wanted this result though having it, I regret wanting it. *iii.* Situations evolve, often unpredictably, because of the material conditions engaged (credit markets, weather), not because of apposite laws or the agents addressing them. *iv.* Planning is frustrated when we lack information about a situation's evolution under the force of our actions.

There is often a prevailing direction to a situation's evolution, though drift is fixed by material conditions, not only by natural laws. Laplace might propose that we identify the laws controlling a situation's development as we engage it, but generational and formal laws tolerate innumerable variations. Memory and imagination are alternate determinants: they collaborate as mind tracks material changes by reformulating its gestalts. This sometimes works, though the novelty or complexity provoked by crossing causal strands is often bewildering.

12. Initiative

Choice is usually contextualized; it expresses an agent's history, perspective, and interests when focused by a current situation. Focus is unproblematic when circumstances are accurately represented by the gestalts directing choice and action: wanting a shirt, I go to the closet where they hang. We improvise when gestalts falter because of frustration triggered by error, or because of confused expectations provoked by conflicted aims. There are three plausible strategies: an inquiry that gathers better information about one's situation; clarified aims; or an interpretation that makes conflict seem coherent. The following is a sample test of hard determinism.

Earth is generous when the first spaceship to Mars discovers a thriving musical culture. The best of Martian composers is puzzled when these visitors give him a piano. He tinkers for weeks before beginning to write duets for piano and local frogs. The music is odd to human ears, but all call it beautiful. Martian history doesn't explain this result; Earth's history all the less. Imagination is the more likely cause: something productive happens in the space where it reconciles the gap between old and new. Starting with available information, rules, and techniques, one analogizes, extrapolates, or generalizes until understanding affords a solution. Whether the context is practical or artistic, this is the power that fills the space.

Hard determinists will respond that originality isn't less determined for our failure to understand it. That is true, but incidental because the question is different: how to understand solutions generated when there is no technique or well of information appropriate to solving them. Determinists may surmise that there were instruments like pianos in Martian culture, though we postulate that there were no useful analogues to our keyboards in its history. They weren't required in the current situation because there as here, inquiry and experiment are sometimes the cure for incomprehension. Contributing the piano exemplifies Mill's method of difference: add something new, then get an original effect by exploiting the freedom to innovate.[23]

Now limit attention to Earth and consider the freedom of people responding to local circumstances. Consider the man deliberating

---

23 John Stuart Mill, *A System of Logic*, Volume 1 (London: HardPress, 2016), pp. 450–63.

when caught in the rain: is it heavy or light; how far is he going; is his coat water repellent? Experience helps when deciding what to do, but judgment and his gestalt are sensitive to circumstances. Having decided to continue without an umbrella, suddenly hearing wind and the crack of thunder, feeling a deluge as the skies open, he changes his mind. His decision is altered by shock, fear, and heavy rain, not by daydreams or the history of his ancestors. Could he have decided otherwise? Given the prospect of a life-changing reward, a treasure just ahead, he would have pursued it. But that wasn't a live option in his perception of the moment; when all his choices were dim or worse, he ran for shelter. Hard determinists are unconvinced: here on Earth, where all the energies of the past and all their effects are inventoried, nothing happens that isn't foreshadowed. But is that so? Our stroller is often caught in storms he ignores when told of bullion free for the taking behind the tree ahead. Why not infer that he would have ignored this threat, too, but for the intimation that this storm might be deadly? Why be surprised, given his fear, that his response was different? This is smart autonomy: the agent who responds appropriately when registering his circumstances.

Hard determinists regard "autonomy" as a temporary *cul de sac* formed by antecedent causes, then reabsorbed by the tide. But this is faulty in several ways: *i.* It ignores the modular character of systems that are effectively self-sustaining, given supportive circumstances. *ii.* It ignores the relative independence of causal strands. *iii.* It assumes that circumstances always impose themselves upon us, though conditions often tolerate alternate responses: chocolate, strawberry, or vanilla. *iv.* It ignores ingenuity, and the interface where established skills meet unfamiliar situations. This is the dialectic that prevents human history from perpetually recycling the same routines. Having estimated where we are, we improvise, test the result, revise, then test again.

Were Google and Facebook written in Tarot cards those many eons ago? Not quite: they were imaginative extrapolations from an established base, including telephones and the internet. Other issues—consciousness and dark matter—require innovations of a different sort. Solutions will come when imagination structures understanding in ways that are currently unforeseen and maybe unanticipated.

13. Productive Imagination

Gestalts make practical situations intelligible: one isn't surprised when served with chopsticks in a Chinese restaurant. Their role in art is different: there, gestalts are ideas directing the organization of an art's figures or words. History is respected, but innovation is prized. Materials are an art's substance; like bricks or notes, they precede it. But there is no organizational principle, no formal cause until the artist imagines it. Listen to the Beatles' "Sgt. Pepper's Lonely Hearts Club Band," then consider that George Martin, its producer, was the principal source of its format. Its raffish qualities had precursors in English music halls but there was no line of ancient conditions responsible for Martin's design; the whole he created exceeded its parts and antecedents. Laugier's forest hut[24] prefigures the rule exemplified in every house, but is there a rule discernible in every novel, sonata, or painting? Understanding is a faculty of rules, but imagination is a faculty that creates unexpected results when it plays with old rules or invents new ones. Where every artist or thinker has access to the same materials, imagination creates wholes that stand apart from their antecedents. Originality has antecedents but no history: Haydn preceded Mozart, but Mozart was different from Haydn.

Finished work inspires others to formulate rules for creating similar wholes, be it music or design, by organizing an art's materials. The rules are a style adaptable by artists less sure of themselves, however subtle. Each vogue has a history: an original master and adherents, then a diminished old age when acclaim has drained a style's vitality. What distinguishes great artists from stylists? Principally, ideas, judgment, initiative, and wit. Do artists of either sort work freely? Most are slow to answer: imagination (rules and materials) direct him or her; the artist is its instrument. But these aren't the artists of Plato's *Apology*, poets inspired by the gods though unable to explain the meaning of their poems. Great artists discriminate: every brush stroke is a choice, one has said. What justifies the inference that imagination can never do more than regurgitate its causes?

---

24 See Marc-Antoine Laugier, *Essay on Architecture* (London: HardPress, 2013).

14. Consciousness

How much do we know of will by way of consciousness; what part is unconscious? Four distinctions are fundamental. We may be: *i.* unconscious after a blow to the head, processing no perceptual information, performing no cognitive activity; *ii.* unconscious in the respect that we perform effectively without conscious attention to the activity, or to obstacles to which we respond effectively (driving successfully while preoccupied); *iii.* conscious of attending to relevant features of a situation: traffic or a child, for example; *iv.* self-aware because a task requires careful attention. (*ii* is preconscious relative to *iii*; *iii* is preconscious relative to *iv*.)

Will is active in the last three of the four postures above: *ii.* One is distracted though effective through successive traffic lights, without awareness or memory. *iii.* Newly attentive, one scans the road for obstacles. *iv.* A new driver, fearing the judgment of an on-board instructor, does nothing to the steering wheel or pedals without anticipating their effects. Why concede will's operation when its conscious markers are absent? Because perception or cognition has activated the voluntary control center in the associative cortex, hence nerves that control muscles and acts pertinent to circumstances. Will is inferred in the cause of the second and third mode; choice and action are perceived (with a slight delay) when consciousness is self-awareness.

Is there more to will than consciousness reveals? Would there be reason to claim having a will if we weren't aware of choosing among alternatives or acting as we've chosen? Self-awareness is an extended window into our circumstances, hence the assumption that will is best seen for what it is when present to self-inspection. But is that so: is it odd that the evidence of will is usually less decisive than an array of flashing lights? Walking in a strange city, arriving at a fork in the road, I decide arbitrarily to go left. I'm aware of making the choice, though it and the act of stepping left are almost simultaneous. Does it matter if an fMRI shows that choosing to go left occurred fractionally before my awareness? It matters, though the implication is benign: electrochemical signals are transmitted in finite velocities. (Consciousness is not a froth where messages pass simultaneously.) Will is opaque, even to self-awareness, but that is true to some degree of every mental state inferred or perceived. None will be fully understood until physiology explains all the expressions and gradations of phenomenal life. In the meantime, details elude us.

15. Choosing Freely

This is our anomaly: we are formed by materiality and our causal history, though free will is essential to the texture, purpose, and moral quality of personal and social life. We could elude the implications of materiality by assuming that will stands outside the stream of causes sufficient to produce its effects. That was Kant's idea: will is free when exempt from the influence of material conditions; choices are made spontaneously from outside space and time. But this is magical thinking, one evoking a time when human bodies were said to be endowed with immaterial souls. What is "free will," if we suppress the inclination to mythologize? Construe it as a metaphor for resources exploited in different ways. Earthquakes and firestorms interrupt the causal tide; mind does it too when inhibiting impulses frees mind for deliberations and decisions that reorient the causal flow.

Hard determinism ascribes the sufficient conditions for every current action and effect to matter's ancient configuration and the laws determining energy's evolving forms. Circumstances are primed; history determines one's every decision; what looks like choice is actually a narrowed focus, one whose only possible outcome is the action taken. Soft determinism demurs: there are sufficient conditions for every event, but one or more of an event's conditions may have no history: those are conditions that arise when the converging causal lineages are those of human agents. Jack and Jill meet as strangers; each affecting the other from the distance entailed by their independence. Each makes space for deliberation and judgment by inhibiting impulses; values and strategies evolve as they test one another. Time will pass before each can expect securely predictable responses from the other; or their coupling will terminate because of mutual disappointment.

Hard determinists would explain the result by inferring that determining seeds were planted eons before; but this would ignore the evidence of current interactions. Why search an indecipherable past for proof of incipient conflict or compatibility when all the evidence is generated by the convergence of independent causal streams? These two don't share a past or parallel preparation for this encounter. Do they fight? One might predict that they won't get along, but that's a guess informed by previous observations. Better to wait and see if they coalesce. That would be the effect of testing one another, not one having necessary and sufficient conditions in ancient times.

Circumstances are elastic; they can be altered, though not by everyone. Rabbits are stuck with habits that make them vulnerable to hawks; we revise practices having effects we dislike. We're liberated when confronting novel or surprising situations because we're free to experiment when having no established response. Addressing a situation with an inappropriate gestalt, we fumble for a time before revising it. Regretting an action, we resist doing it again. Why? Because of a current frustration, not for reasons ascribable to an ancient cause.

Discussion below is focused by rubrics that organize the array of mind's interventions. *i.* First are domains where inhibition is an emergent power. It creates spaces where deliberation, judgment, and choice emerge and stabilize, because they adapt us more effectively to our circumstances. *ii.* Next are novel or surprising situations where self-control is exigent because the effects of choice and action are uncertain or unknown. *iii.* Third are choices whose principal or only effects are personal. *iv.* Initiative and invention are fourth. Their agents are artists, engineers, and all the theoretical or practical thinkers who remake a domain by reconceiving its materials or forms. *v.* Last is a summary of reasons for saying that hard determinism is defeated.

15i. Emergence. Emergence is the effect of complexity: an emergent has properties and powers—stability, life, or mind—that are absent in its proper parts. Emergence is critical to volition because it generates modes of animal response—inhibition, deliberation, and choice, for example—that were previously unavailable. These powers weren't up to us: they emerged in response to circumstances that favored their evolution.

We reasonably infer that the relational capacities of matter's precursors enabled or precluded nature's subsequent evolution. Yet (as above) their dispositions prefigured possibilities for alternate evolutions; they were not sufficient conditions for human properties that evolved with the accretion of later developments: the present was not pre-formed in the past. Hard determinists would agree that successive events of many kinds were required before deliberation and choice could emerge within animals able to inhibit or choose their responses to external stimuli. But all of this is explained, they would say, by successive advances in the causal tide. No steps were jumped; transformations were linear; every change had its sufficient conditions. One may accept this generic account while taking exception to its conclusion; emergence may itself have hard determinist conditions, though it explains the inception of free will and is, thereby, a countervailing step in the determinist evolution of cosmic history.

That is so because living things achieved a degree of freedom from their circumstances when their internal organization created the external barriers, the cell walls of unicellular animals. Those spaces were the protected sites where organisms developed capacities and strategies for sustaining themselves. This was primitive autonomy: needing food, they withstood deprivation by storing energy; stabilizing themselves, they resisted predators and one another. The spaces evolved; faculties that developed within humans—deliberation, judgment, and choice—made autonomy flexible, subtle, and effective. The internal spaces were always natural; their evolution was conditioned by capacities and causes traceable to the origins of the universe. Their consequences in us—deliberation and free will—enable imagination, initiative, control of ourselves, and our circumstances. Will as a faculty has had a lengthy incubation; choices enacted in current situations are often habitual. But sometimes, they express reasons, judgments, or tastes provoked by circumstances rather than history. Histories deviate to some degree because of our choices.

Was the evolution of living things—entities with protected internal spaces—a contingency dependent on the drift of circumstances, or a necessity, given laws controlling the evolution of nature's original conditions? Each of these variables may be construed in either of two ways: *ia.* causal laws are deterministic or probabilistic; *ib.* nature's dispositions, the capacities inhering in its original conditions, were determinable or generically specific (hair that was red, rather than hair that could be variously colored). There are also these additional considerations, and a response: *ic.* self-control; *id.* moral identity; and *ie.* riposte.

15ia. Causal history, and the force of causal laws: Circumstances are tightly predictable, given causal laws; or they embody inexplicable accidents, because the laws are probabilistic. Probabilistic laws violate the principle of sufficient reason: there is no assurance that a set of conditions is sufficient to produce a specific effect. Hard determinism is fatally compromised if this is true, because all or most causal streams are laced with events that seem to have violated deterministic causal laws.

There may have been qualitative jumps in causal history, effects that could not be traced to the determinist evolution of nature's original conditions.

15ib. The character of the dispositions inherent in nature's original conditions: This point is critical, but obscure. The capacities inhering in nature's original conditions might have been determinable, hence susceptible to alternate evolutions, or specific, as seeds (apple or pear) prefigure specific evolutions. We don't have to know which refinement is accurate because buffered animal bodies with interior spaces and evolved interior functions could have emerged on either telling.

Either way—laws that are deterministic or probabilistic, capacities that were determinable or specific—we vindicate the material possibility that free will could emerge in creatures having an external buffer and the elaborate internal functions that emerged when taking advantage of its protection. For having an external buffer gives us time to inhibit responses while gathering information; there was time to deliberate, judge, and choose. This was the likely inception of free will, and, on causal assumptions—whether determinist or probabilistic—the condition for its emergence.

Emergent free will was, I hypothesize, an evolutionary effect; its affirmation isn't the conclusion to a conceptual argument. Laplace might have agreed that monadic creatures having buffered interiors could harbor the development of faculties and strategies appropriate to their well-being. Free will would not be unconditioned, if this were true: attitudes, aims, and information would bias an agent's judgments about personal aims or choices and the conduct appropriate to encounters with people or things in separate causal streams. But that leverage would be as much autonomy, as much free will as fallible creatures could hope or want.

15ic. Self-control: Self-regulation is one of our principal evolutionary achievements. This is temperance made habitual, control made conscious and voluntary. Regulation has numerous expressions. Some are holistic: we stabilize bodily integrity and social relations within sustainable parameters. Other expressions engage particular functions: we discipline thought and passion, oversee the choice of aims, enable planning, direct action, and correct error. Each requires the oversight provided by feedback. Negative feedback prevents organs or modular systems from working at rates too fast or slow for the effective operation of systems to which they're coupled; positive feedback promotes activities supplying motivation or energy for activities of high priority. Mechanisms of both sorts are hard-wired neural circuits that inhibit action or provoke it when target thresholds are attained. Voluntary control makes some thresholds adjustable when set points vary with values and aims. The neural architecture enabling feedback has two levels: the level responsible for muscular activity is surveyed from a higher order where it's twice appraised: actions and effects are measured for efficacy, and for consonance with values, hence conscience.

Regulation is conspicuous when we choose aims, make plans, or formulate reasons for attitudes, choices, or actions (*ici*); and as we practice self-control (*icii*):

15ici. Aims, plans, and reasons: Why do you hold her hand when crossing streets? To keep her from bolting into traffic if the light turns red. Determinists counsel perspective: why emphasize current experience when circumstances would have neither character nor existence without its antecedents? Because the contested issue is the force of history versus current interests and reasons. Our outlook is prospective, not past; the task is urgent, and often without precedent. What's to be done? We reflect and decide. Innovations are usually small, but real. Does it matter to these choices that some of our ancestors were salamanders?

15icii. Regulation, character, and judgment: *Regulation* implies that one is self-directing and -correcting. Much of our control is evidence of habits and inclinations—character—as they stabilize choice and activity. Judgment is the vital faculty when we're confounded by contrary interests or surprising situations. Considering our options, choosing what seems best, we appraise our choices when seeing or imagining their effects. These are consequences for oneself or others, be they partners or bystanders. Who has priority; how do we decide? Personal values make some of these determinations; social and cultural values make others. We accede to a "decent" standard for making decisions, though it varies among cultures and societies. Is there a mean to which all should defer? *Live and let live* is the fail-safe answer when duties, costs, and advantages are weighed.

15id. Moral identity: Choices, their effects and self-control, are the measure of moral identity: what do we choose; how well do we control actions that affect others or ourselves? More than recognition that we are causes having effects, responsibility is the moral posture of agents who hold themselves blame- or praiseworthy for their actions and effects. Responsibility is both a reason for ascribing free will (no one is culpable for effects he or she didn't will or couldn't avert) and evidence of it (soldiers who risk themselves to save comrades). Altruism and self-sacrifice may be explained as instincts acquired without choice, but that leaves much unexplained. Imagine a young man, normally feckless and out of work, who refuses a reward after finding and returning a wallet stuffed with cash. His family and friends are surprised; nothing in his history predicts it. He shrugs when asked to explain: "It wasn't mine."

Responsibility may be construed from the third-person vantage of those who declare what should be done, given a role, rule or law; or the stance of the person engaged. Is his or her moral sense determined, because learned and habitual; or is it sometimes evinced as an expression of choice? One may choose to satisfy a rule newly learned, or to do the same thing without knowing the rule because of fellow feeling. Tightly packed on a subway or bus, we make room for others out of regard for their comfort or ours. Inertia forces some changes; others are voluntary. Are these accommodations generous or merely prudential? Many are both: nothing good happens without cooperation; much we fear happens when it breaks down. This is the moral dimension to self-control. Many actions are routine, yet each is an opportunity to express one's moral perspective. Cab drivers are often aggressive. Time is money; many are determined not to waste it. But sometimes, one rides with drivers who give way to pedestrians and other cars. One driver explained to me that each person has a personal trajectory and often a narrow beam of attention; he makes way, knowing that his passengers will arrive, little delayed, at their destinations.

These are two moral postures, usually assumed at once: how I satisfy my roles and pertinent rules; how I declare myself. The two often cohere. But there are distinct levels of concern: everything done in a routinized way can be informed by regard for its effects. Both perspectives have social utility, though the first is too often a disguise for thoughtlessness. For what's to be done, who is culpable if established tasks or positions are used as shields to obscure their consequences? That happens when roles having pernicious effects are exercised in legally sanctioned ways: judges who impose gratuitously harsh sentences for minor crimes, politicians who argue procedural scruples while ignoring public interests. Moral identity of the professional kind is sometimes perfunctory; the other sort—choice and behavior regulated out of regard for their effects—is the better expression of one's conscience and aims. Consciousness is the private moral space where choices are considered. But are the choices freely made? Only sometimes.

15ie. Riposte: Hard determinists believe that conditions required by these expressions of free will are never satisfied: every current state of affairs disguises the sediments from which they arise. Acting now, we're anchored in the past, though situations evolve, causal history is redirected when circumstances are engaged in ways, large or small, that have no antecedents. Raised in the desert, new to cities, rain, and puddles, I avoid stepping in this puddle when seeing what others do. For if every act has causes sufficient to produce it, the causes for some responses are newly learned.

15ii. Situations that engage individuals with other people or things: Why don't we explain every human initiative and response by citing ancient events? Because the same evolutionary effect that explains free will, also explains history's frequent irrelevance to contemporary problem-solving. Free will is provoked and tested when agents are engaged in situations that are new, surprising, or problematic in any way. That effect is more typical than rare when aims or fears give prominence to states of affairs that seemed innocuous moments before. The situations concerning us locate individuals in relation to other people or things, or they are individual and intrapsychic. Both are complexes of interests, values, contingent states of affairs, and choices.

Consider situations joining two independent lineages: agents who are mutually unknown address one another. Their interaction reorients one or both causal streams when one or more of three considerations affect choice and action: *i.* information about the situation disorients the gestalts of one or both agents because it is new or surprising; *ii.* one or both perceive that their interests are threatened or enhanced in these altered circumstances; *iii.* one or both agents are motivated to act in a way or ways appropriate to his or her interests. Each factor is disruptive in this respect: it provokes thought and choice; do something or nothing.

How does one respond to situations having no antecedents in one's experience? History and habit are a backdrop: they're often inclining, but not compelling. For we have resources that enlarge the array of testable choices: namely, emergent powers—deliberation and foresight—that enable other responses. There are principally three options: leave decisions to random impulses; deliberate on the basis of imperfect information and personal or social interests; or gamble. Each is a strategy sufficient to determine the issue, but none is a cause fully determined by ancient history.

Consider Jack and Jill. Both need freedom to experiment, because neither has sufficient information about the other. Who is he, who is she; what difference does that make to what he or she might do? Hard determinists believe that every current state of affairs obscures its causes without preventing them from determining a current effect. That's partly true. A friend who spoke no Japanese went to Japan with the Navy. He returned with a wife who spoke no English. Incomprehension defeated them. But this isn't an issue for Jack and Jill. They share enough history to clarify misunderstandings, enough confidence to engage one another when neither is sure of the outcome.

Hard determinists emphasize the integrity of causal histories without distinguishing enduring conditions from reacting, adapting agents: DNA is heritable—it has history—as many situations are not. Circumstances established without regard for their human occupants—the Manhattan street grid, for example—are often stable, yet most situations alter perpetually to some degree because of changes in material conditions or those agents. Change is confusing, but also liberating: we can't respond effectively to altered situations if we're preoccupied with those superseded. Adaptability, more than opposable thumbs, is our saving power in situations having no viable precedents. Hard determinism does us no favors by to tethering us to the past. Stifle free will, and you suppress initiative and accommodation.

Unfamiliarity or surprise makes choice risky. Responses are unpredictable when we face bewildering situations; one can't tell what people will do or what their effects may be. Hard determinists invoke causes and causal laws to explain the trajectory and fine grain of these responses, but minds (with information, aims, and values expressed as attitudes) are one of two variables when agents encounter novel or surprising circumstances. The other is the provoking situation: what is it, how is it construed; which demands is it making? Choice and its effects are unpredictable if nothing in one's past anticipates this encounter. Think of Mormons pushing wheelbarrows from upstate New York to Utah when the stock of horses, mules, and carriages was exhausted. What passion enabled them to make a choice for which no ancient history could have prepared them?

Here, in sequence, are graded situations that test choice or ingenuity. Responses are ever more problematic as we're challenged to understand the circumstances we address:

15iia. Social conditioning: Is free will precluded because people everywhere are creatures of their circumstances? As children and adults, the British favor Marmite; Americans like peanut butter. (Children born in one place, but quickly transferred to the other, learn the bias of their new home.) Every day millions of people in either place express a desire for one or the other. Our question—is your choice freely made—is situational and current, not obscurely historical (peanut butter was invented in 1895, Marmite in 1902). Wanting answers, we ask the people choosing: do you have other choices; is anything obliging you to choose as you do? What could we mean by denying that choices are freely made when almost everyone polled says, Yes, there are alternatives, but I want this one? Some respondents can be discounted as addicts. The rest make choices that are conditioned but free: they have choices, there is a context of learned preference but no coercion. Context is ineliminable: there is no way to strip away material conditions that educate us for choice while limiting available choices, and no way to shuck every learned expectation when addressing our circumstances. But there is free choice within these limits: freedom enjoyed when choosing among available alternatives for reasons or tastes of one's own.

15iib. Reciprocity: Reciprocity is situational: it emerges with opportunities for engaging people whose interests are similar or complementary to one's own. Given several options (if only yes or no), we choose among them. Are choices free? Not always: people often seize a desired object when it's available. But imagine an opportunity unavailable until there is access to someone like-minded. Wanting the pleasure of a tennis match, tired of hitting balls against a wall, I agree to play this new acquaintance. Why call my choice free when this is an opportunity I've sought? I wouldn't agree had she played at Wimbledon: I do because this is a match I could win. Free will doesn't preclude causation; it implies exemption from conditions that may have once prevented it. Having the opportunity, I choose it.

15iic. Impulse: Specific impulses—for chocolate or vanilla—are distinguished from the steady purpose or intention that drives living things to engage others while securing and satisfying themselves.

Impulses are often habitual: we act again as we have before. Imagine being asked to choose coffee or tea. One often decides between them, but usually with no pattern to one's choices. Ancient causes may sometimes explain us, but do they also explain this week's random profile: coffee on Mondays, Thursdays, and Fridays, tea the other days (a different order next week)? How would one go about specifying remote causes for this difference? Choosing among alternatives is familiar to everyone who dresses in the morning or shops for groceries. Why is it fraught when the explanation for trivial choices is will's determination by a transient interest or need? I'm drinking tea today because of a recent choice: I'm curious about the taste of leaves purchased yesterday. The relevant history is short.

Impulsive signifies a range of actions, from the automatic to the voluntary, with entries in the middle that are uncertain. Consider the voluntary: I raise my hand as evidence of free will. Why call it willful, implying freedom to choose? Two considerations are pertinent when mind has the power to submit or resist: *i*. Calling an act impulsive implies that brain's causal role is involuntary though brains that evolved by way of our causal history—systems having a complex, hierarchically organized structure—have some degree of self-control. *ii.* Higher-order control sometimes supervenes on behavior that is lower order and involuntary. That control may have greater effect when consciousness augments the brain's power to open or close its hierarchically organized neural gates. What provokes this self-regulating response? There may be reasons of several kinds: belief that the impulse is dangerous, or fear that it subverts an aim.

15iid. Contrarians: Imagine someone who rejects a current standard for reasons of his own. Others tolerate situations that annoy them; he expresses dissent by acting in ways these situations discourage. Which is the better explanation for his response: ancient causes percolating through him, or a sensibility that expresses his distress with socially sanctioned behavior? Is his conduct reactive, implying that choices aren't free when conditioned by sensibility? Or is it reactive but voluntary and controlled: he has reasons—practical, moral, or aesthetic—for resisting conditions he deplores. Is this second response question-begging: why deny that our subject is merely reactive if his reasons are aesthetic (practical or moral), given that sensibility is acquired, during childhood and beyond, without control? Because acquired sensibilities are often revised and refined by people who have their reasons for resisting socially approved beliefs or tastes. Their judgments and self-control put them at odds with people more comfortably socialized.

15iie. Surprised, but steady: We're often surprised, but accustomed to finding useful responses. That's partly because solutions proved viable in other circumstances can be adapted to a present situation, partly because we innovate when necessary or ask the help of someone more adept. We're rarely confused to the point of having to admit defeat, though natural or social disasters sometimes defeat us. This is a plausible example: My room fills with smoke; the door is locked from outside. Surveying my options, I go through the open window, with only a short drop to the grass below. Smoke was the motivator, the reason; the drop to the grass was remembered and imagined; deliberation and choice were quick. Why be sure that my choice had no precedent in my lifetime and lineage? I can't speak for lives previous to mine; what to do in situations like this may be stored in tribal memories. But the sufficient condition for this choice—curling smoke—was singular and current. There were other conditions—some long standing and familiar—but they aren't pertinent to the issue at hand because choices and actions always have multiple conditions. The contested point is specific: are choices made for reasons that are contemporary, rather than ancient.

Each of these provocations provoke several responses:

15iif. Inhibition: **This is a first response, however momentary: we're surprised, something isn't recognized or right; it needs to be identified and appraised. Inhibition is an early expression of agent autonomy: stopping an activity, with or without deliberation, is something we do when realizing that it threatens unacceptable effects. We might explain this response in historical terms: an external cause provokes us before another, internal, shuts us down. But inhibition has evolved in autonomous agents—buffered monads—capable of deliberation, judgment, and choice. I wanted to go but changed my mind; I thought I could do it, but I can't. Acknowledge that situations often provoke these tensions, then ask if ambivalence is reduced or cured by tracing it, without confirmation, to remote origins. Free will doesn't entail the absence of determination; it sometimes expresses itself as the inhibition of impulses and the self-control enabling one to consider pertinent alternatives.

15iig. Deliberation, judgment, choice, and their context: Deliberation is disciplined reflection. Its hypotheses signify possible states of affairs; its aims and plans are directives. Each acquires meaning by way of signs having sense and reference; all are organized using learned rules that promote consistency, coherence, and cogency. Wanting a resolution appropriate to our situation and interests, we test choice and action by considering their imagined effects: what are their likely costs and benefits? Decisions are poor if analysis is shallow; directives are tentative if intentions are ambivalent. Assessments are fallible for reasons that are recent or current, not ancient. But now, when reflection is past, we choose and act or decide that doing nothing is the better way.

Situations with properties that are novel, surprising, or puzzling are the vulnerable chink in the determinist argument that everything current was anticipated in nature's laws and original conditions. Laplace might have said that novel situations resemble traffic jams, cars stymied when none can move because each blocks the others. The jam is unforeseen but it would have been predictable had one known the earlier distribution of cars and the roads on which they move. But this reply is incomplete: original conditions, natural laws, and efficient causes are not the only relevant variables. It ignores complexity—organization—hence the formal causes, the perceived complexity of situations that change repeatedly as circumstances evolve. Determinists likely respond that complexity is merely the assembly of a situation's elements. A traffic jam is a jumble of cars; provide for their configuration by plotting each car's trajectory and nothing remains unexplained.

This analytic perception may seem deep and powerful, but it strips experience and its circumstances of the emphases and forms—the contingencies that give it texture, detail, and significance. For complexities—in health, beauty, and rhythm—are often corporate (holistic) rather than aggregative. Each is a configuration having a distinctive form. Each form is the formal cause that renders the complexity intelligible. An orchestra's musicians play their separate parts in ways that create the complex but unitary effects prefigured in their music's score, though many corporate effects are not foreseeable by plotting converging causal streams because we don't know all the relevant variables or the effects of their interactions. Choreography reduces the variables; we see the evolving shape of a dance; personal health and economies are more obscure.

Situations are complex to some degree; they evolve in ways that are consequential for disputes about free will. Jack and Jill are uncertain about one another's responses; their interactions are tentative, experimental. Hard determinists affirm that their god knows every situation and its resolution; it knows the outcome to every writer's frustration, the evolution of every complexity. Opacity isn't a problem when predicting planetary motions; why does it complicate the relations of situations in which people address unknown or unrecognized others? Because planets and their moons don't misconstrue one another or the sun. People often misidentify a situation's other constituents without clarifying their personal aims or values. Choices and actions are often tentative; responses are often surprising. Uncertainty is chronic. Hence the evolution and emergence of inhibition, deliberation, and initiatives that are tentative. Why suppose that every step was decided long ago, when so many of our cognitive abilities address the need to resolve uncertainties that are problematic and current?

Let's make the argument congenial to hard determinists by rendering two factors in ways they would approve. It's agreed that energy is conserved, so sufficient causal conditions for every current state of affairs embody energy from the ancient cache. And we say that emergent properties—those of a circle, for example—are foreseeable given their generating conditions. Emergent properties are often surprising, but nothing about them is unpredictable if this is true. These concessions entail that current states of affairs are determined by the ancient stock of energy, and that emergent properties are the causal or configurational effects of properties originating in a simpler domain (that of cells or molecules, for example).

Now consider: Jack and Jill are mutually attracted, but mutually puzzling. Why call their future determined when their calculations—tentative, fallible, revisable—are one of its principal determinants? A rigidly determined future looks plausible if energy is conserved and if there are sufficient conditions for all emergent properties, but two considerations are ignored. One is the random factor introduced when agents engage circumstances that are novel or surprising. Neptune isn't surprised by the sun, but Jack and Jill often surprise one another. Why aren't their responses predictable in principle since the beginning of time? Imagine their conversations as each responds to the other in ways appropriate to the other's previous words, not because of ancient antecedents: "Pass the butter," she asks; he does it. The hard determinist intrudes with his principal weapon: everything is predictable; an omniscient god knew what she would say and what he would do. We should understand that a contemporary cause—her request—embodies the ancient lineage while clothed in its current guise.

This is faulty in three respects:

15iigi. All was allegedly decided eons ago, precluding the possibility that a current effect is the result of a cause contemporaneous with or immediately preceding it, though Jack has always waffled unpredictably. Having never met anyone like Jill, he's all the more erratic. His response to Jill has no traceable antecedents in her history, but also none in his.

15iigii. How should we construe the hard determinist reading of this situation: Jill makes a request, and she hears the response of something in her causal lineage (an anticipation of Jack); Jack hears and responds to a request from something in his past (an anticipation of Jill)? Or should we suppose that Jack and Jill are linked in a Leibnizian universe, so her request eternally entails his response? The Laplacian model of hard determinism postulates that independent causal streams perpetually evolve in ways determined by the evolution of their original conditions. Yet little or nothing is said about the convergence of previously independent streams, hence Jack's relation to Jill when nothing in either lineage anticipates their responses to one another. Does hard determinism insinuate a Leibnizian solution: Jack and Jill are already bonded by eternally established internal relations? That would be inappropriate to a problem founded in a Laplacian assumption: that nature is an assembly of lineages, many that evolve and cross while others are mutually independent.

15iigiii. Add that the "omniscient" god invoked to locate sufficient causes for their exchange in ancient history is a *deus ex machina*, a philosophic conceit for which there is no confirming evidence. It seems plausible that our universe may be entirely closed, every next change a predictable (in principle) consequence of some or all that has gone before. But it is also plausible that nature is perpetually reoriented for reasons that are situational and contingent. Emergence may be a principal reason for its indeterminacy. For if each emergent property has sufficient causal conditions, it may happen that effects are imperfectly foreseeable when two emergents, both tentative and disoriented, engage one another.

Is everything exactly determined, given the precise specification of values for relevant variables and laws controlling their evolution? Or do we merely opine that determination is exact because we fear the irregularity of a world where interaction's effects are probable only?

15iii. Situations that are principally individual and intrapsychic: There are three points of reference: *iiia*. initiative and invention in art; *iiib*. resistance; and *iiic*. ordinary decisions. Deliberation is often their context, though impulse is commonplace when making everyday decisions.

15iiia. Initiative and invention in art: Responses to surprise are defensive if we're uneasy, but provocative if we're artists or entrepreneurs seeing opportunities rather than threats. Initiatives express their control of a medium: metal or clay. But could Bach, Cole Porter, or Henry Ford rightly say that his initiatives were his own? Current expressions take contemporary forms, but is that more than a disguise for ancient origins?

Some years ago, a gallery in New York exhibited nineteen (or so) Picasso portraits. All or most featured the head and shoulders of a single male subject painted in shades of black, white, and red. Most differed little from one another; they were, collectively, the record of an experiment in composition. The show might have been described as an historical record: portraiture as paleontology, Picasso's renditions of an ancient form. But that appraisal would have missed the gallery's aim: his ways of construing the form were the only reason for the exhibition. Can we save the gist of the determinist reading by making the same point with a different emphasis: was the aggressive style of the paintings prefigured by a different artist painting or dreaming eons ago? Who would that have been? Consider again the autonomous spaces—the conscious minds—that evolution and emergence have supplied. Most of us fill them with everyday tasks, sentiments, and memory. That jumble provides content for material reworked and refined by productive imaginations: body parts are familiar; artists see them differently.

Nietzsche, writing of eternal recurrence, affirmed that artistic styles are invented, forgotten, and recalled.[25] But something elemental is implied by the distinction of productive and reproductive imagination.[26] For we are, as he also said, creators of values and ideas. Artists innovate unpredictably while embellishing or augmenting familiar melodies, materials, or designs. Anton Diabelli supplied a waltz; Beethoven wrote an hour's worth of variations.

15iiib. Resistance: Imagine someone challenged by an idea or design—a paragraph or drawing—of her creation. Exploratory steps

---

25 Friedrich Nietzsche, *Thus Spake Zarathustra*, trans. Walter Kaufman (New York: Viking, 1954), p. 322.
26 Immanuel Kant, *Critique of Pure Reason*, trans. Norman Kemp Smith (New York: St. Martin's, 1965), p. 165.

were predictable, but now she's thwarted by thought's alien product: she doesn't know how to develop or correct it. This is the impasse of writers or artists stymied by obstacles of their own making. They analyze, probe, or free associate, wanting insights that would leverage a useful change. Not having assured solutions, they experiment or surrender. Is the difficulty exaggerated when the struggle is intrapsychic, both sides occurring in one mind? These situations are remarkable only for pitting minds against themselves; they resemble every situation that confronts a thinker with data exceeding his or her ability to construe it. Resistant content is mastered when we discover an inkling of its motivating idea. Or the idea is obscure in itself, so we try alternate ways of refining it. Success is partial; many first efforts can't be saved.

Finding myself provoked by something of my own making assimilates this example to those considered above: we address other people or things in puzzling situations. But examples of this sort are easily modified without losing their point: we shrink the situation to the scale of reflecting mind by supposing, as often happens, that the ideas to be clarified are conceived but uninscribed. Resolution evades us until initiative succeeds on the back of imagination: solutions dawn as we analogize, extrapolate, generalize, or free associate. Or we leverage a choice by citing a reason: the idea was too complicated; we've simplified it.

15iiic. Personal choices that are ordinary or arcane: Puzzling situations were the point of reference in the section above: how to respond to other people or things when they challenge one's inventory of habitual or prepared responses. There are also the free choices made when circumstances are insufficient to decide an issue. Chocolate or vanilla, coffee or tea? Reality doesn't care which choice it is, when eons haven't been sufficient to fix these outcomes. They occur when history receives a supplement: a determinable (a property or situation having two or more possible expressions) receives a determinate expression because of a decision based on new information pertinent to a reason, interest, or value. Here are two examples: one cerebral, the other anecdotal.

Tycho Brahe made observations from which Kepler inferred that planetary orbits are elliptical rather than circular. The data in Brahe's diaries were previously unknown; his inference was a startling departure from the assumption that planetary orbits are circular. Thought leapfrogged from Copernicus to Brahe, Kepler, and Galileo to Newton: understanding achieved determination (a specific hypothesis with confirming data) when a value (inquiry) provoked an extrapolation that was unprepared by centuries of reflection. Why was that possible? Because the interests, ideas, and values directing inquiry were applied innovatively, rather than mechanically: what could the data imply if not circularity, when each of its variations was long construed as less worth of Plato and God because of being a distortion? Thank Kepler's imagination for exceeding all that previous history had conceived.

Choice intervenes when circumstances allow either of two or more determinations. Decision wouldn't be required if every interest had only one possible satisfier, but reality is determinable in respect to many interests and values, hence to many reasons for acting. Walk or ride, coffee or tea: why choose one or the other? The answer may be habit, but it could be that there is new information pertinent to the reasons, interests, or values shaping one's choices. Wanting something to do, I can't decide between taking a walk or riding a bicycle. Choice decides: I mount the bike, only to realize that both tires are flat. Resolve is quick because desire is flexible; I'll walk.

But isn't choice conditioned by motives that are themselves historically conditioned? That is so but qualified because interests and values are responsive to new information. Kepler was looking for eccentric orbits or willing to consider them; Brahe's records supplied confirming data. The ankle that kept me from walking is better now; I'll test it. Hard determinists resist the distinction between antecedent conditions and our responsiveness to new evidence; they intone a message like that of Plato's *Meno*,[27] though orientations change when information is acquired, not merely repackaged. Could one argue that deviations consequent on new information are never more than responses to antecedent conditions? That would be an inference with a name: *post hoc ergo propter hoc*.

Choice is always a risk, but less so when agents anticipate opportunities once unknown because information has revised our estimates of action's likely effects. Assume that dark matter hides civilizations we shall eventually discover. Their ways will likely be strange to us, though we may decipher them well enough to respond to their messages in ways

---

27   Plato, *Meno*, pp. 353–85.

their agents comprehend. That won't require innate ideas or determinist histories because imagination and inference will have bootstrapped us beyond every current limit. Physicists swooned, then adjusted, when Newton reflected after seeing an apple fall. Something comparable will happen again, probably many times.

15iiid. Disputed variables: We invite confusion when these five variables have contested implications for free will:

15iiidi. Information: Any information that extends understanding of one's self or circumstances is a basis for initiatives that may have no precedent in one's history. The inciting information may concern one's lineage or matters having no precedent within it. Either origin may be decisive in fixing a response to a problematic situation or for determining a determinable's expressions. I hadn't known that my grandmother was a gambler: should I caution my daughter?

Information is a baseline for discussions of free will because this is the least contentious way of escaping the determination of one's lineage. Genes determine many things without being known to the agents affected, but many aspects of one's lineage have no effects unless they're known. Do other variables have an equivalent force, and if so do they have it principally or only because they too are fueled by information that exceeds whatever is or was known of an agent's history? A principal example is the interplay of information and values. Suppose that values are (at least) inclinations to favor or resist a thought or practice, and that new information prompts one to alter an established habit out of regard for value: valuing health, open to the news that speed, sugar, and inactivity are unhealthy, I change. Add that this functional relationship is sometimes reversed: information alters values. Naïve about climate change before learning of global warming, I trade my car for a bicycle.

15iiidii. Reasons: Reasons are justifiers. They are second-order causes: exercise is a cause of health; but citing health is a cause of exercise. Aristotle's notion of final cause is often criticized for its implication that finality is a process directing change, but that understanding is correct when the cause of an outcome is the intention directing it. The condition provoking an intention may have had a succession of antecedents, but many reasons driving it are current: one drinks because thirsty. Could one choose otherwise? That often happens: I'm thirsty, but I'll wait. What makes the choice possible? Muscular—functional—control.

Here too information is decisive. Tomorrow's game has everyone excited, but heavy snow has fractured the roof of the stadium; the game is cancelled, I won't go. My decision is responsive to reasons because my reasons are sensitive to news. The information need only be news to me, not new in itself: I'm surprised by a sequence of red-haired babies, though my wife had chosen baby clothes of a matching shade because she knew the likely outcome. But she's an in-law and not herself affected by the determining blood line; it was information, not inspiration or antecedents, that enabled her choice.

15iiidiii. Values: Values are the set points of the body/brain's positive and negative feedback systems, but also the sensitive leading edge of thought, choice, and action. They impel some actions (call a friend), while inhibiting others (ignore insults). Those rooted in metabolic processes are stable if one is healthy, though they change with illness or age. Others are labile because determined by socialization or information: much of current technology was unforeseeable; wanting it was nowhere in our history.

15iiidiv. Imagination: How could we establish that imagination—invention, analogy, or extrapolation—is more than the quasi-grammatical operation of reconfiguring available colors, shapes, ideas, or words? Suppose that many new musical compositions are prefigured in the eighty-eight keys of a standard piano: for why, if so, aren't they apparent? Because each sequence of notes needs discovery and exposure. A note-sequencing machine will generate occasional phrases of musical interest, but hear the difference when its software program is exposed to bird song or ululating voices. Would it have been musically productive without that information? Only in a random—accidental—way. Why this difference? Because imagination is the power for bringing the brain/machine's innate heuristics to bear on this new information. More than a combinatorial faculty, it is musically sensitive; its innate or acquired aesthetic values make it musically selective.

15iiidv. Functions: Consider the facility apparent in actors, dancers, and athletes: they move supplely; they're self-controlled. Each of their neurological-muscular capacities has operational integrity that exceeds its causal lineage in the respect that each is lodged altogether within agents who control their expressions. Is this the mechanical evolution of complex systems? No: choice and action exceed a causal lineage when impelled by information: one learns Wolof or French, not American English, because that is the content of sounds children hear. Hard determinists emphasize lineages of sufficient causes; they pass over the difference between causes and the determinable capacities activated by information, values, or initiative. There is always history in the beginning, but history is penetrated by accidents, information, and opportunities: one learns baseball, not cricket, because that is the game locals play. The god who sees us at the beginning of life only discerns all we can do given our innate capacities and antecedents; it doesn't see all our opportunities or all we shall choose to do or be.

15iv. Hard determinism is defeated: We have four reasons for discounting the hard determinist claim that there are no expressions of free will:

15iva. Living beings have an inside protected from things outside by a membrane that resists intrusions while filtering information and nutrients. That structure enabled the emergence of faculties for deliberation, judgment, choice, and will. Other animals have these powers to some degree, though not to their pitch in humans.

15ivb. The gestalts with which we address situations express personal orientations, hence histories, but also responses to current situations. They orient us in two ways: creating coherence by integrating the disparate matters thought or perceived and by creating frames in which the difference of figure and ground expresses an agent's dominant values or concerns. A new or troubling situation disrupts a previously established gestalt; starting again, so to speak, a thinker finds his or her way to a different orientation, often one having no exact precedent. A bit of history—information in the previous gestalt—is suppressed. Is the information forgotten? Details may be remembered; the orientation is often lost. This is creative destruction: previous assumptions are a drag on current perceptions, though a radical change in situations alters old persuasions. Yesterday's stranger is today's good friend.

Hard determinism is defeated at the first moment of addressing troubling situations. For superseding gestalts—however fragmentary and confused—disrupt the causal tide. We're challenged to construe our circumstances in terms relevant to our values and interests when they seem unprecedented in our history. What are we to do? Responses may be cautious, or unpredictable and daring to some degree. We deviate from established patterns: forgetting or ignoring standards that were once obligatory.

15ivc. Sheltering within barriers that defend our vital interiors, we are causes that respond to other things or plan our engagements with them. Novelty provokes us. Addressing problematic situations, choosing among a determinable's possible expressions, we rely on information that justifies our reasons, interests, or values. We err sometimes, but the choice is ours.

15ivd. Is there, nevertheless, a way to vindicate hard determinism? Yes: argue, with evidence, that the causal version of Leibnizian holism is valid. (The whole is a differentiated, dynamic entity in spacetime, rather than a complex, static idea in the mind of God.) There are, this implies, no independent causal streams; no encounters such that agents address situations for which they are unprepared. It implies that surprise or apparent novelty are mistaken impressions, and that personal experiments (Jack and Jill) are conceits. For all is entangled; everything is cause and effect of everything else and has been since the beginning of time. But this is a dream, an idea distinct from the more plausible surmise that nature is still marked by the effects of its early history when, prior to its expansion, all was tightly packed. Is it still wholly compressed; or is it true that there are no precedents for many agent encounters because independent causal streams did form and often converge?

16. Last Thoughts

This book has a simple aim: establish within the context of soft determinism that humans have autonomy and free will. Autonomy isn't controversial, every animal has a degree of it; self-maintenance and sociality are common to all. Yet autonomy may be automatic because programmed, hence insufficient to secure free will and all it implies:

inhibition, initiative, invention, responsibility, credit or blame. Many choices are routine; habit explains them. But what decides the issue if assembled causes are indifferent while inclinations are mutually opposed? That leaves deliberation as the source of viable alternatives; choice expresses its judgments, values, and priorities.

Mind was formed by causes; aren't its decisions also caused? Yes, though there may have been little or no germ of current determinants in their antecedents. Composers trained in classical harmonies were disoriented by Schoenberg's twelve-tone scale. History was no guide; their choices were experiments. This point generalizes: anyone facing a situation for which he or she is unprepared responds reactively—without thought—or the response is delayed while interests and values are calibrated. Judicious responses are distinctive and personal because the sensibility that emerged with experience is a dense, self-organizing formation, a barrier to history that generates priorities of its own. Do situations of this sort often arise? They occur whenever speakers await a reply after saying something for which interlocutors have no answers: "Will you marry me"?, "Do you like quantum gravity"?

Freedom is the power to address other people and things in ways appropriate to oneself. This is a creative force, one determining mind's powers in the margin that remains when material obstacles, natural laws, and social rules or roles are acknowledged. Why credit volition with responsibility for one's psychic and behavioral identity? Because this is the fulcrum for initiative, invention, cooperation, or dissent. Is will always free in ways congenial to soft determinism, free because the conditions for choice are internal to autonomous agents? That isn't sure: it's not a contradiction that events in the early universe initiated a lineage still vital in our time, something that infiltrates the internal spaces of some, all, or most people. This concession won't pacify hard determinists because their thesis—nothing is "up to us"—needs more than this possibility to justify it.

Chapter Three

Socialization

1. Conflicted Aims

We say that agents having autonomy and free will are responsible for their effects; yet responsibility is attenuated if individuals satisfy familiar rubrics: grocer, spouse, parent, or judge. For rights and duties are socially bestowed, not privately earned if one inherits status by virtue of filling a role, rather than by creating a singular space of one's own. People often achieve identity by submitting to formulaic tastes and vocations, though some mold identity to a personal design. Imagine older women surrounded by adoring relatives and friends after a lifetime caring for them. Compare their virtue to the self-concern that ignores stabilizing social relations. Though there is a contrary strand to our thinking: man is made in the image of God; all are members of the kingdom of ends. Mill's *On Liberty* is a secular version of our fantasied atomism:

> This, then, is the appropriate region of human liberty. It comprises, first, the inward domain of consciousness, demanding liberty of conscience in the most comprehensive sense, liberty of thought and feeling, absolute freedom of opinion and sentiment on all subjects, practical or speculative, scientific, moral, or theological....Secondly, the principle requires liberty of tastes and pursuits, of framing the plan of our life to suit our own character, of doing as we like, subject to such consequences as may follow, without impediment from our fellow creatures, so long as what we do does not harm them, even though they should think our conduct foolish, perverse, or wrong. Thirdly, from this liberty of each individual follows the liberty, within the same limits, of combination among individuals, freedom to unite for any purpose not

involving harm to others, the persons combining being supposed to be of full age and not forced or deceived.[1]

Most everyone would be happier living at peace with neighbors in handsome, productive circumstances while enjoying a family, friends, and one's talents. The individuals of this dream enjoy both skills and the resonance provoked by their virtuous effects on others; yet these aims conflict because social structures, even Mill's voluntary collaborations, shape individual development and initiatives to their advantage. We drive safely because that's prudent and because laws require it, though this often requires sitting in traffic jams that make commuting hellish for all who do it. This is socialization, sometimes defending, other times vandalizing the lives of its willing collaborators. How else could we satisfy a desire for the autonomy and enjoyment of individual lives, when crowding and scarce resources require laws that facilitate movement or proscribe harm?

This might be our aim: loosen social demands in order that individuals have space to discover their talents and use their opportunities. Collaboration provides the goods and services required to sustain life to a desired standard. Now couple this effect to an additional aim: balance a society's work with tasks that liberate workers to think and choose. Teach varied skills; break up routine with varied responsibilities; mechanize work that's only repetitive. Read Marx, and believe the sincerity of his respect for talent and his regard for the poor.[2] We won't liberate the poet in everyone; we can introduce elasticity into social demands that suffocate choice and self-discovery. Most of agency's effects occur with little premeditation: like kicking a stone. But those identified with a human cause—as parents affect their children—ring with the purpose and values of agency. More than duty, there is passion, self-discovery, and one's humanizing effects on others. Many actions are private initiatives—start a business, take a walk—but many others are social obligations founded in rules or roles. Filling a role is a measure of the habits acquired with experience; we're effective because of stable

---

1 John Stuart Mill, *On Liberty*, ed. Elizabeth Rapaport (Indianapolis: Hackett, 1978), pp. 11–12.
2 Karl Marx, "Excerpts from James Mill's Elements of Political Economy," *Early Writings*, trans. Rodney Livingston and Gregor Benton (London: Penguin, 1975), pp. 259–78.

skills and personal discipline. But why do we persist when conditions oppose us? Is it pride, or the anxious response to socialization and acquired duties: do we satisfy partners who expect efficiency in tasks complementary to theirs?

Imagine that a role's occupant is conscious of the irony in his posture: he's aware that his identity is compromised by the tasks, status, and advantages that consume him. "I accept its duties," he affirms, "but I am not its creature." How does he reconcile that difference? Some roles are chosen, others are inherited or acquired unintentionally: the job taken when nothing else is available. Later, when autonomy and identity are mediated by a role that consumes identity and aspiration, one responds as the person he or she has become. Would one do this job had there been other choices? Perhaps not; many people have roles that were acquired rather than chosen. One infers from Mill's three regions of liberty that he didn't know such people. His acquaintances, or only those he imagined, wanted no abiding obligations to other people. One thinks of them tending gardens, keeping diaries, or dressing for dinner when eating alone. Why do it; or, when a first impulse has passed, why continue doing it? There might be no reason but habit, though the explanation might also be a dreadful moment in social history—a Victorian social purgatory—or an inflexible idea of singular selves.

Is there relief from these extremes: Mill's atomism or the holism that leaves no space for autonomy?

2. Idiosyncrasy

What fraction of purpose or action is rightly ascribed to individuals and their private aims when much is subsumed under socially sponsored rules or practices? Does selfhood—including purpose, desire, and moral identity—have currency distinct from George Herbert Mead's "generalized other,"[3] or from one's roles in a family, business, or team? This question is unresolved since Plato's allegory of the cave.[4] It describes people locked in place while discerning vague shadows

---

3 George Herbert Mead, *Mind, Self, and Society*, ed, Charles Morris (Chicago: University of Chicago Press, 2015), p. 440.
4 Plato, *Republic, Collected Dialogues*, eds. Edith Hamilton and Huntington Cairns (New York: Pantheon, 1961), 514a–517e, pp. 747–49

on the wall before them; they ascribe character to the shadows while coordinating their interpretations. Adjusting those stories to make themselves mutually intelligible—learning to tell the same story—they see the same things: I know who I am by knowing what makes me recognizable to you.

But is that all I know myself to be? Kant and Hegel agreed that passions are too feeble a basis for personal identity. Often verging on the chaotic, feelings make us opaque to ourselves. One supposes that Kant and Hegel were equally impatient of personal fantasies, however generalized. Like Plato writing of the Forms, their ideas of selfhood invoke the universality of reason, its content and virtues. Kant located selves within the kingdom of ends where each thinker realizes his or her rational nature by affirming the categorical imperative;[5] Hegel's *Phenomenology of Spirit* supersedes particularity and contingency by introducing a trajectory that buries individuals in layers of universality and necessity.[6] Alternative formulations save particularity by affirming it (as Nietzsche did), or by making individuality the emergent effect of sociality. So, Mead argued that I know what I mean or intend (hence who I am) when knowing how I would respond to your responses to me.[7] A succession of actions—each a response to the other and an anticipation of the other's likely response to the first—locates both agents within this evolving dialectic. Other accounts are less ingenious but more straightforwardly social: children learn the language and habits of their caretakers, then the rules and roles of a community. They are comfortable among themselves and recognizable to adults by virtue of knowing society's constraints, including their duties and the spaces left to choice. Rules are observed because deviants are ostracized.

Is personal identity altogether subordinate to one's social identity? Am I a cipher when shorn of socialized habits and roles? Each of us has powers—muscular, artistic, or intellectual—made determinate when imagination and initiative shape determinable roles and opportunities. The idiosyncrasies of one's powers and inclinations are obscured when

---

[5] Immanuel Kant, *Groundwork of the Metaphysics of Morals*, trans. Mary Gregor (Cambridge: Cambridge University Press, 1997), pp. 41–42.

[6] See G. W. F. Hegel, *The Phenomenology of Mind*, trans. G. B. Baillie (New York: Harper, 1967).

[7] George Herbert Mead, *George Herbert Mead: On Social Psychology—Selected Papers*, ed. Anselm Strauss (Chicago: University of Chicago Press, 1964), pp. 50–51.

tastes and desires are subordinate to the norms, duties, and roles that secure and support us. But socialization also has disruptive effects, not least because of a discomfort that all feel to some degree when obliged to satisfy rules or roles designed to fulfill holistic or abstract interests. What dare I be when situations oblige me to construe myself in ways that suppress an abiding idea of myself? How do I relieve the pain of wearing shoes made for no one in particular?

Philosophers obsessed by the obstacle of verifying other people's intrapsychic experience emphasize public criteria for private thoughts and feelings. They construe our uniformities as evidence that privacy and idiosyncrasy are extinguished for want of intelligibility or because altruism makes us self-effacing. Verificationist bookkeeping ignores private differences, as if they were nothing at all, though privacy and interiority may be inexpungable. There may be more within us than public criteria acknowledge: thought and feeling may be lurking, careful not to ruffle the surface of public talk. Bluetooth, mind to mind, would dispel all doubts—I know what you're thinking—but that technology is a step away. The demand for public verification is, all the while, quixotic: we have tastes and desires unknown to others, as well as talents unknown to ourselves. We are conscious, often self-conscious, but never directly observed by others because one's companions are obliged to infer what they can't perceive. We might construe behavior as the test and essence of selfhood, were it established that mind's content reduces to amorphous feelings or percepts. But that misdescribes mind's faculties and content: perception is often clear; thought and plans are often cogent and precise. We have the surmise—credited to Kant but familiar since Plato—that experience is organized by schemas—rules—that differentiate thoughts or percepts while configuring them in ways appropriate to an aim.[8] Someone who makes his way, wordlessly, into a bank vault by picking the lock proves the clarity of his thinking.

Listen to what people say; hear their word choice, and the precision with which they say it: acknowledge that you know how they think. Though something more, something provocative because disruptive, is also apparent. Kant distinguished reproductive from productive imagination: one uses schemas to recreate tableaux of sorts previously

---

[8] Kant, Immanuel, *Critique of Pure Reason*, trans. Norman Kemp Smith (New York: St. Martin's, 1965), pp. 180–87.

experienced; the other prefigures experiences that may have no antecedents. Everyone has memories, most of them jejune. But there are also people with ideas that are remarkable or merely odd; these are the artists Nietzsche celebrated. Most move among us like unobserved comets passing Earth, though some are acknowledged as they revise our ways of thinking, doing, or making. Publicity corrupts its artists when society requires that innovations be framed in terms comprehensible to popular tastes. Hence the social cycles of inertia and renewal: we're somnolent when practices and persuasions are reduced to a lowest common denominator; we awaken to new ideas. Some practices cycle mindlessly—buttons on a sleeve, skirts above or below the knee—others evolve when gifted individuals, artists and others, breach a society's boundaries by extrapolating to possibilities unknown.

Reconsider a time of stasis; notice that homogeneity and conformity were more the result of suppression than the absence of difference. We speak a common language but interpret it with nuances peculiar to ourselves. A few of us paint, think, or play in ways that others are slow to perceive or understand, yet wit takes ideas and practices in surprising directions; we generalize, analogize, or extrapolate to outcomes that were unforeseen. People resist these changes, then embrace them; sociality covers over the breach, hardly conceding that anything has changed. Yet look more closely at the ways people think and act; see all that is distinctive in their ways of construing and expressing information or performing familiar tasks. Individuality is a constant imprint on thought and practice, though we satisfy the demands of organization and cooperation by ignoring it.

Are these real differences or only a libertarian fantasy; where is diversity in people doing common things while having common thoughts? It flourishes under the veneer of a regularizing gloss. We learn different content or subtly different abilities because of different orientations or interests, or because we vary in our capacities for acquiring information or skills. These are obstacles to socialization and evidence for autonomy, because each of us is a barrier to uniformity. Idiosyncrasy suggests that people are autonomous to this degree: we acquire information and skills in ways calibrated to our perspectives, aims, and capacities. Hence this all but ineliminable conflict for everyone living with others: we can't learn current doctrines, tastes, or practices without suppressing something vital in ourselves.

We are formed by our societies without being their creatures. My barber described his mother to me earlier today. She's eighty-four and lives alone in a village outside Palermo. She has a bad knee; her short-term memory is poor; but she presides over a domain—her home—and won't compromise her autonomy. Having visitors, she climbs a ladder in her garden to pick fresh fruit for their breakfast; they return to New York finding that she's hidden all her monthly retirement money in their suitcases. Why? Because caring for her children, in her way, is her vocation.

Is it vaguely ridiculous that old people insist on their autonomy? A principal choreographer died a week ago at eighty-eight. He was in his hospice bed on his last night, silent and immobile, when the hospice doctor visited him. May I ask you several questions, she asked? No response. May I ask you two questions? Still no response. Are you in pain, sir, and if so, where? The choreographer rose out of his bed: "You are my only pain." The doctor called his dance company the next morning to say that he had weakened overnight and might die during the day: "Except that in his case, maybe two weeks." He died that day. (As told by the company director.)

3. Talent

Talents aren't known until there are opportunities for their education and expression. This coupling is tricky because cultures are specific and proud; why search for talents unknown or anomalous with established practices: there's no demand for a Caruso or Michael Jordan if no one sings or plays basketball.

Agency embodies an essential irony: we are autonomous, though our actions are unintelligible, illegal, or ineffective if they fail to satisfy social interests or standards. This discrepancy expresses two constraints on agent talents: what we do—tasks we inherit or acquire—and the fact that standards for doing them well are socialized. Speaking intelligibly to others requires that one use a language they understand. The performance condition requires skill; the social condition requires the reciprocities of people having similar skills. Differences are suppressed because we have interests and needs that individuals can't satisfy alone: a shortstop plays his position by adjusting to the styles of his teammates; intimates speak to one another in ways that each has learned to hear. Differences persist because we speak a public language while using it in distinctive ways.

Social energy falters when old patterns and the habits defending them are the only defense against stasis and decline. Add the costs of personal frustration and the loss gains urgency. Society as much as its members often needs regeneration, but what's to be done when identifying and cultivating unknown powers seems thankless? Three steps are incumbent: *i.* Regard everyone as a luminous space, a center of mostly unsuspected talents or inclinations. We needn't pretend to know those energies or their details; it's enough that we acknowledge the possibility of achievements that express unknown abilities. *ii.* Let tolerance for difference abet early learning in practices that are standardized to some degree: including reading, mathematics, or play. Encourage improvisation directed by a question: what would you like to do today and what tools do you need for doing it? Let teachers sometimes observe children rather than instruct them; see what is done when we don't know what it is or how to direct it. One of New York City Ballet's premier male dancers was raised on a Navajo reservation in New Mexico. Imagine the tolerance and insight of the parents who encouraged him. *iii.* Let adults show patience and respect for inclinations that seem odd or unproductive in one another. Let people grow when they seem past the age of growing.

Why do societies change, often radically, when socialization is a persistent stone that weighs on the imaginations and practices of its members? They're altered by circumstances—economies, governments, wars, or climate—and by individuals who rise unbidden with effects that were nowhere anticipated.

4. Interiority

Interiority is two things: a resonant private space, and the educable sensibility that fills it. Individuals vary: singularity shines through because interiority never yields entirely to the demands of collaboration or social discipline. Behavior is sometimes uniform—we cooperate or submit—though we hear the same messages differently. Interiority is indestructible so long as one retains an autonomous nervous system that filters information in ways conforming to one's values, attitudes, understandings, and desires. The system may be suppressed or manipulated, but its resistance is evidence that interiority has force and form. Words used to characterize it—*character*, *personality*, and *sensibility*—are allusive but superficial because the experiential side is the only one clearly perceived or understood; its physiological structure is inferred, not inspected.

Gaston Bachelard's example of interiority—he compared houses to homes—can't be faulted.[9] Most houses were never one's home; they evoke no memories and have no meaning to visitors who see only a structure and its furnishings. Those are markers to one for whom the house was home, but she looks past them, remembering how things were used, with whom, and when. The structure may be serially repurposed across the history of its occupations; but home is a fixture—specific but different—in successive biographies. Someone new to a house looks on passively; former residents are alight. For sensibility is a tripwire. Its design and construction are subtle and idiosyncratic, with meanings, aims, and persuasions superimposed on temperament: we're sanguine and steady, or edgy and reactive. The array of its variations has values too diverse for easy reduction to the simple means prescribed by rules, roles, or generic identities. Though people submit to common standards because submission is rewarded, and resistance is punished; or idiosyncrasy is sedulous and safe because it's ignored by social demands and identities. Yet homes aren't better if all are equipped in the style of a transient motel. So is experience diminished if generic identities strip members of purpose and vitality. Do we want what we separately need? Or do we desire the same things irrespective of their worth? Is interiority allowed to breathe?

Homes want furnishings; interiority needs cultivation. Children won't cultivate thought, feeling, or skills if parents and teachers don't show them how they're acquired. Watch anyone skilled in a task and ask how he or she has come to its mastery. There are self-made craftsmen or athletes, though most learned discipline from a teacher. This is the anomaly of our differences: having distinct talents and separate private spaces in which to enjoy them, our talents acquire form by incorporating the ways of our culture's socialized pursuits. Being athletic, one learns the games of his or her community; liking music, we learn its instruments. Individuality takes form as the student incorporates a social resource. Instructors represent this aspect of local culture to subjects who embody

---

9 Gaston Bachelard, *The Poetics of Space*, trans. Maria Jolas (Boston: Beacon Press, 1964), pp. 7–8.

their social messages in ways that are self-transforming. This is the alternating cycle—back and forth—as a society slows to teach, then advances on the skills of those it has taught.

Why is interiority elaborated in some, but ignored or suppressed in others? Is it odd that all a team's players are distinctly talented and trained, while advertisers treat their fans to the same vacuous messages? This division is costly because it creates a society of mutually unintelligible castes: people who enjoy their educated skills or tastes, and those satisfied by generic distractions or rewards. My analogy—woods to societies—fails at this point because sustainable ecosystems are usually coherent: relations among their niches make them mutually sustaining. That is not so where respect for interiority is reserved to people who are well-educated and financially secure or to those who are socially entrenched because they perpetuate class traditions.

Do we educate for generic efficiencies (everyone learns to read) or the cultivation of each member's personal taste and judgment? The first ignores our differences; the other makes us mutually estranged (you like languages, I prefer math). Disparity is expected with educations sensitive to our differences, though routines calculated to enforce uniformity—boot camp and rote learning—punish the variability of those instructed; we live by many of the same rules without living in the same ways. Nodal causation somewhat mitigates these effects because its regularizing norm—live and let live—tolerates individual variation. People controlling their individual talents and lives will be different. Tolerance mitigates mutual impatience.

5. Social Space

Walk along a beach on a clear day when space seems void of limits; we don't see its geometry or intrinsic force fields. Social space is like that when we move through it unopposed. Compare playing a game that invokes a nest of regulations: there are rules of the game, including the roles and responsibilities of team members; regulations that limit fraternization; regulations prescribing the character of relations between opposing teams (penalties for aggression); and regulations proscribing or prescribing conduct appropriate to any social relation (saying *thank you* or *hello*).

Walking together seems unproblematic; walking down a crowded street is only one or two steps less constraining than playing a team sport. For regulations enable collaborations by articulating the social spaces where they form. This idea—articulated social spaces—amplifies the idea that human societies resemble a stand of trees. For if the autonomy of each tree is qualified by forest ecology, so is the autonomy of human agency qualified by the layered regulations that constrain activity and collaboration in a densely occupied social space. Think of people uncomfortable in big cities. Disliking the noise and agitation (what locals experience as energy), they're disoriented by the vague apprehension that the social space is informed by layers of constraint. They intuit that each person, resident or visitor, has only a narrow path within the system of regulations that define his or her space. Don't tell these visitors that the freedom of city residents is greater than any they know. For their city is a plenum of opportunity. Yes, it embodies layers of constraint, but also systems and domains that teach and incite the passions and talents of its residents. There is disruption when artists and entrepreneurs alter aims and perceptions, but a city excited by diversity and organized for business pauses and stabilizes. Private lives are less hectic in quieter cities, but Athens, Venice, Paris, and New York are instructive: agitation is productive.

Notice too this offsetting tension: the social space of regulations is an ethos informed by three "transcendentals": the good, the true, and the beautiful. This is the culture of Plato's cave: emerging from darkness, we rise in light that enables and impels. We satisfy social scruples and maybe these ideals because education and opportunity foreclose doing otherwise. Consider goodness, because its value is pervasive and least contested. Activity creates and sustains it by way of the reciprocities established and the effects achieved as work is done. Friendships, families, and neighborhoods, businesses, schools, and communities are the spawn of activities initiated when people are interdependent and effective, but needy. We often appraise agency's effects by citing gross material changes: washing clothes or painting a fence. Though salient examples would have us consider one another. How are we altered, partly by things we do, partly by our bonds to partners? This is moral resonance; it has memory and extension. We create webs of moral conscience without knowing how far or deep they go. People respond when news spreads in morally resonant communities: someone falls in the street; others stop to help. An expert at making prostheses responded to pictures of amputees in a distant war by making limbs for its victims; his effects were magnified when other makers volunteered their help after learning of him. Hospitals, police, and firemen embody these values.

Truth is instrumental; no plan enhances its success by misrepresenting an activity's aim, partners, terrain, or resources. Yet true answers to these four questions exceed practicality because none are more essential to our nature and self-understanding: What am I, or what are we? What is the character of other people and things? What is my, or our, place among them? What is it good to do or be? Other questions may also seem urgent: Is there a god, if so, what is its nature, and how are we judged? Every inquiry has one of these topics as its generic directive; truth is their animator. Now beauty. Moral goodness requires our engagements with one another; the inquiries seeking truth are propelled by accumulated insights. Some things are beautiful in themselves; others require the imagination and skill of single artists. They would be largely mute without the styles in which they train, though artistic genius is mostly autonomous in the rare people having it. They elaborate on traditions or exceed them, without explaining why they've deviated, or how observers should regard their innovations. We accept a tradition's gaps without being able to explain, or even notice them.

Too much preoccupation with the good, the true, and the beautiful is likely to sabotage any project they inspire. We ignore them because they aren't perceived as relevant to all that's pedestrian in everyday life or because too much concern for them makes us clumsy. But these are the vectors animating social space. Are they "transcendental," implying an origin out of nature? Not really. It's our need and aspiration, individually and collectively, that drive them.

6. Normativity

How do regulations acquire their force? The threat of punishment is one reason, though most people are motivated by an urgency that evokes the collective interest and passion of Rousseau's "general will," not by fear. We respond to the requirements for effective sociality by acknowledging its layered conditions. Some concern the tasks or roles appropriate to an activity's aims or participants: drivers and their passengers. Others determine one or another dimension of the social context where the activity is performed: students and teachers; parents and children. Some are legislated; others are well-marked, though usually informal. Habermas has emphasized the shared interest in procedures that enable coordination.[10] John Dewey's idea of privacy—it binds individuals sharing an aim—combines this regard for collaboration with that of efficacy, tolerance and respect.[11]

What is normativity? Kant ascribed it to an *a priori* imperative, though it has the simpler basis intimated in Aristotle's remark that man is a social animal: we need and are, mostly, comfortable with one another. Discomfort is sometimes real; violence is our pathology. But we defer to bonds and regularities that enable safety, efficacy, and well-being. There is normativity in all the practices sanctioned by mutual deference.

7. Socialization

We accommodate ourselves to a society's structure and aims as we go our separate ways. The result is socialized autonomy: singular persons sharing the common forms of thought, cooperation, and sensibility.

7i. Socialization is the public bath where personal differences are nuanced or suppressed. It has four primary modes: *ia.* We commit ourselves to friends, spouses, or partners. *ib.* Thought, feeling, taste, and behavior conform to local standards. *ic.* We choose or inherit roles in families or businesses, cities or states. Roles differ with one's occupation or aims, but here, too, we learn practices that normalize relations and tasks: playing midfield or third base is roughly the same, whatever one's team. *id.* We satisfy local laws: whatever direction you're going, whatever your destination, traffic laws are mostly the same. Idiosyncrasies are submerged, without being extinguished.

---

10   See Jürgen Habermas, *Theory of Communicative Action: Reason and the Rationalization of Society*, Volume 1, trans. Thomas McCarthy (Cambridge: Polity Press, 1984).
11   John Dewey, *The Public and its Problems* (Athens: Swallow Press, 1954), pp. 15–16.

7ia. Commitment: We bind ourselves to others in passion, duty, or as partners sharing an aim. Individuality is submerged or suppressed in each of these modes, though it shapes our ways of performing standard tasks. Does passion express affection or lust; am I committed to this team, this game, or to my salary? The actions of people doing the same things for different motives may look the same, but individuals, and sometimes their partners, know the difference.

7ib. Local standards: Predictability and safety, productivity and civility require that we do ordinary things in recognizable ways. Yet standards are satisfied in ways sensitive to local differences. I once went miles out of my way after seeing the sign for a prize-winning ice-cream store, only to find that vanilla was the one flavor sold.

7ic. Roles in associations and organizations: Associations are assemblies of people having a shared interest; members usually have the same or similar duties and rank. An organization's members are distinguished by their functions: doctor or nurse; student or teacher. Each of an organization's roles has distinctive duties and freedoms, so aspirants educate themselves for the tasks to be assigned. Applicants are often required to pass a certifying exam, though not one so standardizing that it eliminates personal styles or idiosyncrasies. Cab drivers are often terrifying, though all have passed an exam.

7id. Laws: Laws standardize practice without effacing distinctions introduced by lawyers or accountants speaking for their clients. Regularizing behavior doesn't eliminate private interests.

7ii. Socialization may have either of two aims: obliterate difference or manage it. There are societies of both sorts. Both tell us how to behave, what to suppress. Both relegate autonomy and idiosyncrasy to three places: *iia*. inclinations; *iib*. the choice of vocations; and *iic*. an altered perception of sociality.

7iia. Inclinations: We want and like different things. Every economy able to produce more than the rudiments of well-being responds by supplying a variety of goods and tastes: bread for those who want it, but butter and jam, too.

7iib. Vocations: Vocations are often inherited; those chosen are expressions of inclination, opportunity, or need. Every vocation, whatever its origin, introduces us to a version of sociality that is focused by a practice, task, or aim. Each is distinguished by its ways of binding agents doing the same or complementary work: parents to one another and their children; buyers to sellers. Every such relationship is a collaboration; each requires give-and-take to succeed because partnership in complementary roles is a negotiation. But cooperation drains autonomy when participation is obligatory and terms are rigid. Agents who have little or no freedom to define their roles must, nevertheless, establish viable relations to partners in complementary roles. Think of teachers and their students, soldiers and their officers. The roles are determining, but there's latitude for accommodation.

7iic. An altered perception of sociality: Socialization is often construed as a homogenizing process: we acquire generic identity as fans, workers, or citizens. But there is a different way to understand us: neither generically nor by way of the organizing rules or roles that make us anonymous. Nodal causation is the critical difference. Episodic causes occur many times a day, some in predictable sequences, others randomly. Most are incidental to an agent's identity: we close a door or turn off the lights. Causation of this other sort occurs, as noted in Chapter One, when many agents preside at once within assembled domains. Trees are nodal: each nurtures and defends things living within or around it. An ensemble of trees—a wood or copse—is an ecosystem in which each tree affects others while sovereign in its space.

Human societies are more like forests than we imply when reducing their members to single agents or homogenized classes: Jack or Jill; men or women. Trees are rooted: each stands amidst a changing ensemble of others, or alone. Humans approximate these ensembles when each participates in associations or organizations distinguished by their aims or traditions. Think of these as alternate canopies, each having its style of affiliation, all posing specific constraints—rules and roles—on the tasks and freedoms of their participants. Each ensemble assigns some degree of freedom to its participants, but none—a saving grace—eliminates idiosyncrasies that distinguish agents from one another. Citizenship is usually more permissive than church membership; friendship is less constraining than a priesthood. Participating in several assemblies at once, we alter our expectations and behavior accordingly: some are flexible; others demand responses that are prescribed and specific. Why are trees a cogent analogue in these variable circumstances? Because each affects others, while having latitude to secure and nourish itself.

Personal differences intrude everywhere, though philosophy tells homogenizing stories. Mill's *On Liberty* and Hegel's *Philosophy of Right* define our dialectical extremes, one for the individualism that sets us apart, the other for the rationalism that makes us indistinguishable. Both are caricatures. Look for social texture, and you find diversities they obscure. Every person is a persistent source of effects that overlap those of other nodes. Together, they add dissonance but also variability and viability to the whole. This is true of particular undertakings, and of generational trends. Mapping a society from above, one sees centers of intense activity—families, businesses, or schools—distributed in low-density savannahs. Look closer, and you see individuals active in ways that satisfy both themselves and their reciprocally related partners, not isolated persons or generic ciphers. Sameness from a distance is difference close up, because the sustaining activities are a function of motivation and individual skills.

Sociality construed nodally is liberating because it acknowledges that an ensemble's constituents—its people and their relationships—vary in character, purpose, and effects. Their differences don't incite hostility if tolerance and laws normalize social life. Activities once perceived as disruptive or inane are digested in the stabilizing flow of fruitful diversity. Hip hop isn't grand opera; many people are indifferent to both.

8. Collaboration, Cooperation, Command

Consider these three modes of sociality: *i.* people having common or complementary aims plan a way of achieving their aims; *ii.* they choose or inherit roles within that design; then *iii.* cooperate to achieve its aims. Having a specific role entitles people to command the work of partners who supply their information or resources; it obliges them to satisfy those who await successful completion of their tasks. There is also the benefit achieved when a society's members respond to imperatives in the work of its thinkers and artists: they digest ideas or products with feeling or understanding sufficient to incorporate or reject them.

8i. Collaboration: "In the beginning," said Locke, "when all the world was America,"[12] one could go to a trackless wilderness and carve out a space in which to live without having to defend against the jealousies of people like those Hobbes described.[13] But life would be hard. It's easier when tasks are shared by specialists, each doing his or her part better than a single person doing all of it. Collaboration implies either or both of two activities: participants formulate a design that synchronizes the tasks or interests responsible for completing a project, or they coordinate their work while doing the tasks required to finish it.

8ii. Cooperation implies the reciprocal accommodations of the people (or machines) performing a project's tasks. Agents make themselves accessible to those from whom they take unfinished work, and intelligible to those to whom they pass it when their part is done.

Collaboration and cooperation are two aspects of the reciprocities essential to the formation and work of productive systems: families, schools, businesses, or states. Little of any complexity or social value is achieved without them; hence the pressure on individuals to participate, to conform. Glaring exceptions—cubist painting and Beethoven's late quartets—are apparent, but they too are works created in the social dialectic of thinkers who elaborate their differences when provoked by history and their peers. *8iii. Command*: Agency is confusing because of looking these two ways: it implies the autonomy of individual agents, while making them responsible for behavior that satisfies social norms. Am I entitled to a voice of my own, or am I an instrument responsible for sustaining Mead's "generalized other"? Agency loses its personal force if every action is calibrated to whatever passes as social duty or momentum. We cherish the idea of freedom without realizing the exemption it promises from systems and regimes that suppress tastes, talents, and the social relations enabling their expression. Command is saved for dreams; we retreat because the insecurity we fear is closer at hand than the success of initiatives we imagine.

Watch people going to work in the morning, then leaving at night. See them patient and sturdy, then exhausted and depressed. Some enjoy

---

12 John Locke, *The First and Second Treatises of Government* (Cambridge: Cambridge University Press, 2018), p. 92.
13 Thomas Hobbes, *Leviathan* (Cambridge: Cambridge University Press, 1996), p. 89.

their work, but many do not. Could we be more secure; better used; more autonomous; better able to fix vocations for ourselves? Is there no way to reduce self-alienation in the regimented societies where self-identity is mostly social identity? Could there be incremental changes that make economic and social organization responsive to individual initiatives? Rather than dread the time when technology reduces opportunities for human employment, let's encourage the progress, already centuries old, that liberates workers from dismal jobs. Give substance and status to autonomy; relieve the stress of work by discovering, educating, and exploiting talents. Societies transformed by art or thought would sometimes feel anarchic: people going every which way. But there would be less anger, less despair, fewer people feeling that no one cares who they are or what they're worth.

9. Cities

Generic talk of men or women, workers or management obscures their identities by effacing significant differences. Homogenization is hard to resist because generic abstraction is easy, and because it's often appropriate: a subway's many riders are mostly faceless; destinations are different, but all need an efficient service. There are three versions of urban socialization. Two are apparent in cities where *gemeinschaft* and *gesellschaft* are competing modes of social organization.[14] A third style maximizes autonomy.

Gemeinschaft—community—implies the intimacy of people bound by beliefs and practices focused by religion, vocation, or shared pride in a team. Tribal meanings inform participants who recognize and defer to one another; all find solace with those who understand the world as they do. *Gesellschaft* signifies rationalized systems where efficient housing, transportation, and bureaucracy bind workers to their jobs. Efficient services supply basic needs, but anomie saves residents from obligations to unrecognized neighbors. Anonymity reinforces privacy; it makes interiority a principal resource. Yet *gesellschaft* reduces the motivating force of interiority: sensibility is devalued because it's not

---

14 Ferdinand Tonnies, "On *Gemeinschaft* and *Gesellschaft*: Conclusions and Outlooks," *Perspectives on Urban Society: Preindustrial to Postindustrial*, ed. Efren N. Padilla (Boston: Pearson, 2006), pp. 92–99.

easily monetized or managed, and because it has no social cachet to people who shun its cultivation.

Urban attitudes look these several ways: to rationalized neighborhoods and services; to ethnic communities that preserve traditional beliefs and practices; and to the vocational communities of musicians, dancers, writers, or artists. Georg Simmel stressed the interiority of residents who enjoy cities where the conditions for work, transportation, housing, food, health, education, and governance are rationalized. But his "metropolitan man" goes everywhere to listen or gawk.[15] His motives are expressed *sotto voce*: forgive us if we enjoy all that is quaint nearby. These sophisticates are consumers; they live in towns where critical functions are reorganized on efficient principles, but they enjoy difference, and imagine that paying for lunch helps to sustain it. Their cities have trajectories like that of Jane Jacobs' neighborhood in New York's West Village as it passed from neighborly community to urban efficiency. She lamented the loss of low buildings and local streets, but her perspective was transitional: relations to her neighbors were business like; all were committed to defending their turf from threatening intruders. Frequent reference to "eyes on the street"[16] was less a profession of community than fear that their neighborhood would be violated.

Louis Wirth described a deeper interiority where vocations are enabled by the efficiencies of technology and professional services:[17] we sacrifice the warmth of family doctors if local medical practice is competent and reliable. Effects magnify when cultivated professionals enrich schools, concert halls, and galleries by supporting artists who have come to their cities for jobs, training, or excitement. This is socialization of a singular kind: go where others challenge you to learn what art can be, while you write or paint in ways of your own. Artist communities are the unplanned genius of city density: members cultivate their skills under the direction of teachers and fellow workers, while propagating creative spaces of varying sizes and intensities. Communities assemble spontaneously in neighborhoods where rents are cheap, and cafes want the trade of artists who challenge one another while exchanging ideas.

---

15   Georg Simmel, "The Metropolis and Mental Life," *Perspectives on Urban Society*, pp. 134–44.
16   Jane Jacobs, *The Death and Life of Great American Cities* (New York: Vintage, 1992), p. 56.
17   Louis Wirth "Urbanism as a Way of Life," *Perspectives on Urban Society*, pp. 134–44.

There are academies where training is sustained and formal, but also schools where experience is the teacher. International finance is one of those; its complexity requires bankers, lawyers, and accountants who perfect their skills while working with one another. These many centers—of business, invention, ballet, or sport—justify the crazed title of Rem Koolhaas's early book, *Delirious New York:* delirious because of its energy, diversity, and unpredictability.[18]

Most of city life is ordinary rather than distinguished. It isn't usually inventive or intense: predictability and safety require that it be so. Yet the steady pursuit of everyday life is not ordinary or uniform: people trained to satisfy social norms distinguish themselves in small ways. Personality shows because one dresses a little differently, or one does his work with a distinctive twist. Some train drivers on the New York subway pull smoothly into stations; others lurch. Is that intentional, or the effect of poor control? One isn't sure, though standing passengers stretched forward and back know the difference. For nothing is regularized to the degree that effective instruction and command would have it; we don't learn the abstract standards, or we resist them in the name of idiosyncrasy. Military discipline often crushes personality, though some armies encourage it, because battlefields aren't training exercises: initiative is required when situations aren't predictable. City dwellers are adaptable because city life isn't always routine. You shake yourself when something irregular happens; you stop to help or walk away.

The third style of urban socialization is here in the distinctive array of one's interests and duties. Residents are socialized by having to make choices of their own for work, housing, or friends. People living in smaller communities fear the homogenization of city life; they see mass transit and traffic jams, they feel the energy, but dislike the mutual indifference. Confused by residents who choose new tasks or duties when overburdened already, they see excess where residents see opportunity. The city churns; and every resident endures episodes or conditions he or she dislikes. But residents experience and experiment with local diversities. All have tastes, inclinations, and an acquired personal rhythm: how much can one tolerate; what does one enjoy?

---

18 See Rem Koolhaas, *Delirious New York* (New York: Monacelli, 1997).

10. Disequilibrium

Imagine a situation in which two conditions are satisfied: every person discovers and cultivates a talent before taking a job that exploits it. Better still, each functioning adult has a space in which to enjoy his or her talents while having a vocation that is socially useful or, at worst, innocuous. All resemble the autonomous medieval goldsmiths about whom Marx fantasized.

These conditions are ideal. In biology, they would be sufficient for life-sustaining health; here in human experience, these are conditions for psychological and social health. Distributive justice requires that equilibrium—talents educated and enjoyed—is a condition achieved by all a society's members. This is an unrealizable aim, though justified because we need an ideal: we can't fix a broken arm without considering the shape of those intact. Equilibrium implies that several personal conditions are satisfied: we educate talents whose exercise gives pleasure to the agent, while earning a decent standard of living and the respect of others. The athlete is paid by his team while working with mates who value his play; the lone artist has the respect and financial support of people who value her work. Complexities ramify, usually to the disadvantage of equilibrium, so we ignore them in order to sketch and justify the ideal.

Imagine being secure in a job that exploits a highly developed skill. One has financial and institutional support for work that is socially popular (sport) or tolerated (humanities professor). There is no gap between a preferred activity and one's job. Work is sometimes frustrating, but persistence and skill eventually succeed. Compare the disorientation of people who cannot say what they do, except to tell where they report about matters whose significance eludes them. They are paid; efficiency may have earned them promotions. Yet it isn't clear to them that their product or activity serves more than a rhetorical or cosmetic aim. Wanting something visibly worthwhile, they find it in themselves, not because of a deeper insight into ultimate values, rather because a productive talent has weight that's absent in job titles and made-up vocations. Marx was succinct: we want work that exploits a talent we enjoy using; control of the work we do; credit for doing it; and financial support that enables us to continue using the skill while caring for those for whom we're responsible. These satisfactions are mostly private; few are sources of great wealth, though securely employed carpenters, gardeners, or violists are admirably placed. Why? Because they discovered and refined a talent, and because they've escaped lives of frustration appeased by distractions.

Equilibrium is therapeutic; it resolves the tension created when people are confused because of wanting self-expression in circumstances that reduce them to jobs, debts, or responsibilities they can't ignore. Yet this characterization may seem false; people of all ages want affiliation and recognition in styles approved by their cultures or societies; the benefits lavished on others are rewards they want for themselves. Unrealized talents occasion no regret when people like their jobs, clients, and fellow workers: an unsuspected skill for speaking Dutch has no cachet in a society where no one else speaks it. Promotion, respect, a steady income: these are rewards with immediate satisfactions. Do these effects compensate for the failure to plumb some part of oneself? They are a compensation, if one doesn't realize having talents whose cultivation would be transforming.

Why does equilibrium seem alien? Because achieving it is an accident in circumstances never designed for personal advantage; only a small fraction of adults do what they want to be doing, given their talents or skills. Why aren't more people favored? Because society is a machine organized to defend and sustain the majority of its citizens in ways that promote the stability of its government, economy, resources, and bureaucracy. Are most adults beset by duties that can't be foresworn short of bankruptcy, child desertion, or divorce? Why be surprised that deep gratification eludes us or that we persist as health allows, hoping all the while that our children may do better?

Disequilibrium has several causes. Population density, primitive social services, oligarchy, prejudice, and economic organization are slow to relent. Freedom *to* is sometimes lauded as the most desirable power of all. Though modes of production and conceptions of well-being require forms of organization that largely preclude the discovery or cultivation of personal talents. We see ourselves as workers of a kind having effects of a kind; we're appraised for work we do, not for work we might have done if significant talents had been discerned, educated, and used. Many factors—industrial organization, labor unions, media, and marketing—consolidate these emphases, though there are other ways of perceiving who we are, and what we might do for ourselves and one another.

Is there a plausible way to reconstrue ourselves and our circumstances? The analogy proposed above may be liberating. Construe human societies on analogy to forests: each tree matures under the protection of the forest canopy, while providing cover for life within, around, and under it. See human autonomy as intrinsic and inalienable, while acknowledging that there is no effective autonomy without social rules, roles, vocations, and resources. We can't be autonomous apart from societies that nourish, protect, educate, and employ us. Established ideas reject this middle ground: we are generic ciphers intelligible to employers, marketers, and ourselves by way of the work we do or things we buy.

Change will be conceptual before it's material: we won't honor ourselves or one another until we integrate this schizoid perception so both parts can breathe. Each of us knows him- or herself as a singular mix of thoughts and feelings, aims, and anxieties; but also as a person having generic roles and duties. How do we join incongruent identities without distortion? How can I be perceived as a node in a social ecosystem, perceived by others and myself as both autonomous and responsible to people or things dependent on me? This will be slow to happen because each person's access to desirable material goods depends on a narrow vocational focus: doing this, whatever it be, to get what the agent and family or friends need or desire.

There is also a conceptual failure, one having a long history. We emphasize *freedom from* but say too little of the factors or influences from which we want relief; we say even less about *freedom to*, its preparation and aims. The Enlightenment sought liberation from dogma and authority, both religious and royal. Having achieved these objectives, it left the choice of one's aims to personal discretion. Why this tolerance? Because *democracy* came to have an extended meaning. No longer restricted to a notion of sovereignty—government by the people—it became a generalized permission: let everyone decide his or her aims and means, given respect for laws that serve the public interest. Nothing in this formulation urges a more careful consideration of who we are or what we need. Those are issues safely ignored when we skip forward several centuries to an economy that dazzles us with goods and services that were once unimaginable. Can we alter this point of view if we suppress its frustrations? That's not likely when conditions for change are so much weaker than the constraints and inducements holding us in place.

Chapter Four

Autonomy

1. Minerva

A feral cat loiters at my open garden door. Living in the rough has made her canny; she knows the neighborhood and its opportunities. She hunts alone, she prowls. Like us, she sees her prospects through a conditioned lens: food, where it is, how to get it. Minerva has never been inside this house, but provoke her with a smell, look away, and she'll bound inside. These are conditioned responses: DNA honed by experience. But consider any first entry into a house she doesn't know. No established practice explains it because there is no habit specific to this house: she hasn't been here before. Just now, she lingers outside, moving a little in response to every motion of mine, awaiting a move that would override her natural prudence. Seeing food or smelling it, seeing the doorway clear, she would enter.

Would that express a decision? No less than my decision to enter a provocative door. Would it be an act of will? It would in this respect: conditioning has shaped her response to opportunity, but she doesn't chance entering unless a signal provokes her. Having that sign—my distance from the door—she would strike. Where is freedom? In her flexible power for responding to me and the door. No, you say, she doesn't decide; she isn't free; she responds to every stimulus with trip-wire efficiency. But this is a reply from the old behaviorism: we too react quickly sometimes, expressing a decision by way of an action. Describing ourselves in this way would ignore cognitive and volitional faculties for which there is abundant fMRI data. Is there equivalent evidence that

© David Weissman, CC BY 4.0   https://doi.org/10.11647/OBP.0197.04

cats deliberate when provoked; do they reflect and decide? Not with our complexity, but they are canny.

This one reconnoiters for minutes, circling left and right. Will I interfere? Not sure of my response, she waits. When I move, she bolts. The calculation is hers; the action is her response to an altered situation. Why call it less than free? Because she's a cat? That underestimates her; it flatters us.

2. Semantics

Autonomy is ambiguous because of its core meaning. There are three ways to construe it: having power to decide what is done, how, and why. Each implies some degree of control. Having that power is a condition we often satisfy—calling a friend, making lunch; hence the persuasion that one is often autonomous in all three ways. That impression dissipates with the realization that control is attenuated by limits on resources, opportunities, and the array of aims that are viable and socially approved.

3. Assertion

Autonomy at its core is always personal and private. Intelligence is conspicuous in the work it does—its expressions are often available to public view—but one sees a finished product, not its genesis. Sensibility is disguised or concealed, but everywhere relevant to the history, habits, context, and tastes of the person engaged. Does everyone at a family gathering have the same feelings and opinions as every other? Are their differences exposed? Surely not. Would they be neutrally perceived if expressed? No to that as well. Yet autonomy wants resistance. Apparent success is misleading when it seems effortless: too easy, we say. Add that we lose passion if nothing opposes us. This is autonomy in its other dimension: more than a condition having ontological implications—exemption to some degree from determination by conditions distinct from oneself—autonomy is a psychological demand, one whose intensity varies with personality. Its measure is a continuum with social comfort at one extreme and the force and challenge of Nietzschean will at the other. *Comfort* implies safety, acceptance, and whatever benefits derive from hewing to established practices. *Challenge* implies risk and the intensified clarity that comes with making careful decisions quickly.

These two are principal markers of the purpose that is agency's keel. Every living thing is self-regulating, an aim augmented in humans by the desire to wrest some degree of control and direction from the homogenizing effects of nature and socialization: how do I emerge from the crowd if only to declare myself? Ideally, one sets and sustains a path of one's own; but circumstances often divert us. Life is the trace of successive recoveries: control reaffirmed after one or more lapses. Or opportunities and resources oblige us to make tolerable bargains for others or ourselves. Resolutions of both sorts express the insistent demand for personal control. Imagine the torture of people permitted no degree of autonomy, then the blame and anger they turn on themselves. Social policy from Locke to Rousseau, Kant, Mill, and Dewey is thought's healing response: each a way to make space for oneself.

Autonomy expresses itself in thought, sensibility, and action. All are socialized, though socialization can't ablate thought or sensibility because its means are inefficient—the "generalized other" can't think or feel for me—and because individuals resist the uniformities it prescribes. Socialization reduces discord by bending us to common practices, but we resist crude uniformity. Dresses vary because women don't believe that one style or color flatters all. Punishment has to be severe if people are to accept a regime that limits their powers. Rebellion is a moral or political response to repression, but also the will and animal spirits of people who won't be caged.

Purpose resembles uniform rectilinear motion, in the respect that intention, action, and cause are agency's signature properties. The impulse is largely physiological, though encouraged or repressed by societies that sanction a range of acceptable aims. Its persistent strength is a measure of the force or reward required to satisfy or suppress it, though intensity isn't always apparent because we're easily distracted by status or material goods. One way of naming social pathologies lists the ways of suppressing autonomy by diverting purpose.

Action's social control has several expressions. Some are benign: geese in flight are self-propelled; geese in formation are socially constrained. Crowd control is another example: people move left or right because directed: we go as ordered. Other versions resemble herding but differ in the degree of latitude reserved to traffic agents. Their laws constrain the choice of vehicles (cars, not horse carts), without specifying the make of one's car or its destination. Grammarians require that poets know syntax, rhythm, and an inventory of words, all of it restricting though the poem is one's own. These are material, social limits on autonomy when a driver's fantasy and a poet's control of her thoughts and feelings are their contrary. Mill's *On Liberty* speaks for the artist's residual power to romantics who conflate initiative and self-control with unqualified freedom. Yet every child grows to maturity in a society and culture where skills are acquired in local pursuits. Cricket stars are rare in Japan because the game is isn't much played there.

Socialization enables collaboration: it exploits our differences and the autonomy they enable as we work together to produce complex effects. This is socialized autonomy; it has graded expressions. Consumers express their identity and independence by the things they buy or places they go. Control is sporadic; there may be little direction to impulses that come in no predictable order. Self-regulation is more demanding when single-minded careers never deviate from vectors established in work or school. Though we resist: we try to set a pace and direction of our own in contexts we don't fully control. A job is taken or lost, one is pregnant without intending it; but there is autonomy in the ways that episodes are construed, coupled, and exploited. Who is fully autonomous? Ragged artists, unpublished authors, street musician playing their songs. The rest of us are compromised to some degree.

4. Self-Identification

Choosing or declaring one's identity would seem to be one of autonomy's inalienable powers. Given the city, religion, or school of my loyalty, am I also empowered to decide who I am? The question is vexed because the basis for personal identity is contentious. Is it established by an array of contingencies—address, body-type, memories—or by the idea and feeling that I know who I am? Do I sometimes check the contingencies to confirm the accuracy of that self-perception? For people sometimes feel that the body they inhabit is false to who or what they are. Is identity fluid and changeable, adjustable or revisable as one chooses? These issues are often decided by sociality and convention:

we are as others see us when certain traits are thought to be definitive. Though there are surges of anarchy when people affirm an identity they've chosen.

Is there a truth to the matter, or is identity a choice or aspiration? How tall is she? There's one answer for a measurement in bare feet, another in heels. Why is one measure determining, when both are actual readings? Because we have a practical commitment to nature unadorned: male or female, appearance or reality. People falling between these camps for reasons of mixed parentage or biology are denied the comfort of rigid designation and words signifying their differences. What are they to do? Suffer ambiguity or invent language that signifies emergent identities.

Confusion resolves if we acknowledge that personal identity has several elements: one part is material; another is social; a third is self-declared; a fourth is aspirational. (The third and fourth conflate if the identity declared is the one desired.) Why should this matter if all are free to emphasize whichever element they prefer? It matters because of the discomfort aroused when the first and subsequent factors are decalibrated. Why are we bothered? Because consensus is comforting: we're happier when hostility abates because all agree on the classification of types regarded as consequential: gender, race, or religion, for example. These are traditional social fault lines. Rigid expectations soften as some categories vaporize (because of intermarriage, for example). Let them go; let people choose partners and identities while old ideas molder quietly. Choices founded principally in transient enthusiasms may subside; they can be respectfully acknowledged while principal expectations fall back to stable differences.

Let there be coherence in these two perspectives: my self-perception and—more difficult—my comfort with the idea others have of my identity. There will often be disagreement about one's entitlements or moral posture, but people would be happier, less conflicted if they were perceived as they wish to be.

5. Collaboration/Contention

Most things we value require partners. For *interdependence* is the more accurate characterization of our lot; it qualifies the fantasy of being able to do all that we wish without companions. Choosing partners is one of autonomy's prerogatives, though committing to them limits one's freedom of action.

Collaboration is the sensitive middle ground where autonomy merges productively with socialization. There are many sites of attunement, all discovered by trial and error. We know some conditions for finding them: a corporate activity must have aims that are comprehensible and shared by participants; requisite skills must be coordinated by an efficient plan, then supported by appropriate resources and oversight. Collaboration works when participants who are skilled and mutually respectful know their aims and effects. They know when deviations are efficiently corrected; they're gratified when effort is acknowledged. Singing in a chorus requires a trained voice and accommodation to others, hence the chagrin if a chorus member quacks like a duck in the middle of a song.

People joined in pursuit of shared or complementary aims are Mill's third region of liberty; their reciprocities structure the privacies Dewey described.[1] More than things they do or make, those relations alter the participants. One is smarter for having to answer a partner's questions, emotionally enlarged by having to consider his or her feelings. One needs only a single friend after the age of four or five to know that autonomy is qualified by caring for a friend while wanting his or her esteem. But this is true as well of one's socialized aims. Descartes' *Passions of the Soul* characterizes a thinker who always looks within for his bearings.[2] Compare the participants in Dewey's privacies: they are centered while expressing personal attitudes that bind them to partners in undertakings they share. Parents amidst their families, team members in a game: all act autonomously when fulfilling their social commitments. Far from Cartesian isolation, this is resonant participation in communities one values, large or small. Collaboration is social glue: work is accomplished; people are transformed. Autonomy is compromised, in the respect that aims, information, and emotions—attachments—are altered. Will, too, may be subordinate to group aims—I do it because we do it—though conscience and self-regulation are a final defense against subordination. Socrates was exemplary: unable to defend either of the available options,

---

1 John Dewey, *The Public and Its Problems* (Miami: Swallow, 1954), p. 15.
2 See René Descartes, *Passions of the Soul*, *The Philosophical Writings of Descartes*, Volume 1, trans. John Cottingham, Robert Stoothoff, and Dugald Murdoch (Cambridge: Cambridge University Press, 1985), pp. 325–404.

he would do neither: "[T]he other four went off to Salamis to arrest Leon, and I went home."[3]

People vying for partners, resources, and opportunities are sure to provoke the resistance of competitors. There are two problems here, each with a partial solution: how to distribute resources in proportion to need; how to make opportunities visible to all when perspectives and interests differ. Add the competitive juices that excite competition, and the vanity that comes with success. Discord is one of autonomy's principal effects. America celebrates freedom of choice and pursuit; discord and litigation are costs we're slow to acknowledge.

6. Regulation

Regulation is distorted by the "no-harm" principle affirmed by Mill's *On Liberty*.[4] It seems benign in realms where agents have nearly infinite space to pursue their aims (the implication of Locke's phrase: "when all the world was America"), though it's naïve and reckless in cities where crowding, scarcity, and complexity make many private choices consequential for other people. What must be added if Mill's formulation is to be viable in societies where people in close proximity adversely affect their neighbors without knowing it? Kant's two-part answer emphasized inhibition and a principle: let everyone inhibit doing what all can't do without subverting the possibility of that action; no one should steal because trust and cooperation would founder, chaos would ensue if all were to steal. He characterized this rule's satisfaction as the supreme condition for social morality, but its actual purport is more spartanly utilitarian: this is the critical condition for practical coherence in a complex society. It requires that individuals be self-restraining when a thought experiment—universalization—shows that behavior of a kind (stealing) would sabotage productivity or communication if generalized. Though we invoke inhibition much more often than those times when a maxim is discarded because it can't be universalized without contradiction: actions are inhibited (without this test) because their effects—violence, cruelty, or dishonesty—are plainly inimical to this or that person, or because there are better moral choices.

---

3 Plato, *Apology*, 32d, p. 18.
4 John Stuart Mill, *On Liberty* (Indianapolis: Hackett, 1978), p. 9.

Autonomy is restrained in both these ways: inhibition and laws. Policy is canny when it chooses one or the other because of the problem to be solved. Inhibition is the choice of agents who foresee their likely effects; they prefer having the responsibility that goes with foresight and choice. Yet those defenses aren't always sufficient: drivers need traffic laws because they often can't see the complexity of the traffic through which they move. A visiting Martian might conclude that we can't be trusted *en masse* to regulate ourselves individually. Though we do that unproblematically in most domains where societies require that behaviors such as dress or sexuality be routinized. Those are spaces where inhibition is control enough because of convention, personal discipline, and the fear of being ostracized.

7. Oversight

There is no apparent way to release the talent and spontaneity of all a society's members. Social complexity and our material needs guarantee that most people will remain cogs in an economic machine. Yet the interdependencies making us productive are altered by technology, social policy, and circumstantial changes in climate and resources. Clarity about our values gives us leverage when changes are made. Three such values are determining: *i.* control of one's actions and effects; *ii.* freedom to enjoy the sensibility and skills that distinguish us; and *iii.* the coherence, productivity, and safety of our relations to one another. These values would be conspicuous in communities more like the trees in a copse or glen, but they are no less desirable in our hardscrabble industrial societies. *7i. Control of one's actions and effects*: Find ways to organize productive activity so that adults exploit their powers for self-regulation; anticipate and defend their resistance to overseers who ignore personal abilities and differences. Technology facilitates these aims by automating tasks that are arduous, boring, or demeaning; by distributing managerial authority to small affiliated bands of self-organizing workers; and, when feasible, by enabling people to do their work from afar. Let people decide when and how to work, if they can quickly transmit what they've done to those needing to see it. Liberate workers from conditions that make them less productive by breaking up the routinized spaces where work is done. These are familiar solutions to chronic problems.*7ii. The discovery and expression of one's sensibility and skills*: Everyone has several or many talents, most of them unknown because there is no opportunity to discern them. How many potential musicians never learned to play an instrument because none were available? Expose children to opportunities, support them as they search for ways and means suitable to their abilities: know that everyone who speaks any language could have learned every other. Expose children to tasks and experiences that cultivate their tastes. Trust them when they respond to some things, never to all. Don't assume that adults have outgrown their earlier enthusiasms. People too stiff and embarrassed to sing or dance may renew passions long forgotten. *7iii. The coherence, productivity, and safety of one's relations to others*: These are virtues that mustn't be compromised by too scrupulous a regard for autonomy: we sacrifice some degree of self-control for these other values. But this is often a two-edged sword: lose yourself in regimented social bonds or retreat into an isolation that sucks one's energy and self-regard. This is a puzzle created by our principal forms of employment: most of us can't make ourselves financially secure without surrendering the autonomy we prize. Our industrial economies have run away with us; recovering control of them is a condition for having control of ourselves. But this isn't news.

Where is oversight in this picture? It comes in two ordered thoughts: how do current economic and political organizations affect the lives of their worker/citizens; what would suit us better? These are the questions of every economic and political reformer since the eighteenth century. This book has a narrower focus: where agency implies freedom, what should count as stable expressions of autonomy? Three seem critical: discovery and cultivation of one's principal talents and inclinations; ample chances to use one's skills; and the opportunity to know and enjoy the collaborations of like-minded people. Are these aims frustrated, sometimes strangled, by social and economic realities? Some people know these frustrations, and work to reduce them. It would be a good thing if everyone were mindful of the obstacles and committed to their reduction. But this implies social mobilization and action by people who are already busy and, in our time, not always unhappy.

8. In Itself, For Itself

One feels centered when activity is a personal choice unrestrained by rules or roles, though one may feel it, too, when satisfying a law's requirements or a manager's demands. How do we know that the sense of acting on one's judgments and choices is an expression of personal autonomy, not the comfort experienced by satisfying laws, roles, or a superior's approval? There isn't a sure sign of the difference, though a reliable sign is the observation that family members, colleagues, friends, or neighbors have priorities and trajectories different from one's own. Having made our choices, we go our separate ways. Yet autonomy—freedom to and from—is so avidly affirmed that people are convinced they have it when a closer look would show that our claims to freedom are often rhetorical. People who come to understand this are prey to political cynics. We want to save freedom from their suspicion that autonomy is a chimera, short of the heaven where *On Liberty* is the biblical text and duties to others are always limited and chosen.

Chapter Five

Moral Identity

Personal identity has several principal markers: the structure, look, and skills of one's body; intelligence and sensibility in their several modes; purposes; and moral identity. Moral identity, absent free will, is the function of social roles and the accidents of one's circumstances: the bills one pays. Acknowledge free will, and autonomy explodes: no longer the creature of my circumstances, I am responsible for roles I choose and for responses to situations I deplore. Kant worried that will is the only power one controls when intentions are thwarted by the complexity of the ambient world. But this is the burden of moral identity: each will shows itself as a distinct voice amidst the sea of contrary aims, inclinations, and deeds. Moral identity without free will is a mask one can't shed; with it, the moral will is a force directing action.

Moral postures drift over a range, with variations as frequent as the virtual points on a line. My concern is the difference made to this variety by free will, an issue complicated by the two perspectives from which it's discerned: the self-perceiving subject and his or her observers. These perspectives are imperfectly aligned. Both see moral identity as it evolves, but their judgments may not cohere: observers formulate an idea of an agent's behavior while inferring his or her intentions; the agent challenges their view with his own. Integrating memories of his motives and actions, he reconciles their effects with his values, telling a rounded story that excuses his faults. Subjects usually credit themselves with meaning well; observers aren't so sure.

We may suppose that moral identity is intrinsic, like height and weight, or that it's assigned, like reputation. But neither is accurate. This chapter argues that we acquire it in four ways: *i.* by acting on behalf of one's needs and interests; *ii.* by one's choices and behavior when duty-bound to others; *iii.* by choices and actions resulting from participation in a society's tribal or public life; and *iv.* by an agent's self-appraisals. Which of the four dominates? How do they integrate and evolve over time? The chapter has four sections: one for each of these perspectives. The fourth reverts to the first: the perspective of agents assessing themselves while confused by moral ambiguity.

1. Three Perspectives: Agents

Vulnerability makes us self-interested, but dependent on others for resources and conditions that make us secure. This dynamic has contrary tensions: self-interest can't be altogether disentangled from one's relations to partners and public concerns. Moral solutions are responsive to both, though the concerns of others sometimes oppose one's own.

1a. Moral will. Personal identity is established with a name, address, and (in the United States) a Social Security number. Self-interest, closer to one's existential core, is a desire to live as needs, talents, or inclinations prescribe. Why call these interests moral? Because their expression is the authentic voice of the person having them, and because well-being is compromised when that voice is suppressed. Why is their expression a task for moral will? Because self-expression is, before any other function, will's task. That role is disguised because personal traits and choices emerge in cross-currents where they encounter three other centers of moral gravity: the trajectories of other people, organizations, and established social practices. Agents' responses to them are legible if they live in societies having well-established rules and practices: all of us observe the traffic code, but some cars are flashy and new; others are plain but serviceable. How much diversity is tolerable in a society that prizes coherence? There is an inclination to understand what other people want or do by seeing them in the context of standardizing rubrics. But what's to be done if moral intelligibility founders for want of socially agreed styles or desires?

Social confusion doesn't confirm the moral value of laws or imperatives, though their absence is notable because anarchy is a likely result when agents are deprived of guidance. This is our quandary:

avoid incoherence, demand uniformity when moral ambiguity makes it likely that conceptions of self-interest will vary; or tolerate differences that defy rules or laws when circumstances and inclination provoke distinguishing responses. We're generous when conceding that relationships vary; why not extend this freedom to individuals whose attitudes and practices vary from accepted norms while respecting Mill's no-harm principle? For there is a middle ground: those who do no harm to others can safely be allowed to fulfill ideas of themselves, given our understanding that offense is not harm. Others need feel no right or obligation to impose their tastes or scruples on people having inclinations different from their own. These intruders may tell a story justifying their interference: it's what their god requires. But this is a rationalizing excuse for their inclinations, however they're explained or justified. For why, fear aside, should people tolerate those who hinder or abuse them if their actions are not harmful to others?

Moral will, so construed, is the power directing one's intentions so far as they express one's interests, talents, and the rules establishing social coherence. There is also this other understanding: it interprets moral will as an expression of self-identity and resistance. Often focused by vulnerability and grievance, it responds with anger or pride, given evidence that some personal aspect of race, gender, religion, or ethnicity isn't acknowledged or respected. This is personal and moral identity as they pursue social recognition or esteem by way of political action. The coupling of diversity and democracy makes this demand justifiable and unavoidable, but my focus is different: it emphasizes moral will as the voice of agency. Grievance in the face of insult is one of its likely effects, but not its principal expression. That ground is agency: deliberation, choice, and action as they satisfy one's interests or needs while expressing one's intellect, sensibility, and duties.

1b. Judgment. Moral identity is a function of the judgments provoking choice and the will directing action. Declaring our needs, values, and reasons, we appraise our circumstances, choose our partners, and act. Judgment is quick if the cost of alternate choices is slight or if there are other choices to make and work to do; though responsibility is qualified when social values and interests supply convenient rubrics. Deliberation slows when choice is confounded by options that are mutually exclusive:

stealing is bad, caring for others is good; though Robin Hood's moral standing was ambiguous because he did both. What is one to do if feelings of duty, guilt, or fear intensify because costs are considerable either way? Resolution comes with judgments that are safe because conventional, or with choices that promise bountiful effects though costs are high or unforeseeable. Both inclinations establish a moral profile: others safely predict what we'll likely do, given that will is constrained by habit. Soft determinism acknowledges this developmental limit on choice without yielding to the harder version: judgment's determining conditions form within the deliberating agent as he or she responds to evolving circumstances, not only to affects more ancient (DNA or social caste, for example).

Judge and *judgment* are two of those allusive mental action terms that are freely used but hard to substantialize: we often affirm or deny one or another aim or plan without knowing how mind/brain does it. Judgment seems unproblematic when events are sharply defined, emotion is plain, and social directives elide with personal norms. Though it often happens that reflection provokes conflicting emotions while exposing complexity in one's interests or situation: the pity and terror expressing the moral conflicts and intellectual complexity of Greek tragedies are emblematic. Social practice eases resolution by supplying formulaic answers, but complexities multiply. Having few conventional rubrics but many problematic situations, each of us makes judgments that express his or her singular moral posture.[1]

Moral posture is an agent's cognitive-affective balance in its prescriptive, imperative mode: it develops over a lifetime of making and acting on one's decisions, then appraising their effects. Yet history is not so determining that agents can't deviate in ways confusing to observers: that happens because complexities evolve and because emotions change as we see and weigh them differently. Inclinations make us predictable, but insight is liberating. Altered gestalts impel altered judgments. Hume declared that reason is and ought to be a slave to the passions.[2] He ignored judgment's context: the understandings (accurate or not) that provoke and disrupt emotional responses.

---

1   David Weissman, *Hypothesis and the Spiral of Reflection* (Albany: State University Press, 1989), pp. 187–89, 195–96.
2   David Hume, *A Treatise of Human Nature*, ed. L. A. Selby-Bigge (Oxford: Clarendon, 1978), p. 415.

1c. Privacy. Which actions are authentically one's own when so much we do is determined by context, rules, and roles? There are principally three possibilities. First is Descartes' affirmation—I am, I exist—a discovery repeated in the second couplet of a John Lennon-Paul McCartney song:

> Would you believe in a love at first sight?
> Yes, I'm certain that it happens all the time.
> What do you see when you turn out the light?
> I can't tell you, but I know it's mine.[3]

What is the sense of "me again" accompanying every experience? Is it direct access to mind's formative power when creating experience; or is this the experience of resonant sensibility (hearing music, feeling the wind)? Is one of these two the authentic test of selfhood? Or is there no direct measure because self-awareness is always compromised. For I only know myself when discerning the degree to which I satisfy pertinent rules or roles. This would entail that "It's mine" is always socialized; I know of myself only what observers know of me.

Lennon, McCartney, or Sartre[4] wouldn't agree. Each would likely insist that he is never rightly perceived by others. They hear a voice or acknowledge his vocation when all should look past the message when listening for the messenger. But what could that mean: are we looking for the existential core or the raw, unschooled sensibility? The core isn't observable to third parties; even the person conscious of him- or herself can only say "me" or "me, again." Are we nevertheless close to the existential truth if we imagine a person remade by a different education and circumstances, as if his or her untutored sensibility might be identified when abstracted from its historically contingent formations? The verificationist dilemma is here: what could we know of capacities and inclinations that would have emerged had education or opportunities been different? We turn away from innate capacities out of regard for the only evidence we have: namely, observable achievements. Presented with unschooled children, teachers make the plausible

---

[3] John Lennon, Paul McCartney, *The Beatles*, "With a little help from my friends," *Sgt. Pepper's Lonely Hearts Club Band*, Capitol Records, June, 1967, © Northern Songs Ltd, England.

[4] Jean-Paul Sartre, *Being and Nothingness*, trans. Hazel E. Barnes (New York: Citadel, 2001), pp. 52–53.

assumption that education will transform them as surely as water boils when heated. This becomes a strategy and doctrine: knowing little or nothing of our children's unformed talents, we defer to education's likely effects. Ignoring innate variations, hence the distinctive private spaces they condition, we forsake the idea that we educate raw capacities. Opportunity and motivation may expose talents that education ignored, but most students will never know what they might have done or been.

Our narrow focus seems reasonable because teachers don't have access to student talents, apart from practices that hone student skills. But this is a narrow window, one responsible for our cramped perception of human nature, achievement, and satisfaction: we see what's done, hence the skill for doing it, not what could have been done. We teach the average skills appropriate to effective social and economic roles; we're careless with people having skills or imagination out of scale. People who could do more are suppressed or marked as troublemakers. They fight back or struggle, then capitulate. We say little about a student's nature because nurture is the only way to reveal it. Closer analyses of DNA may fill this gap when its structure is correlated to practice and behavior, though our emphasis on conformity provokes a question we can't answer: is deficient behavior evidence of insufficient capacity, poor training, or resistance?

Agency, properly extended, would signify unknown wells of capacity in the undifferentiated many. It would acknowledge people frustrated; those who believe that something of worth in themselves is unexplored. Why honor or nourish an unknown; why extend the idea of agency to acknowledge inferred powers unless circumstances are propitious to their cultivation and use? Our habitual response is careless; most cultures ignore the intelligence of women without acknowledging that anything valuable is lost. It's easier to suppose that the uneducated are uneducable. But two costs subvert us while unacknowledged: the loss of useful skills, and the frustration of people who feel unfulfilled or cheated. Privacy is a sanctuary, but also a trap, a place to which one comfortably withdraws, unless it's a site of grievance. People perpetually denied the opportunity to express themselves are rankled by disappointment, however well disguised. This is costly: calculate all that's lost when fractions of a population are furious or demoralized when their talents are ignored.

1d. Idiosyncrasy. Kant assumed the affinity and good will of people who share values and circumstances; his imperative would reduce conflict among agents who may provoke it merely because of complexity, confusion, or competition for scarce resources or opportunities. But those are not the limits of our differences. How are agents to be cut from the same moral cloth when each has a character developed from a specific history, an intellect formed by certain challenges, and a sensibility cultivated in disparate cultures or domains? Why be surprised, given resources that qualify us for judgment, action, and reflection, that we are morally variable while satisfying society's common tasks or loyalties?

Why suppose that people who vary in either way will apply the categorical imperative with the same results? Is lying always the same violation; does it imply the same community-destroying effect if you construe it as purposively spreading misinformation, while I regard it as strategic subterfuge? Kant was aware that personal desires and moral perspectives diverge; his imperative would make them cohere without violence. The imperative needn't be applied in ways that suppress variety because difference—wear clothes that suit you—doesn't always provoke conflict. It doesn't suffocate personal and situational differences until construed as the demand for a framework of universalizing rules. Never be late, no disloyalty, worship no other god; let everyone show his or her commitment to the local community by respecting its rules. This is good sense when the rules are traffic laws, though Kantian uniformities violate moral sense in other circumstances. Don't feed this child, until everyone in your situation could feed whom? This child, some comparable child, or all children?

Is there a common ground for morality when we abstract from the idiosyncrasies of people or their situations? Kant ignored variability and ambiguity by supposing that moral identity has a simple condition: wills are true to a rational standard—consistency universalized—if they satisfy the categorical imperative. Morality of this sort resembles a pure note, low-D or high-C, rather than an octave located somewhere on the scale between them. Why so many notes? Because moral identity is fluid as we move in and out of complex situations where significant aims and virtues conflict: choices have good effects while motives are confused and information is imperfect, or we're clear headed and well informed though satisfaction of one value requires betraying another. Societies cohere morally because participants agree about the values and aims appropriate to everyday affairs, not because all have the same response to situations perceived differently.

What is the least society requires of me as I make decisions appropriate to my aims? Kant's aim was a rule that inhibits choices and actions sure to sabotage the possibility of community, hence the freedom of individuals otherwise going their separate ways. Coffee or tea? Your choice because neither threatens community. His standard—adherence to a principle that would inhibit community-subverting choices—isn't cogent if action is to be efficacious in two domains that don't always cohere: the community where cooperation makes us productive and rules mitigate conflict, versus the private lives of that society's participants.

A law requires that one stop at red lights. Every Kantian would observe it, but what should a man do when driving his pregnant wife to the hospital moments before she delivers? Private interests are often threatened by universal laws; does a logical standard (consistency) override individual welfare, especially when inconsistency (violation of a universal) is the only cost? What good does the universal serve if not the distributed well-being of those it covers. If the driver collides with other cars when going through a red light, we have a disaster that focuses a moral dilemma; but if not, we have a logical conflict—the universal and its exception—misdiagnosed as a moral conflict. Does this imply that individual, situational choices always trump social/moral universals? No, it affirms that universals have no moral authority apart from the instrumental value achieved by promoting stability and reliability when individuals negotiate social complexity at minimal cost to themselves, their partners, and neighbors.

This pragmatic test is sensitive to the variability of people, their capacities, situations, and attitudes. Violinists play together in a section that sounds as one when its virtuoso yields a little to the slower speed and articulation of his partners. Theirs is a difference of skill; moral variations have different conditions. Their bases are the coupled faculties—principally intellect, sensibility, and self-control—responsible for the moral identity acquired as we choose and act. Intellect discriminates and integrates; sensibility is feeling and taste, a cultivated power for perception and delight that responds as quickly to people, sport, or circumstances as to ideas, music, or food. Where all see or hear, it is sensibility that explains what we look for and enjoy. Self-control is founded in habits and attitudes that routinize thought and will as they respond to ordinary tasks and circumstances. This is character, our stabilizer.

Acknowledge this range of powers for discriminating one's interests, feelings, needs, and aims, then consider the diversity of roles and rules, partners and circumstances where these powers are brought to bear: why is it plausible that this diversity of motives and circumstances should yield to Kant's simple rule? Isn't it too simple when everyday life requires the coordination of two sometimes conflicted aims: maximize social stability, while facilitating individual choice and well-being? Kant deferred to his rational ideal—universality and consistency—though his standard is crippled by contrary aims (save the young or save the old when you can't save both) and by social interests at cross-purposes with individual needs and abilities. He rightly feared personal choices that sabotage the possibility of choices that are coherent when generalized, but societies are not defenseless: people know and discount their liars; banks raise interest rates to cover losses from borrowers who renege on their loans.

Moral identity is the product of an unstable coupling: it emerges when personal idiosyncrasies are formed by roles, reciprocities, and vocations while disciplined by laws and traditions. A singer's talent is formed by her teachers, then by her parts and partners. She learns scruples appropriate to rehearsals, performances, and critics. We might describe her ascent to universality with Hegel, but that would lose all the detail of her history: how could she sing any role without drawing on the particularity of moral intuitions acquired as a maturing woman in a culture that biases experience in ways peculiar to itself? Yet there are also countervailing, stylized, and generic forces. For much we do is learned, when established structures or traditions limit our choices. We speak our parents' language, learn their virtues, and think largely as they did. Accessible vocations are those of one's society, so one's job is likely a variant of those common or familiar to one's neighbors.

Roles one acquires entail a moral posture for which practitioners are responsible: being a lawyer, nurse, or lifeguard carries moral and legal duties specific to these roles. Does this imply that the impression of personal choice is an illusion? This isn't the whole burden of responsibility because every such duty is less than the weight of moral identity. Josef Mengele was doubly culpable: because he violated his oath as a doctor, and because conscience didn't countermand his sadism. Moral identity is the inhibiting force that intercedes when roles or circumstances encourage behavior averse or abhorrent to morality.

1e. Constraints. Rules, laws, or vocation give us social standing, hence some degree of respect, while disguising the anxiety—shared by all—that deference to rules is prudent because we are vulnerable and all the more fragile because competitive. We learn these two constraints: give everyone his or her due; live and let live. Collaborate when doing so is mutually useful; find viable bases for cooperation when interdependence is acknowledged. Are there discrepancies in nature or society that embellish some while degrading others? Rebalance life's chances if the answer is yes. Finding causes but no justifications for these differences, finding them sustained by embedded inequities, we challenge or correct them.

This is moral identity of the second order, moral identity as it amends the unregulated effects of the morality governed by rules or roles. People accepting this responsibility justify the trust of their fellows, for this is the posture of those who participate in Rousseau's general will: it wills the good for all. We acknowledge that others want well-being as much as ourselves, and that many won't likely achieve it if we are not personally and collectively self-regulating. There is no guarantee that altered practice, personal or social, will not have other malign effects, but it is practical wisdom that deliberation and experiment are conditions for altering the unintended effects of personal or social behavior. This is the morality of creatures whose lives are managed by their powers of self-control, not merely by whim, accident, or the unforeseen effects of complexity and conflict.

The morality described here has three constituents and an override. Inclinations are the point of reference: what do I want to do or be? How do I go about doing or being it? Next are my roles, their tasks and duties. Third are the practices, rules, and laws that constrain social relations. The override? Acquiring foresight; practicing inhibition. We modulate one of the three when its exercise distorts one or both of the other two: we relent, for example, when a partner's vulnerability supersedes his or her role and duties. Which of the three is usually determining? Ideally, there is balance among them: we are effectively socialized while distinctively ourselves. But this is smug when said, and easier said than done.

1f. Interiority. Which duties are determining? Morality's three social anchors (the relations of intimates, relations that are commercial/ vocational, or holistic) suppress autonomy in the name of affiliation, reciprocity, loyalty, efficacy, or safety. Resisting them makes one alien or an outlaw, yet individuality can't form without psychic space. Nietzsche described its genesis in a passage quoted more fully above:

> Meanwhile the organizing 'idea' that is destined to rule keeps growing deep down—it begins to command; slowly it leads us back from side roads and wrong roads...it trains all subservient capacities before giving any hint of the dominant task, 'goal', 'aim', or 'meaning'.

Interiority is our sensitive core. Favored pursuits give it purpose; meanings and taste give it valence. Interests are common, though inclinations are personal: I'm at peace with myself when doing this well (whatever it be). "To thine own self be true" is advice from the center.

Where does interiority form? Farms or a town—Dewey in Vermont, Emerson in Massachusetts—are likely sites. Cities are oppressive to those who hate congestion, but they liberate initiative and experiment in people who prize anonymity. Urban complexity intensifies specialization and competition: one needs quick wit to discern opportunity, then education, connections, or money to seize it. Abilities are honed for specific tasks in law, finance, medicine, science, government, or education, but all who succeed are distinguished by intellectual and emotional autonomy. Communities of professionals are, in the best of circumstances, self-monitoring and self-correcting. Each of their commercial, industrial, or cultural spheres has a discipline where behavior is reliably safe and steady. But these vocations are loci of privilege and advantage, not the only sites where privacy resonates. No one escapes interiority, because human physiology guarantees it: everyone seeks a clear path through his or her near-world. Public policy is challenged because no social order of any scale does for all what cities do for some.

1g. Meaning. Personal identity is often fixed by the accidents of birth and one's circumstances, though the array of identities available in principal cities is reminiscent of the masks and costumes offered in popup shops that open before Halloween: one chooses what to do or be from an array of personas. Trajectories that were once unimaginable are now familiar and tempting. But duties are askew, moral identity is unstable when core loyalties are misaligned. Before, character, church, and commerce assured that people would have habits and expectations likely to change slowly, if at all. Now, when irony or cynicism makes commitment less assured, we do what we're afraid not to do, or we do it because it's advantageous. Where commitment is shallow and willed, we use laws and inducements—money, status, or threats—to enforce it.

What explains this shift from disputes about practical priorities—pay the grocer before paying the electric bill—to seismic shifts of attitude regarding one's obligations to families, work, the church, or state? A principal reason is that practical interests aren't a sufficient basis for distinguishing the zones of moral concern. More than life-preserving, each taste or affinity is also life-affirming, because infused with meanings that justify or explain one's commitment. Why be loyal to this spouse or team? Because each positions the agent in a firmament of meanings. Loyalties would be unintelligible or unworthy without them. For meaning is one of the two ways we locate ourselves in the world: is this Jerusalem, Riyadh, or Rome; a city with a mayor and a street plan, or the place where human history acquired significance? Visitors from Mars need warning signs or maps; but there are no maps for people who have lost their faith. Where do they go when the signs of personal and moral identity have altered or lapsed?

Meanings, like practical needs, color-code our circumstances: this, not that—apples, not stones, are edible; this, not that, is my child or church. Moral identity is an array of vectors illuminating the people, things, practices, or tasks we value. Their worth is often doubled: eating is a devotion, an opportunity for thanking our god for his beneficence: work, as in medicine, is the duty of care. But this balance—need or significance—is unstable. We dress for warmth and propriety, with or without regard for style. But fashion may be our over riding aim, so we're careless about discretion and safety: she wobbles on six-inch heels.

2. Three Perspectives: Nodes

Nodes are steady sources of effects that create, sustain, or affect other things. Agency is nodal because human alliances make us dependent on one another, but also responsible to and for one another. Systems too are nodal: families, businesses, and states have consequences for constituents, others, and themselves. Socialized autonomy, zone morality, and tradition are three venues where nodality is morally consequential.

2a. Socialized autonomy. Morality is often construed in either or both of two ways: one makes regulation personal and private by pitting reason, judgment, or discretion against impulse or appetite; the other uses law and punishment as a guarantor of acceptable behavior when self-control isn't reliable. These strategies have converging aims: subordinate desire for the sake of personal discipline and public order; enhance safety and productivity by regularizing individual actions and their effects. We justify our rigor by saying that people are often reckless.

This, number twenty-two of Jonathan Edwards' *Resolutions*, is a sample of attitudes that may have been common in 1723 when America was mostly a frontier:

> Resolved, to endeavor to obtain for myself as much happiness, in the other world, as I possibly can, with all the power; might, vigor, and vehemence, yea violence, I am capable of, or can bring myself to exert, in any way that can be thought of.[5]

Self-love was familiar to Augustine, Descartes, and Spinoza. All affirmed it as a universal instinct, though Edwards reduced sensibility to grievance and self-assertion. This is autonomy unmoored from the reciprocal causal relations that sustain productive activity. They embody negative feedback: argue too forcibly and friends ask you to stop. Hence the equilibrium where interiority—deliberation, judgment, and choice—defends autonomy while acknowledging shared aims and one's partners.

---

[5] Jonathan Edwards, *Resolutions: and Advice to Young Converts* (Philipsburg: P and R Publishing, 2001), no. 22, p. 2.

The analogy of a previous chapter—woods or a copse—is useful here. Each tree has roots, trunk, and foliage. Each is physically autonomous and responsible for effects on things of the sphere it creates and sustains, but all owe some part of their well-being to the environment established by the ensemble. Extrapolate to people in social environments: individuals establish families, neighborhoods, businesses, or states that nest and overlap, creating environments where individuals are relatively autonomous while mutually sustaining.

This contrariety—autonomous but mutually affecting—expresses off setting pressures. We know and hardly disguise our personal aims and frustrations, but all is discounted when familiar accounts of social activity emphasize standard responses to generic circumstances. Individuality is only numeric difference: we are young or old, buyers or sellers. Vocations, genders, and fads have a similar effect when invoked to classify us indiscriminately. This isn't foolish if similarity is all that matters, though the effect is pernicious—idiosyncrasy loses relevance—when individuals are stripped of all but generic agency: I am whatever marketing reports say of me. But is it true that my aims and values are only those of my kind?

We may blame that implication on laws and the conditions for social coherence, but they don't, in themselves, justify this Procrustean bias. Laws that coordinate complex activities are essential facilitators; traffic laws, for example, separate moving cars for their mutual safety and efficiency. There are many such techniques for separating agents having an identical aim: different keys for the locks of different homes. Yet separation and safety, like traffic lights, are means, not ends. Every individual has an essential devotion to his or her well-being, but also tastes, inclinations, and signature ways of satisfying common aims. Each is a node from which multiple effects ensue, some intended, not all controlled.

Trees in a wood are overlapped by the roots and canopies of their neighbors. Effects proliferate because reciprocity relates each node to some or many others. There are opportunities for doing as one likes, but sometimes the whole is a plenum where each space is confined by other spaces and their occupants. Late for an appointment, I stop a cab that stalls in traffic: autonomy languishes because qualified by events. No agent fully controls him- or herself, because all respond to circumstances and other agents. Each has a trajectory; but all are encumbered by genes, history, aims, and circumstances.

Psychic posture is the social product of these powers and constraints. It has character, attitudes, intellect, and sensibility, but its shape is elusive; like a rough surface, it reflects light in several directions at once. Steady when seen from one perspective, it has a different cast if one steps left or right. This variability is apparent in communities of every size, though most conspicuously in cities, because their complexity enables diverse choices while restricting autonomy. Each precinct is a complex of niches where choice is qualified by restrictions imposed by partners, neighbors, rules, laws, or local customs. Residents usually restrict themselves to the familiar streets of home and work, though local transport facilitates ventures into neighborhoods where they encounter people whose attitudes and expectations differ from their own. Nothing untoward usually happens because public encounters require behavior that is reliably benign throughout the city. Suppose, however, that a rider mistakenly leaves a bus or train at a stop different from his own. The neighborhood is unfamiliar, people are different. Uncertain that the attitudes and look of his local neighborhood are acceptable here, he treads carefully. If diffidence is a bad idea, swagger would be reckless. How do we bind disparate neighborhoods and tribes if one travels abroad merely by taking a city bus?

Is moral identity always local, so postures amicable in one precinct look belligerent when addressed to visitors from another? Several responses soften apprehension and avert conflict. One is repression or disguise in people who are careful not to betray their differences. Are they guarded out of respect for others; because difference is punished; or because one represses traits that elude social approval? Conflicts are sometimes provoked by the reasonable fear that opponents would deny us life or the means to live, but one may be prudent without being defensive or belligerent. Why not acknowledge that otherness is usually benign; grant what others need to live, then consider issues that still divide us? Many disputed interests assure that conflicts will be hard to solve or never solved, but this attitude would mitigate disputes if conscientiously practiced. It isn't encouraged because of fear, and because we imagine that a first strike will devastate the other side.

Though usually it doesn't, so conflict intensifies until we destroy one another. States and corporations do this to one another; people do it too.

Conflicts are envenomed by personalities whose self-esteem requires their control of others. There isn't always redress for the worst of them, because their victims are intimidated or seduced. This too is socialization, though its pathologies are complementary: the autocrat needs deference; his admirers find courage and standing by identifying with their shameless guide. Their relationship is the inverse of agent-health. The autocrat's psychic autonomy is often crippled; he's desperate for admiration. His admirers want self-esteem but can't achieve it without attaching themselves to one who sees evidence of his worth in their rapture. Compare contrarians or conscientious objectors; both reject the autocrat's blandishments because they dislike thoughtless consensus. Contrarians reject views that may seem plausible, because they feel entrapped by collaboration. Conscientious objectors reject affiliation because they're offended by ideas or practices that seem false or perverse. Neither can tolerate an autocrat's wiles. Yet socialization is, quixotically, one of autonomy's conditions: we're free to be ourselves, doing whatever is distinctive about us, in the company of people with whom we collaborate.

2b. Zone morality. Zone morality signifies moral interests and codes that apply in four domains. One is the zone of autonomous moral agents; the three other zones are morally consequential social relationships: systems that are core, vocational/commercial, or holistic (civil, statist, or tribal).[6] Each is a node, hence multiply consequential; every agent participates in zones of all four kinds. Core systems are families and friendships. Interactions are regular; members are mutually familiar. Roles are well-defined but supple and diverse: one is a younger sister, parent, or friend. Transactional relationships—in stores, work, or school—are normalized by formalities specific to a task: student and teacher, customer and clerk. Each responds to the other in ways appropriate to his or her roles. The relationships of totalizing systems—states or religions—are more detached: there are civic, criminal, and commercial laws, religious rules and rituals.

Every such relationship is moral by virtue of its fulfillment conditions: namely, the causal reciprocities that bind a relationship's participants.

---

6 See David Weissman, *Zone Morality* (Berlin: Walter De Gruyter, 2014).

These are systems that embody the two kinds of feedback: negative and positive. Negative feedback implies both a range of viability, and a response by one or more of a relationship's members if that range is exceeded. So, buyers and sellers continue to do business while prices rise or fall within a range, though business is disrupted if prices exceed that range at either end: buyers stop buying if the price of goods exceeds their limit; sellers stop selling if it drops below a limit. Each advises the other if the rise or fall exceeds their tolerance; business resumes when the price falls or rises to a range that is viable for both. The control on positive feedback is steady satisfaction: people pour into a rising stock market, as miners rushed to California when there seemed to be endless gold in mountain streams. How is morality embodied in causal reciprocities? It establishes the satisfaction conditions for a relationship's members: this (whatever it be) is what each participant need do to maintain an exchange relation to his or her partner.[7] Each has the same message for the other: be honest and consistent; give me what I need to maintain our relationship. Disappointed expectations—no more gold—quash feedback of both sorts.

Core systems satisfy basic interests and needs. Moral demands vary among families or friendships, but certain duties and attitudes structure the feedback relations common to all: receive support but take care that you also give it. Commercial or vocational relationships are narrowly functional: their efficacy requires that participants satisfy their roles: buyers and sellers, students and teachers. Obligations are stark: work for a salary; study for a grade. Corporate—holistic—relations are typically prefigured by its rules or laws, then expressed by its practices. A strong church or central government reduces conflict by imposing its rules. A democracy responds by encouraging participation in forums where competing claims are argued and negotiated; its legal procedures promise fairness. Systems of both sorts encourage the consistency that promotes social stability and predictability: coordination is eased because actions required are those expected.

Imagine that nothing breaks the rhythm of a small community: population and resources are stable; people are productive and mutually respectful. Members are predictable and safe when circumstances are

---

[7] David Weissman, *A Social Ontology* (New Haven: Yale University Press, 2000), pp. 50–52.

benign because all defer to the mores prescribed by local stories and rituals. But this isn't uniformity. Members acknowledge their different interests and attitudes: young and old, men and women, shopkeepers and their customers. Variability expresses the paradox that stability is fluid to some degree as practices alter with circumstances, meanings, and one's perspective. There is diversity, but social diversity, like that in art or music, can generate harmonies or dissonance: practicalities cohere, or they're mutually inimical because of scarce resources, political discord, cost, or inefficiencies. Shall our town pay for schools or transportation; unable to agree, we do neither.

What is stability's ground: its structured zones—families, businesses, the state—or the autonomy and discipline of its citizens? Abraham Lincoln, or the Union Army? The answer is surely both: no stable systems in any zone without people to sustain it. What percentage of the population does it require? Numbers vary with circumstances, but we know when the number is too low because basic systems are degraded: schools, marriages, or businesses can't fail everywhere without affecting every system coupled to them. Now consider that the practical foci of social zones are augmented and distorted by the personal zone. Its focus is oneself: what do I need or want? Practical decisions that were fraught when social zones were the only focus—work or family—are intensified by guilt or lust. Which has priority if I want an expensive dinner when my children, or the neighbor's children, need shoes? We may allege that choices are principled, though evidence usually reduces to the practices historically favored by the local community. Does local sentiment affirm that neighbors are responsible for the welfare of other people's children? Because if not, one isn't blamed for ignoring them.

The four zones fill most of the space where morality is invoked, but not all of it. There are, for example, casual or chance relationships that seem to fall beyond all the zones: someone trips on a leg carelessly extended; cars drench a pedestrian when turning a corner in the rain. But these are not anomalies; they fit the corporate, totalizing zone where reciprocity requires the recognition of others' dignity, and a standard of behavior like that of Mill's no-harm principle. For we are often in mutually affecting relationships with people who are otherwise unknown. Those occasions provoke the obligation of care: knowing that we may affect people adversely, many of them unknown, we control what we do and how we do it. Discretion at these extremes expresses our tacit self-regard. For we, like Descartes, Hume, Kant, and Mill, ground morality in an idea of ourselves and our deserts before generalizing to all who are like us. This, like the idea that we are souls made in the image of God, expresses the secular hope that there may be empathy and safety in the presence of difference.

2c. Tradition. Tradition is history learned osmotically: we absorb its beliefs and practices while hearing its stories and performing its rituals. Its lessons and meanings tell us who we are; its history distinguishes us from those who are alien because they don't share our memories. This is tradition from the inside, the warmth and comfort of the tribe. But tradition is fragile. Clothes, haircuts, or sociality distinguish sects in secular cities where other visible differences have lapsed. Nor does history survive in many people beyond loyalty or aversion. This is a significant loss to societies where traditional stories and practices were the moral glue infusing young and old with standards, permissions, and prohibitions. Communities reduce to aggregates; the analogy to forests of separate trees is ever more accurate when anomie[8] pervades us. We reduce to ourselves, hence the vulnerability of people having free will: responsible for what we choose and do, we can't hide behind social identities we've renounced. Women once expected men to open doors for them; men expected patience from women less tolerant of their foibles. Each is somewhat disappointed in the other; many of both won't defend the old way

3. Three Perspectives: The Whole

Agents perceive that each is one of many, and that the whole is an interest distinguishable from those of individual agents, core and intermediate systems. All are helped or hurt by totalizing interests: divine grace or climate change, for example.

3a. Kant and Hegel. Kant's emphasis on will's autonomy pries individuality from the tide of unconsidered choices. Sovereign wills exhibit their freedom by withholding assent from practices that can't

---

[8] Emile Durkheim, *Emile Durkheim on Morality and Society* (Chicago: University of Chicago Press, 1973), p. 145.

be universalized without contradiction: pay your bills, don't lie. Kant's intention was sober: limit diversity at the point where it subverts order and productivity. He knew that people go different ways, but Kant is ambiguous: which has priority in his thinking: order and uniformity, or freedom and difference?

This uncertainty is intensified by several dubious assumptions: *i*. Kant assumed that contexts where decisions are made are often enough alike to be considered identical for the purposes of universalizing a maxim (a rule or plan for prospective action). But are they identical beyond a superficial inspection? Imagine three people waiting on a station platform when there is space for just one additional passenger on the arriving train. What's the next step: should no one board; should all the current riders descend because only one can board? Which of the three should have priority—the person going to work, another to a movie, a third to a doctor—if urgencies differ? This example is no problem for Kant, you say, because these differences disqualify their situations as identical. Alright: suppose each of the three is going to a doctor, though for ailments of different severities. Still not identical? Refine them more: each suffers the same illness to the same degree, but in different parts of the body. Identity is elusive. Is it secured by considering candidate mental states; are agents enough alike to be considered identical when comparing their aims, values, and history? Surely not: the interests and motives of one may be unlike any other. Circumstances may never be the same. *ii*. One may never have information sufficient to know that an action would satisfy Kant's imperative, because observable effects ramify forever, while others, some immediate and nearby, are never observed. I don't know the totality of my effects, pernicious or not, when testing a maxim. *iii*. Kant's test for consistency is too simple: do nothing that everyone in situations of a kind can't do without contradiction. You order chocolate, I order vanilla: this seems coherent, though conflict is a short distance away if the choice of either entails bankrupting costs for the other. *iv*. Kant's examples—credit and lying—mislead because they are narrowly chosen. Imagine a culture where people hesitate to marry anyone their parents oppose. Would the culture teeter if one person were to violate parental wishes? Would confidence plunge were five to do it? Would credit or honesty cease if several or many were to cheat or lie? We know that doesn't happen, because credit and communication persist though some people ignore Kant's imperative.

Kant's argument for withholding assent derives from Descartes' fourth *Meditation*: don't affirm any maxim that can't be consistently universalized by everyone in circumstances like those of the agent; inhibit the will until reason is satisfied that all the implications of a proposed action are clearly and distinctly perceived.[9] That formulation frees will of its immediate social burden (other people's expectations) when its freedom of action is reduced to two possibilities: don't choose because the categorical imperative isn't satisfied (a maxim's implications aren't clear and distinct), or affirm a choice that satisfies the imperative, however banal (everyone breathe).

This outcome evolved when Hegel evoked reason to control sensibility. Kant required only that the cacophony of desires be regimented by employing the imperative to eliminate the maximally destructive effects of contradiction: no trust if all can lie, therefore, no collaboration. This could be elaborated with a series of *ad hoc* prohibitions, each alleging a risk to social coherence if generalized: no gambling, no adultery, no fast driving. But social control requires measures more systematic. Hegel supplied the rationale: reason should introduce a suite of laws, rules, and roles.[10] Max Weber's efficient bureaucrats were Hegel's clerics: they could be trusted to rationalize any public service that seemed disorderly.[11] Kant (like Mill) tried to honor the autonomy of individual moral wills; let them do as they wish up to the point of violating the categorical imperative (or Mill's no-harm principle). Hegel supposed that we are imperfectly moral or free until private wills have achieved the perfected coherence, the righteousness of the Absolute: moral laws are to conduct and conscience what natural laws are to nature. The latter are known; the former are willed. Nature is created as the Absolute entertains and affirms ideas that nature embodies; we internalize the moral law by affirming and applying it. The convicted murderer is elated on the way to being hanged because he acknowledges that this sentence locates him accurately in the moral order of being; there is no gap, no discrepancy between his desert and his will. This is theology repurposed as ethics:

---

9   René Descartes, *Meditations on First Philosophy*, in: *Discourse on the Method and Meditations on First Philosophy*, ed. David Weissman (New Haven: Yale University Press, 1996), pp. 84–90.
10 G. W. F. Hegel, *The Phenomenology of Mind*, trans. G. B. Baillie (New York: Harper, 1967), pp. 384–89.
11 Max Weber, *Economy and Society, Volume 2*, eds. Guenther Roth and Claus Wittich (Berkeley: University of California Press, 1978), pp. 1381–461.

human consciousness loses its finitude by rising to the consciousness of the Absolute; will is relieved of moral error when godhood is achieved by consciousness thinking itself: I desire only what reason and a god's law would have me desire. What is moral autonomy in our less exalted human domain? Just the affirmation of laws that socialization prescribes: the Ten Commandments, for example.

Kant might have deplored Hegel's coercive morals and their implications for personal differences and freedom, though their shared emphasis on the universal applicability of mind's transcendental faculties is reminiscent of Plato: normative reason ought to prevail over ephemeral personal impulses. Kant's divided account of mind—an ego that is empirical and/or transcendental—entails that will, too, is ontologically complex: one part is responsible for motor action; the other makes decisions from outside space and time. That dualist formulation (one that locates mind both in the world and out of it) obscures the circumstances of people having scanty information and imperfect self-control but demanding partners, exigent duties, and scarce resources. His emphasis—reason is noble, desire is base—loses its categorial force if reason is understanding, a faculty that sorts, organizes, and appraises information through the narrow window of need and opportunity. Kant's holistic emphasis—what all should do—is an aristocratic interest, one that abstracts from the urgencies and vulnerabilities of improvident people. He left no moral space for those whose choices are forced.

3b. Justice. What can justice be to those for whom autonomy is a principal value? Does self-love trump justice? For everyone is self-concerned: all have memories and plans focused squarely on themselves. What's to be made of other people, if one's purposes are foreground, while their concerns recede into obscurity? Where is the middle way between Hegel's absolutes, and the variability of inclinations, priorities, and states of affairs?

Justice requires perspective: all can say, with Descartes, I am, I exist. Each has a claim on resources needed to satisfy wants and aims; their satisfaction usually requires the competence and support of other people. We come to acknowledge that each person has duties and aims comparable to one's own, and that cooperation is usually the only way to satisfy all. Mutual tolerance is nevertheless slow to gel if every day is a competitive struggle for partners and resources: *Live and let live* isn't compelling while defending oneself from someone who doesn't believe in it. Forbearance comes more easily if one starts with ample opportunities, and a network of family and friends. There, where collaboration is assumed and empathy is generous, distributive justice seems easy because partners are recognizable versions of oneself.

Is it preferable that we cite empathy rather than prudent self-interest when defending the laws and practices of a just society? Fellow-feeling is critical to its emotional tone; but implementing a just distribution of rights and resources doesn't go well if equity is widely resented. Distributed rights and benefits are resisted where factional advantages make Kant's starting point—the Kingdom of Ends—unintelligible. Rousseau made unanimity—an equal voice for every participant—a condition for founding a society that originates in the general will and a social contract.[12] But people preoccupied, vain, competitive, or tribal don't accept the equalizing implications of saying "I am, I exist." Distributive justice is their *bête noire* because agency is solipsistic: one doesn't see beyond the clash of people opposing one's anxiety or indulgence. Or a circle of entitlement founded in tribal meanings—of loyalty, purpose, or belief—establishes the only reality acknowledged.

Injustice is endemic. Why is it tolerated? Because of solipsistic fantasies, greed, and the pleasure of controlling other people. But also for this reason: corporations, schools, or teams are organized for the efficient production of goods or services: not everyone is qualified to play third base. Is it good enough that outcomes are unequal because talents and opportunities aren't equal? Marx was prescient: "From each according to his ability; to each according to his needs."[13] This is contentious at times of scarcity. But suppose that productivity is ample, and that education and opportunities inspire discipline and deter free riders. Why isn't this a reasonable policy in favorable circumstances? Why on this condition would we, why do we, tolerate the indulgence of some at cost to many?

4. Reflection. Ardor and frustration are well distributed at all three levels: individual, nodal, and the whole. Failure is sometimes useful if one acknowledges complexities we can't avert.

---

12 Jean-Jacques Rousseau, *The Social Contract and Other Later Political Writings* (Cambridge: Cambridge University Press, 1997), p. 57.
13 Karl Marx, *Critique of the Gotha Program* (Rockville: Wildside Press, 2008), p. 27.

4a. Self-regulation. Kant had emphasized that action's effects exceed will's control. Moral responsibility starts here, where agency is causality and causal power includes self-control. Others hold me responsible for acts chosen and performed when I could have acted differently, or not at all. I am, on these occasions, praise- or blameworthy for effects that accrue (absent extenuating conditions: "you couldn't have known").

Learning to play the piano requires self-control: where do my fingers go? Roles in businesses and families require it, too: we learn what to do, with whom, where, and when. Many tasks are difficult, but each has lesson plans or directives that ease the way. The self-regulation appropriate to moral identity has heuristics, but no book of instructions; rules are generic, though moral perception is specific and nuanced. We learn it by considering action's effects, their costs, and beneficiaries. The surgery was a technical success, but the patient died: was it worth doing? This isn't a calculation for which there are *a priori* answers. Appraisals inform a discipline's procedures, as they're improved or proscribed. But equally, each is a moment of self-reflection in the negative feedback loops that monitor individual choices and actions: is this a procedure I should be doing?

Self-regulation is capacity and opportunity disciplined by oversight—inhibition, deliberation, judgment, and choice—given information about partners and resources, costs, and benefits. Most choices are made without this conscious inventory, though we imagine being able to justify our aims and values. Hard determinists suppose that this persuasion is window-dressing; we may be self-inhibiting for historical reasons, but not because self-regulation is a response to opposition or opportunities discerned as we assess a problem. This was the question of Chapter Two: do acquired abilities enable us to address novel or surprising situations; or is every solution conditioned by the tide of previous responses? Oversight and control are a test of this dispute because they exploit skills acquired as we learn to regulate ourselves in distinctive circumstances: learning the skills has a history, though any occasion for applying them may have no precedent in one's experience. Why did you turn left? I saw a gas station.

Deliberations provoked by oversight are three dimensional: forward, current or lateral, and past. What is our aim, and the plan for achieving it? How do we mark our progress? All this is prospective. We also look to the rear: what have we learned? Reflection spreads laterally as we consider the complex webs of mutual dependence that condition progress: what are we doing, how, and with whom? We know the partners directly engaged, while ignorant of supply chains unknown and unimagined. Are there duties owed to partners more remote, debts we don't recognize or pay? Oversight enhances efficiency; it covers these bases to some degree, while reducing costs to those affected, near or far.

Regulation appears in a different light when oversight is contrasted to stubborn persistence. Peirce described four methods for fixing belief.[14] Authority, *a priori* intuition, and scientific method prescribe or correct private opinions. Tenacity, the most primitive of the four, is fiercely personal. Adherents resist revision or correction because they know or imagine no better way, though tenacity needn't be crude: Edwards' "vehemence" and Napoleon's mastery were memorialized in William James' "The will to believe."[15] Persistence sometimes works: circumstances are transformed, facts on the ground are created when tenacity is allied to initiative and imagination. Notice too that action sometimes resists oversight, and that tenacity is action unadorned by prudence and regulation. For their relation expresses the suppressed tension between action and its control. We discount the pleasure children have when banging on a piano's keys; we want them to learn how to play. Yet we're aware of a competing interest: regulation is inhibiting; we lose spontaneity and power. This is tenacity's beauty (and often, its abuse): it sets agency—unrefined, honest, and bold—apart from its critics and controls.

4b. Responsibility. Consider the phrases *responsible for* and *responsible to*. Every agent is responsible mechanically for causing its effects. *Responsible to* has the additional implication that agents are responsible to those requiring justification for one's choices and actions. Demands and responses would be rhetorical if hard determinism were correct, because there would be no preventing the effects of a causal lineage. No one would be responsible for his or her effects, or responsible to anyone

---

14   C. S. Peirce, "The Fixation of Belief," *Collected Papers of Charles Sanders Peirce, Volumes 1-VI*, eds. Charles Hartshorne and Paul Weiss (Cambridge: Harvard University Press, 1934–1935), paras. 377–87, pp. 223–47.

15   William James, "The will to believe," *The Writings of William James*, ed. John J. McDermott (New York: Modern Library, 1968), pp. 717–35.

for justifying them because we, no more than wind or weather, would have freely chosen them. Yet there are forks in the road, situations large and small that may go different ways. People discern and seize these opportunities, making choices undetermined by their causal histories.

Morality enters the flux of causal activity when effects are determined, all or in part, by our intentions, actions, and the range of our control. For then, there are questions: Who is affected, how? What are our duties to them? Answers simplify our judgments of people and their conduct when perfect overlap—doing effectively what is beneficial, reasonable, and prudent—would be perfect virtue. Yet this is an unreasonable aim, given that it requires finesse, appropriate resources, and omniscience about the character and range of one's effects.

Tornados are responsible, but not culpable, for their effects. We are both: being responsible, we exhibit our moral identity by regulating ourselves. But there are ambiguities. Here are two sets of questions—distinguished as *4bi-viii* and *4bix-xiii*—and possible answers. The first set is pragmatic: *i.* What are intention's morally legitimate aims and concerns? *ii.* Which effects should we foresee? *iii.* Do available controls prevent unwanted effects? *iv.* How should we choose when an intended action will probably affect other people or things in disparate ways, some to their disadvantage? *v.* What are agents' duties to those adversely affected? *vi.* Effects ramify; how far does responsibility extend into remote, unforeseeable effects? How far should it extend? *vii.* Should we limit intention or action when foresight and control are known to be insufficient? *viii.* What is one's responsibility for social behavior one doesn't approve and can't prevent?

My responses tilt in the direction of prudence and responsibility. This is a consequentialist inclination, one sensitive to effects that ramify unforeseeably in complex situations. Reckless behavior sometimes punishes many people, including the agent responsible. Cooperation and the general will require the personal discipline that would reduce these effects.

4bi. What are intention's morally legitimate aims and concerns? Actions that enhance well-being or minimize harm to those affected.

4bii. Which effects should we foresee? Those normally resulting when people act as intended in familiar circumstances. We also extrapolate: what could happen?

4biii. Do available controls prevent unwanted effects? Some controls—inhibitions—are internal; other—laws, circumstances, or unwilling partners—are external. Acting many times a day, often carelessly, we assume that conditions are amenable to the actions intended, and that adequate controls are in place. But we aren't surprised that action misfires for want of personal care, or that circumstances weren't suitable to choices that seemed reasonable when made.

4biv. How should we choose if a considered action would likely affect other people, things, or ourselves adversely? We drive cars knowing that the pollution they cause is bad for us and the climate. We choose a short-term advantage—easy transport—for a long-term cost to health and the environment. Prudence would have us make other arrangements, though individual drivers aren't equipped to alter large-scale solutions (roads and cars) for distributed private advantages (driving as one chooses). Measures of harm for personal choices (opening an all-night bar) are often shallow and self-interested. A tolerance for pain and disruption—for oneself or others—is partly cultural: the more we value initiative, the less we calculate its effects.

Why are we reckless? Partly because action leaves so much unchanged, and because we lack graphic evidence of middle- and long-term effects. There are no pictures of cancerous lungs on cigarette packages sold in the United States. Tobacco companies don't want us to see the risk.

4bv. What are agents' duties to those adversely affected by their actions? Foresee the damage, when possible. Repair or compensate for it when foresight was too little or late. Courts and insurance companies have rough measures of the compensation appropriate to damaged people or things. Action is careful in proportion to the knowledge that agents will pay for their carelessness. But this is legalistic rather than principled: foresight and actions based on reasonable assumptions are a more stoutly moral defense

4bvi. Effects ramify; how far does responsibility extend to unforeseeable effects? How far should it extend? Every action has effects that exceed our ability to track them, but that isn't an excuse for ignoring the likelihood of effects we can anticipate. What happens if children aren't educated? Nothing grave tomorrow, but severe costs for days to come.

4bvii. Should we limit intention or action when foresight and control are known to be insufficient? What should be done when future effects are undecipherable? Socrates advice was plain: don't act if you can't see far enough ahead to confirm that action's implications aren't malign. But this advice falters when the effects of inaction are unacceptable. A patient needing surgery dies on the operating table: should the doctors have proceeded? The risks were known; there was no good answer.

4bviii. What is one's responsibility for communal behavior one doesn't approve and can't prevent? What is one to do when society has policies or practices one opposes? This is sometimes the effect of being a minority when the majority prefers a different course. One may be patient: experience and judgment may alter opinions when the issue is next considered. Though decisions may never be corrected because the majority always favors what was done or because it never considers that its actions have effects that are pernicious and irreversible. Personal responses may be no stronger than irritation; but what if they rise to moral outrage: what should such people do? Demonstrate; try to rouse others. But what if those who respond lack the social or political influence that would alter policy or practice? Is there a point at which moral outrage may be regarded as protest enough? Is one excused of responsibility for practices one opposes if one has expressed indignation?

Dispersed individuals, vulnerable, and afraid alienated but mostly passive, are no challenge to complex systems acting for reasons that are tribal, economic, or political. Organization alone may frustrate moral judgment, as tyrannies and slave states do. But organization alone is not always the issue: America abuses immigrants at its southern border despite being democratically organized. States and societies of its design are more consistently benign because their procedures were designed for equity. Yet government and bureaucracy are moral agents of the second order. Designed to minimize the harm they do, they regulate but can't always control people responsible for official choices. Does the state do horrible things in our name because of officers protected constitutionally from our strictures and remorse; are we complicit in their crimes whatever our reservations? We're trapped in a political system designed for good will and self-correction. That design betrays us if elected officials and constitutional controls are too lame to withstand willful leaders.

Questions of the second set are more theoretic: *ix*. Am I responsible for anything I choose to do or be, given that DNA, circumstances, and educational history are decisive for all I do? *x*. Is moral responsibility additional to causal responsibility? Is the moral burden incrementally different from the causal burden? Are there are extra-material principles—whether natural or conventional—supervening on our actions such that the morality of an act is founded in the satisfaction or violation of these principles, not merely in the act or its material effects? *xi*. Moral responsibility is uncertain when circumstances are complex. A first cause is sometimes hard to identify. Who started the quarrel that eventuated in a death; for what reason? *xii*. Are we praise- or blameworthy for a moral difference if we haven't chosen it? Stepping in front of a car saves a child's life, because the driver sees me, the adult, when he hadn't seen the child. But I, too, hadn't seen the child or acted on her behalf. Do I earn moral credit, or only recognition for my causal role? Is choice the desideratum: the act is moral only if chosen when its effects are foreseen? *xiii*. Is moral education additional to education that prepares one to make causal differences? *xiv*. One defers to authorities because of their power. Is that because power is their right; because power is intimidating; or because we believe that authority is virtuous?

These are questions that might be asked of any intention, action, or effect. The range of possible answers is indeterminate because each of the variables has a range of finely differentiated values. We are saved these large numbers because circumstances, partners, resources, and laws usually reduce to the small range of values acceptable within a culture or tradition. Stray outside approved values and you risk slipping into zones of infinite reproach. You didn't know that your mother-in-law was allergic to scotch? Should you have asked?

The diversity of variables and their values is not the end of moral trouble, because choices and actions are complicated by layered contexts of zones and meanings. Two are conspicuous: contrary demands are made by two or more of the core, vocational, or civic zones, or by the interpretive frameworks (church and school, for example) that infuse choice with significance. One yearns for simplicity when actions approved in one zone or framework are condemned in another. Kant supplied direction, but his imperative is not the solution when zones or meanings are mutually confounding. Not every conflict is resolved when all participants tell the truth.

4bix. Am I responsible for any part of what I am or do, given determinist strictures? This issue resolves in two ways: hard determinists believe that there are no free choices; the soft version affirms that information, values, and interests—not ancient precedents—are determining when emergent capacities for imagination, thought, or language address situations for which history has no responses. Why call ahead when late? To alert someone waiting for me. But why is she waiting? Because we agreed to meet, not because our meeting was foreseen and arranged in ancient times. The hard alternative requires that every agreement between independent beings express a synchrony established at the beginning of time. We're to believe that history perpetually resolves its complexity, all its parts in harmony. If I call, she's forewarned. Though hard determinism implies—when conflated with Leibniz's internal relations—that I needn't bother to call because, consciously or not, she's alerted already.

Purpose and responsibility might be adult fantasies: make life significant by instilling a sense of duty and contingency; encourage us to believe that what happens is up to us. But this explanation is more troubling than reassuring: designing and executing nature's harmonies would be enormously expensive in attention and effort. No agent less powerful than an omnipotent god could do it. Agree with Descartes and Leibniz that a god is the only cause, and there is no obstacle to saying that we have no responsibility for anything. The alternative is less theological: it explains our adaptation to current circumstances by citing emergent powers, current circumstances, and each person's intentions, skills, information, and scruples. They enable the choices and actions with which one responds to the ambient world. Are we deceived by trying to master time, circumstances, and our nature; why believe that we live into the future if all of us are playing out a history we can't override or redirect? These are silly illusions if each of us is a complicated windup toy. But we resist the idea that every current causal relation is the present moment in trajectories that meet or diverge because of a cosmic design or its determining natural laws. There is this simpler explanation: interventions in situations unforeseen are calculated, controlled, and often effective. All are enabled by agents who do or can inhibit responses while calculating the action most likely to satisfy partners or themselves.

4bx. Is moral responsibility additional to causal responsibility? Is the moral burden incrementally different from the causal burden? Local peasants catch rabbits on the lord's estate. The groundskeeper does it, too, but they're guilty of theft; he does it with the sanction of his job. Is this a conventional difference founded in social norms, or a qualitative difference in the act, its performance conditions, or its effects?

Probably the greater part of moral activity is in the habitual performance of one's duties. There is no difference between the moral and causal aspects of choice and action in these cases: parents care for their children; people work as colleagues or partners expect. Seeing one or the other, causation or duty, in the work they do is a function of perspective. Though a difference is sometimes visible: effects fall short of an agent's duty, because childcare is haphazard; or discrepancy goes the other way when friends or neighbors exceed reasonable standards of care. Actions often satisfy social norms because people learning what to do typically learn behavior prescribed by a norm. They may hardly register that standard behavior is also the standard for satisfying one's duty. Social norms are usually sufficient to achieve desired effects—children are nourished and schooled—though effects like these aren't so elevated that morally committed agents can't do better.

This issue—the relation of moral to causal responsibility—is also pivotal in discussions of free will. Causation acquires its moral face when voluntary action or inaction affects people or goods they value; the moral side is effaced if the two elide. Theologians exculpate God when explaining evil by supposing that finite souls have free will; more than causes, we have judgment and the ability to discipline our passions. Evil is our fault.[16] What would be implied if we didn't have free will? There would be no distinction between actions and effects that are causal, and those which are both causal and moral or immoral, because we would have no power to intervene in the causal tide. Hard determinism would befall us. Hence the challenge of Chapter Two: confirm the distinction between causality, *simpliciter*, and moral causation without invoking immaterial souls or Kant's transcendental ego.

Someone feeling himself pushed accidentally inhibits the inclination to push back when all are standing in a crowded subway car. Live

---

16 Thomas Aquinas, *Selected Philosophical Writings*, ed. Timothy McDermott (Oxford: Oxford University Press, 2008), pp. 286–316.

and let live, we think. This is the vow of people competing amiably for resources, opportunities, or space; though mutual hostility is also possible, and sometimes expressed. Which is the viable response? Either may seem appropriate given one's circumstances, but neither is extra-material because each is a coping strategy designed to maximize one's advantage now or over time. Nor is the choice immaterial if judgment is mistaken: you respond to an elbow without retaliating only to be knocked down. We make decisions based on information and values that include safety and well-being. Self-defense—a moral power and cause—is their adjunct. Morality sometimes rides on the cause.

4bxi. Moral responsibility is uncertain when circumstances are complex. Moving toward the exit, you step on someone's foot. Was there space to avoid her; were you being careful? Yes, I lost my balance when the bus stopped abruptly. Fixing responsibility is straightforward when an effect has one sufficient cause—"You called"?—though not when several or many causes would have been sufficient to produce an effect to which one's action contributed. Uncertainty is challenging for agents who take responsibility for making the difference at issue; it's an opportunity for those who wish to disguise their effects. We limit these ambiguities by reducing choice, hence responsibility, to rules: what do they require; what was your role; did you act as the rule prescribed? Discerning what was done under the aegis of rules enables us to assign responsibility to the participants, though most tasks engaging several or many agents are accomplished with discipline, but without rules. People shopping in a busy market go their separate ways while employees stock the shelves. Who is responsible when people slip and fall because customers tracking slush from outside have made the floors slippery? Not individual customers? Not the management that mopped, and spread sawdust? Moral responsibility isn't easily apportioned when there is no rule for dividing it. Three issues stand out in circumstances where any judgment or choice is plausibly challenged: *bxia.* judgment; *bxib.* duties near or far; and *bxic.* inhibition:

4bxia. Judgment: Everyone is active to some degree in situations of various kinds. Some actions and effects are morally indifferent, but all may have consequences that are morally sensitive. Those are effects on people, their interests, or the environment. What's to be done, or averted? We appraise our circumstances, consider our values, and rank our priorities. Choice and action are quick because habitual, or slow because we deliberate when circumstances are complex.

Practical experience values safety, predictability, cooperation, and mutual respect. Rules and rule-bound practices defend these values; behavior is moral to the extent that it satisfies them. Many such rules are formulated and imperious, but many more—thanking a cashier, holding a door for the person behind—are subtle and familiar, but uncodified. Deontologists want us to know that rules of both sorts may have few or no exceptions, yet there seem to be no occasions when one or more values aren't compromised in situations where two or more conflict: sustaining one, we concede the others.

Rules are the standards on which we rely when deciding what is permissible, but how do we decide what to do when applying a valued rule would violate a valued practice (telling the truth at cost to an honest man)? This is the task of judgment: having learned relevant values and the means for satisfying them, we rank competing interests or values. Is this determination any kind of demonstration? No, other people, with other interests, would decide differently because they disagree about circumstances or likely effects, or because they rank interests differently. Acknowledging this variability, respecting other choices, we make our judgments and act accordingly. This is the "situation ethics"[17] disparaged by people who prefer the severity of exceptionless rules: they never lie. And one agrees: truth-telling is a condition for cooperation, efficacy, and social stability. Yet there are other values. Hence the ambiguity of moral choice: what is best to do when serving one value violates another?

Evolution is slow, but change is often quick: will is free to experiment within the domain of elastic rules at the frontier, where circumstances are uncertain or unforeseen. This is morality in a Nietzschean space, where agency creates, tests, and justifies its choices. Old rules are adapted to new situations; or we adapt to circumstances of our making when new practices stabilize our altered conduct. Consensus forms, most of our life-sustaining values survive, but we're unsteady. How much change can we anticipate; is it likely that the remote effects of current actions

---

17 See Joseph Fletcher, *Situation Ethics: The New Morality* (Louisville: Westminster John Knox, 1966).

will be appraised with material, moral, or aesthetic values like those approved today? Will our heirs rue effects that seem desirable to us?

4bxib. Duties near or far: Agency is moral in the respect that intentions and behavior are responsive to the interests and well-being of others and oneself; purpose is steady as we try to make circumstances favorable to partners, duties, and our interests. Most tasks are common to all; crystallized norms—rules, laws, roles, or traditions—stabilize behavior, while making it predictable. Yet solutions vary with circumstances and change with technology and aims. Choices appropriate at one time, in one locale, may be unsuitable later or at any time in another place. Are there also duties to people and things remote in space or time, duties incurred because they or their interests are helped or harmed by things we do? Uncertainty about this moral burden is a reason for agency's variable focus: here and there, short term and long. We may try to anticipate our long-term effects but doing that effectively requires knowledge of circumstances that may not resemble any we know.

4bxic. Inhibition: Some things shouldn't be done because rules, roles, or traditions preclude them; learning what to do and how to do it, we also learn when not to act. This is the essence of Kantian morality: do no harm to the conditions for sustaining community. There is also a margin for choice where care and control—prudence, respect, or discretion—override inclination or opportunity. Which is suppressed: action or the thought or desire motivating it? None but the agent may know which is inhibited or why.

4bxii. Are we praise- or blameworthy for a moral difference if we haven't chosen it? Imagine that a careful driver strikes a pedestrian who runs into traffic without warning from behind an obstacle making him invisible to traffic. The driver is a cause of the accident, though he bears no moral responsibility for it. This is an example of the difference between *agents* and *agency*. Agents are causes, whatever their character and whatever the character of their effects. Agency is causation with purpose, responsibility, and control. The driver had no intention of causing an accident; driving carefully with no control of its victim, he had no responsibility for hitting him (though vehicular law rules otherwise).

Kant warned that one never controls the effects of one's choices, hence his belief that will is the only power we control.[18] This ignores the considerable evidence that agents often produce intended effects. For we are nodes: rightly praised or blamed for our intentions, choices, and actions.

4bxiii. Is moral education additional to education that prepares one to make causal differences? Military training is the inverse of medical education. The Hippocratic Oath infuses action with moral concern for those whom doctors treat; military education reduces concern for enemies. This difference expresses the contrary values that frame human interests and action. We educate for this diversity: doctors to heal us; a military that defends us. Fact and value seem fused; students and trainees are discouraged from distinguishing them. But one can distinguish them: soldiers herding prisoners, like doctors working for violent regimes, are encouraged to avoid excess. But moral discretion is fraught: how does one inhibit the dominant impulse required by the work one is recruited to do? There may be no recourse short of refusing the job.

4bxiv. One defers to authorities because of their power. Is that because power is their right; because power is intimidating; or because we believe that authority is virtuous? Constitutional authority is assigned to people filling offices within the system of relations prefigured by a state's foundational laws. Their authority extends only to the particular duties of their respective offices; it terminates when they leave office. The character of their authority—its force and applications—is manifest in the founding plan or its elaborations. It may have been designed with the purest of intentions; though a state's officials sometimes misconstrue their authority as a right to interpret its applications in ways that violate its aims. We the citizenry hesitate: we're respectful of the state's authority; we don't want to believe that its officers are outlaws abusing their positions. But we're skeptical: we know that authority is not essentially virtuous. We need to be willing and ready to use constitutional means to control or terminate officials who believe that legal authority is a weapon defending personal interest.

---

18   Immanuel Kant, *Critique of Pure Reason*, trans. Norman Kemp Smith (New York: St. Martin's, 1965), pp. 474–75.

4c. Empathy. Relating to other people often feels mechanical; there's something to be done, little time to do it. Partners are utilities: work goes better because they're efficient; or we're annoyed because they slow it down. But there is a contrary impulse, one that may hardly show: we're sometimes attracted to other people out of affection, sympathy, or respect. Emotionally binding responses are an evocation of core relations to family or friends. Some people believe that this response is prefigured in every mortal's deference to his or her god. Though explaining it doesn't require an appeal to the supernatural: one is more likely to recognize feelings in others if comfortable in oneself. Some cultures formalize warmth for others in the salutations exchanged between buyers and sellers when entering or leaving a shop: each acknowledges that the other's dignity is more significant than a possible sale. People dismayed by the harshness of city or business life often look for ways to intensify the exchanges of feelings; this is the "spirituality" of which they speak. One achieves it with others, but equally when it's provoked by nature, music, or poetry.

Sentiment is the moral engine of Mill's *Utilitarianism*, though empathy is purged as a moral motive in Kant's *Groundwork* and (for all but its dedication) in Mill's *On Liberty*. Judgment is its necessary condition, given the risk that sympathy will be perceived as naive or weak.

4d. Conscious/unconscious. Self-awareness is often missing when choices are made and action ensues, but should we infer that our frequent experience of choosing because of intending or acting because of deciding is always illusory? Careful studies suggest that consciousness is incidental to many actions and their initiating decisions.[19] But it would be odd if this were always true. Conceding that introspection is an imperfect lens into mental functions, granting that its evidence is often misdescribed, is it sure that consciousness is always misleading or incidental? Does evolution usually do things in vain? This question isn't evidence or an argument, but it should make us suspicious of claims that introspection is always unreliable. Is that also true of percepts, dreams, and headaches?

Moral identity is precarious because it's suspended between motives that are often unconscious and one's awareness of rules, roles, or

---

19   See Daniel M. Wegner, *The Illusion of Conscious Will* (Cambridge: MIT Press, 2002).

laws. One recalls Plato's characterization of the man who feigns good intentions while having no interest in any benefit but his own.[20] Social harmony requires that he be controlled, though moral identity is cosmetic if appetites control him while he feigns submission to social rules and practices. This tension is identical to the one that unsettles autonomy: does moral identity pivot on attitudes and behaviors society prescribes; or is it qualified and revised by each person's understanding, sensibility, and interests?

Freud's three-part distinction—Id, Superego, and Ego—tracks this dilemma. *Id* signifies subconscious drives and desires that would sometimes be destructive if expressed; *Superego* indicates their controlling social constraints; *Ego* implies acquired powers for self-regulation.[21] These three trace a Hegelian triad: thesis, antithesis, synthesis. But the progression implied is too facile if conceptual only: for how does Ego achieve autonomy if independence is suppressed by mechanisms of social control? Freud also alerts us to another issue central to moral identity. The story I tell of my moral posture is an aestheticized summary of my history; one that reconciles and justifies, often without acknowledging costs, fault, or motives. How accurate is it to the unconscious motives and passions that energize my choices and actions?

It isn't surprising that disagreements about selfhood are commonplace: self-perception (self-persuasion) may vary considerably from the motors of agency. There is, however, this control on a story's accuracy: does it square with the evidence known to observers? How close is one's impression of his or her moral posture to theirs; which is more accurate if there's a discrepancy? Conflicts are frequent: others see my actions and effects; I counter by citing my intentions. But disputes can be resolved when actions misfire if there's accord that agency is a cause having effects: what went wrong: plans or motives? We learn what to fix, what to avoid.

How accurate is the perception of one's moral identity when many of its triggers are unconscious? The discrepancy seems reduced as one ages: there's less one does that's surprising. But the implication is alarming: selfhood is real, but elusive; we have moral identity, but only

---

20   Plato, *Republic*, 364a-365b, pp. 611–12.
21   See Sigmund Freud, *The Ego and the Id*, trans. Joan Riviere (New York: Dover, 2018).

a distorted idea of the attitudes and values provoking us. Hence the persuasion that moral identity resembles an unbalanced three-legged stool: one leg is the characterization of people who accurately predict what I'll do, given situations like those previously observed; another is the rounded moral story—the apology—I tell of myself; a third is the uncertainty of future behavior given the unpredictability of responses that elude repression in situations that surprise both myself and those who observe me.

4e. Equity. Anger and alienation are often the effects of having talents but no opportunity for discovering what they are, or how to use them. Compare the many people educated to high standards. Ambitious and capable, neither threatened nor angry, they relate amicably to others while pursuing aims for which talent has prepared them. Marx imagined the initiative and autonomy of medieval craftsmen. We learn as much by watching someone carrying a double-bass down subway stairs; doing it is clumsy, but he knows where he's going. Self-alienation would be minimized if talent and training were matched by opportunity. Frustration would be reduced because personal depth, initiative, and self-regard would be cultivated and acknowledged. No economy we imagine can be as productive as we desire while responsive to the particularity of all its members. But the burden shifts: how do we compensate the many people whose autonomy is sacrificed to the organizational features of the economies we have? Are there no substitutes, no supplements, for goods, stories, and games? Is the unconscious a sink where Ego atrophies because punished, bribed, or afraid?

Would we be bland if all were saved from the distress and confusion that come when talent and purpose are blunted or denied? Only a little. The opposition prefigured in Freud's dialectic—Id or Superego—would be largely drained, but life might seem too generous, too forgiving. Less ambition might entail less discipline, with no guarantee that one's judgments or choices would cohere.

4f. Self-appraisal. How well am I doing it; how do others see me; is this what I should be doing? Commentary may be distracted and forgiving or careful and severe. It's impelled by a desire for well-being or by the anxiety that one's actions are substandard or damaging to others; let me see what I'm doing, the better to control it and myself.

People lacking self-awareness seem decorticated; they resemble windstorms with no measure but their impact.

Aristotle construed well-being as happiness:[22] one achieves it by tempering appetites, establishing viable relations to other people, and using one's skills. The result is *eudaemonia,* a steady feeling of well-being. Discovering and educating one's talents seems a topic better suited to morale than morality, though both are relevant, because well-being is a perpetual aim, a duty to oneself and a hope that's slow to yield. Happiness is often conflated with pleasure for the good reason that the words signifying them often have the same referent: "Are you happy? Yes, I'm pleased." But the two are sometimes distinct. Imagine a parent awake all night with a child whose temperature rises inexorably. She prays for relief until it comes: his temperature falls quickly; he stirs. His mother would be exultant if she weren't so tired.

John Stuart Mill distinguished three kinds of happiness/pleasure: animal, intellectual, and moral.[23] Animal pleasure and its sources are familiar to all. Intellectual pleasure is different in kind. The pleasure that comes with sugar or drink is intense, addictive, distinguishable and separable from its sources. Intellectual pleasure is lambent, hard to isolate, and always dependent on the continuing support of the activity promoting it. Do you like algebra or poetry? You don't get the pleasure they provoke without engaging them. Moral pleasure is, again, different in kind: there is no pleasure, Mill wrote, like that of taking responsibility for the well-being of another person.

He ignored two other sorts of moral happiness, both implied by Aristotle's remark that happiness is the accompanying tone of activities that use one's faculties appropriately. Powers include those common to all—perception, thought, feeling, and will—but also one's talents. Athletes are never so alive as when playing their favorite game; but that is also true of card players and pilots. Hence this other source of happiness: imagine a nurse who dreamed since childhood that this would be her working life. Doors opened, chances fell in line, and now, close to retirement, she looks forward and back declaring herself content, no regrets, the ego ideal of her childhood long ago realized and sustained.

---

22 Aristotle, *Nicomachean Ethics*, in *The Basic Works of Aristotle*, ed. Richard McKeon (New York: Random House, 1941), 1095a, p. 937.
23 John Stuart Mill, *Utilitarianism* (Indianapolis: Hackett, 1979), pp. 7–12.

The well-being Aristotle described brightens her days and relations to other people. She's happy; they see it. Animal pleasures are episodic; they come and go. Happiness of this sort abides. But this isn't everyone's state of mind. *On Liberty* is oddly abstract; there is hardly a phrase that evokes fellow-feeling or responsibility. Yet there is an exception: Mill dedicated the book to his late wife in paragraphs having a confessional quality all but unknown in modern philosophy.[24] Death is deplored for many reasons, but one most affecting is the wound to happiness: there will be no personal renewal in the presence of a beloved child, partner, or friend. Why is it moral? Because one is diminished: grieving for another, but also for oneself. An agent reasonably asks of himself: Am I happy? The answer depends in part on the perception of his moral posture. How is it appraised; how does one measure the morality of his intentions, or the actions they provoke? There are two criteria, one social, the other personal and private. The answer is a function of the two, though their sum is problematic because their separate estimates don't always cohere.

4g. Guilt. Moral identity is also weighed by this other variable: how are others affected by my aims and actions; am I virtuous? Granting that plans don't always go as intended, how much guilt lodges in the design of my aims and their likely effects? We're saved embarrassment because conscience is often rigorous: guilt or inhibition flashes *stop* when passion, advantage, or one's job says *go*. Descartes' *Meditations* has a complementary emphasis: suspend beliefs or practices whose truth or cogency is unsupported by evidence; are they accepted as true or moral merely because one affirms what others say or do? Descartes refined his warning in three words: *doubt, deny, refuse*.[25] Renounce laws and practices that make life predictable, while having no other justification.

Skeptics make others uncomfortable: what motivates them? Contrarians predictably oppose whichever thought or practice draws their attention. Conscientious objectors are more detached: unmoved by innocuous things, they challenge whatever violates their principles. The rest of us are stolid; we honor personal scruples and social duties without excessive calculation. A question that objectors might put to

---

24 John Stuart Mill, *On Liberty* (Indianapolis: Hackett, 1978), p. 2.
25 Descartes, *Meditations*, p. 66.

the rest of us is the inverse: what would we have to do—what must be done in our names—for us to grieve or feel guilty for harms others suffer? This is two things; how to accept public responsibility—how to be known—for acts harmful to others; and how to let that responsibility penetrate one's sensibility—I helped do this. Public responsibility is easier because no one is likely to turn on a neighbor and blame him for effects ascribed to both. We take cover by hiding in crowds, where guilt or grief seem reduced because each is saved from feeling the weight of the moral burden, a load further reduced by face-saving confessions of weakness. How guilty could I be if I had no power to prevent the event, and have no way to avert its recurrence? Distress intensifies in people who dare to stand alone; those are the conscientious objectors who feel guilty merely by virtue of living in societies responsible for effects they deplore.

4h. Moral ambiguity. A will is moral, whether its effects are good or bad, when it controls a person's aims and actions. An effective moral will is, accordingly, the measure of one's moral identity. What does she want; what does he do; where, when, with whom, and why? Answers may vary, as when turning a kaleidoscope radically alters the display. There may be several reasons for the change. Four are principal: *i.* Rules or laws sanctioning behavior may be inconsistent. Endorsing one bars the other: be generous, except to enemies. Conflict is apparent in the relations of the various zones: respect for fellow-believers; scorn for those who don't share our beliefs or practices. *ii.* Autonomy differentiates agents who satisfy the same rules or practices: some people drive slower than others, because of their concern for the safety of all; others do it to frustrate the drivers behind them. *iii.* Intentions change: I no longer want the car I thought I needed. *iv.* Altered circumstances provoke the realignment of interests and values: diminished health makes one more tolerant of others moving slowly.

These are independent variables. Their complexity doesn't foreclose prediction; agents are typically consistent or regularly inconsistent. But they do complicate an observer's expectations. Does she know better than I what she'll do? How pressing is her aim; will she compromise a principal value in order to succeed? Moral ambiguity is sometimes the guise of people whose self-interest is their dominant value; other values shift opportunistically with circumstances and the promise of personal satisfaction. But ambiguity is also characteristic of those whose respect for others is unqualified; they, too, choose and act in ways that alter with circumstances and changes in themselves.

We live amidst the moral anarchy that comes with dislocations of family and local life, opportunist business practices, and bad luck. What would I do if the local police began beating the homeless or arresting law-abiding immigrants? I'm not sure. A simple formula—Kant's, for example—promises virtue at the cost of relevance: don't do anything that everyone in your circumstances couldn't do without contradiction. Never lie; never sabotage the likelihood that you will be believed when telling the truth. What if I sometimes want my lies to be construed as truths? One never knows—to the point of logical certainty—the actions Kant's rule would approve, given the conflicting demands of overlaid moral zones, and the obscurity of effects that trail off in several directions.

Not having an *a priori* rule to direct us, we revert to modest declarations of practical wisdom. *Live and let live* is a principle of charity: others, too, have interests; don't subordinate them when pursuing your aims. *To thine own self be true* declares that responsibility can't be extenuated: do nothing that would violate your sense of right. This formula is aspirational: it assumes a degree of self-knowledge, rectitude, and control that eludes us when virtuous motives conflict: help others, help yourself. Join the two, and we have attitudes favorable to social peace. But notably, these are slogans directing us in situations for which we have no *a priori* cure.

The solution for social complexity is Darwinian and adaptive, not Kantian. Solutions arise when choices and actions satisfy consequentialist calculations: where accidents are bad for all concerned, we settle on efficient ways of averting them. Ambiguity acquires its second-order, conceptual gloss when philosophers comment on established societies. Compare, for example, the ideas of freedom and responsibility in Rousseau's *Social Contract* and Mill's *On Liberty*. Both assume that societies do or should operate within a framework of rules and rights established by the democratic processes regulating assemblies of free people. Their disagreement about the moral identity of a society's members is, however, a point of confusion among us. Are we free because we participate in communities that enable the formation of specialized talents: musician, cook, or surgeon? Or because we are social atoms liberated to do as we please up to the point of harming others? Do we imagine being unencumbered by duties to others, or regard partners as the necessary adjunct to needs and talents we're ardent to satisfy and express? We could disperse for lives uncompromised by duties to others, but wouldn't that frustrate the wish to be a parent or spouse?

Autonomy wants a solution to these contrary impulses and ideas. We don't expect it will be cheap: freedom without community, liberty without duties. There will often be occasions when judgment is stymied by having to adjudicate between duties to others and duties to oneself. Observers are confused if we do one or the other in no predicable sequence. But this is judgment, decision, and will showing themselves in complex situations where one has multiple interests and duties. Like muscle, they atrophy without use.

4i. Truth. Two notions of truth have implications for morality and identity. A sentence that's meaningful because it signifies a possible state of affairs is true if the possibility obtains: 'There's a cat on the mat' is true, if there is a cat on the mat (abstracting from the context of the utterance: when and where). The sentence is satisfied by a state of affairs correctly represented by the sentence. The other notion—*being-in-the-truth*—requires an interpretation that bestows significance or purpose on a belief or practice: idealizing one's family or school, for example. Everyone invokes truths of both sorts; we value our friendships, and dress for the weather. Yet these notions are sometimes acutely opposed. That happens when all of reality is consumed within the meaning-bestowing narrative of a social class or nation. The schism is plain when religions, like philosophy, ask basic questions: what am I, or what are we; what is the character of the reality we address, and what is our place within it; what is it good or bad to do or be? Religions are cosmologically and ontologically ambitious, so it matters that religious narratives provide a context for all reality. *God did it* is an all-purpose explanation.

Moral identity may be grounded in truths about our material circumstances, and commitments to valued others; or in truths expressing one's dedication to tribal or religious beliefs or practices. Neighborly relations may be moral in either way: because of interdependence and mutual regard; or because our orienting story requires that we respect one another. Yet agents may be confused: where should they look for information or guidance when performing practical tasks: to circumstances and people experienced at solving problems, or to those who interpret our meanings? Is pregnancy a biological function, with deep personal significance; or is its meaning enlarged by the prospect that a god has created another soul? Is farming a practical art requiring persistence and skill; or one best achieved with prayer? Both, you say. But which of the two is less reliable?

Why say that identities of both sorts—practical or pious—are moral? Because each enables agents to appraise their choices as good or bad, right or wrong. Yet the two seem categorically different. Being-in-the-truth expresses one's estimate of the moral equilibrium in a god's world, and the steps required to honor or sustain it. Truth as satisfaction or correspondence seems bloodless and aloof by comparison. An array of truths tells us where we are or have been, while seeming to have no implications for moral identity: acknowledging someone's pain is not, in itself, an offer to reduce it. But this persuasion mistakenly supposes that the moral transparency of being-in-the-truth—gods want good works—is also required of truth as correspondence. Its moral implications are not so close to the surface.

Peirce understood truth as the successful outcome to inquiries that test hypotheses: a sentence or belief is more likely to be true if there is empirical evidence of the effects predicted. We alter failed experiments; mistaken hypotheses are reformulated or abandoned. Why do either? Because truths reporting actual states of affairs are the steady condition for effective engagements with other people and things. Action is contrary to intention if misinformation about partners or resources motivates behavior that violates morality because detrimental to them or oneself. There was once a popular song: "I didn't know the gun was loaded."

Truth as correspondence is instrumental; we can't negotiate our relations to other things without it: a call for help draws me to the person calling, not to a Ouija board. It is unsettling that that so many of the "truths" we affirm and defend are dogmas having no cogency apart from the beliefs and practices commended by their supporting stories. It is morally significant and causally effective that I know the loyalties constraining belief and behavior in my community. But there is also an overriding moral interest in the character and existence of things independent of anything said or thought about them: the health of one's children and friends, for example.

Truth-telling of both sorts has a social context. William James imagined an ethos where every individual is free to imagine and commit himself to a cosmic story of his or her invention: see, for example, his *Varieties of Religious Experience*.[26] Doing this exhibits our liberty, though it requires vast tolerance because it makes us mutually unintelligible. Truth as reality-testing has a different social sanction, one apparent when people coordinate their aims and work. That's not possible if we don't agree about the facts at hand, because collaborations are embedded in testable, mutually acknowledged assumptions about matters relevant to our tasks. We trust the speeches of people who regularly tell the truth because that coheres with our knowledge of them, and because truth facilitates the ordinary pace of communication and practice. We're disoriented by talk laced with error: what is there to do when every other assertion misdirects us? And equally, cooperation is disrupted when partners disoriented by one another's world-views struggle to identify aims and states of affairs about which they agree.

Collaboration is perpetually sabotaged by our inability to distinguish these notions of truth. The flag is raised, we sing the national anthem: thinking of our history and ideals, we affirm our solidarity. Anyone feeling otherwise shouldn't be here. A church's congregants and fans of a team have similar feelings. All share a commitment to a practice, garb, song, or prayer. Responses are true to their feelings or beliefs; but why speak of it as truth? Because meanings locate believers in sentiments and expectations where many things are plain: I know who and where I am; what it's safe to do and be; my allies, hopes, and prospects. A newspaper reports that a team's fans are less affected by wins than losses. Hopeful already, fans suppose that victories vindicate their loyalty: all will go well. Losers feel sabotaged: things aren't going well; events aren't as they seemed or promised.

These two ideas of truth are prefigured by a passage in Plato's *Euthyphro*: "Is what is holy holy because the gods approve it, or do they approve it because it is holy"?[27] The first implies being-in-the-truth because one defers to the preferences of the gods, an authority such as a priest, poet, or statesman. The second invokes truth as the outcome of inquiry, be it the inquiries of the gods or the reality-testing

---

26 See William James, *The Varieties of Religious Experience* (New York: Penguin, 1982).
27 Plato, *Euthyphro*, p. 178.

of people who coordinate their work while sharing an aim. Morality for people who acquire identity with a belief or practice can be many things: perhaps loyalty to a city or team. Religions and ideologies are more comprehensive: each prescribes right practices and a conception of reality. There are books to learn, but also ideas to quarantine, attitudes to disparage. How do believers justify their beliefs and practices when nearby alternatives are familiar? By citing people who believe and act as they do. Why is this a decisive test? Because conviction intensifies when mirrored by others. Why trust them? Because other believers are an objective measure of my beliefs: that others see what I see is evidence for the truth of beliefs we share.

Is there no middle ground between the truths of reality-testing and those postulated by meaning-bestowing interpretations? There may be accord about actions encouraged or proscribed, though reasons diverge. All is sacralized—murder and theft offend the gods—or laws and rights are conventions justified by their effects. The first encourages reverence; the other expresses the practical history of people joined by their deliberations on social comity and its conditions. One construes law as divinity's plan for creating order; the other sees order as the effect of prudent management.

Which is the preferred idea of truth when moral identity is its focus: truth as a set of favored meanings; or truth as an accurate characterization of what one is and does? Meanings may be flattering but unreliable: this devoted fan tithes his income and knows all the words to the national anthem. Compare truth as correspondence: it promises honesty without comfort. We prefer that weather reports be accurate; we're less comfortable with unvarnished accounts of ourselves, though sobriety requires it. Why be sober? Because, by and large, we want accurate information about ourselves and our circumstances. Though "by and large" doesn't cover everyone. It may not cover anyone all the time: self-perception is often self-persuasion. But is it acceptable that stories informing one's identity are false?

Agency falters without the resistance that nature and society provide. But that is not the lesson philosophy has drawn. Its principal voices in modern times were romantics: Mill's *On Liberty* largely removed us from society after Descartes had expelled us from nature. Freedom was the prize, after centuries of ecclesiastical and political oppression;

imagination would be our free space. But that was a mirage; too many fantasies lack substance or coherence. There are many things we can't do, and don't imagine we can. Immersed in a world of other people and things, we act in concert, often to avert having to act alone.

Why should anyone care about this subjectivist romantic tradition, philosophy teachers apart? Because the existence and character of the opportunities and obstacles we encounter are the everyday realities of people we address. They don't construe themselves as brains in a vat, or egos in the void. Circumstances are sometimes confounding, but people have some degree of freedom when ranking and pursuing their aims. Frustration doesn't hurt as much if one can imagine tasting the flavors one prefers, but should we lose the difference between reality and fantasy, between making a difference or enjoying a dream? There is always a tension between facts known to inquiry and the meanings dear to significance-bestowing stories. But did we intend to alter the balance at cost to reality and our place within it? Bold staring eyes were once philosophy's signature; truth was our motive. Was that a mistake?

Afterword

Agency is fundamental to all we are and do, whether its context is thought, feeling, or action. But philosophy has no coherent view of agency because Descartes inverted the idea of it before Kant and Hegel transformed his version of the *cogito* into the transcendental ego and the Absolute. The idea was further distorted by three issues considered here: Subjectivists reduce agency to the circle of conscious experience while believing that mind thinking itself is its principal or only activity. Behaviorists restrict the evidence for intention to the data available to observers: seeing me cross the street, they tell what they've seen and how they construe it. Hard determinists affirm that agency is only a vehicle for energy that flows from an ancient past to a distant future. Nothing, they say, is up to us. These are not the three postulates of anyone's unified theory, though their convergence deters commentary that would deepen and extend our self-understanding. Where no topic is more fundamental to human reality, we purge these muddles, then emphasize autonomy, control, collaboration, and appraisal. This is agency responsive to others and itself.

Bibliography

Anscombe, G. E. M., *Intention* (Ithaca: Cornell University Press, 1957).

Aquinas, Thomas, *Selected Philosophical Writings*, ed. Timothy McDermott (Oxford: Oxford University Press, 2008).

Aristotle, *The Basic Works of Aristotle*, ed. Richard McKeon (New York: Random House, 1941).

Bachelard, Gaston, *The Poetics of Space*, trans. Maria Jolas (Boston: Beacon Press, 1964).

Brentano, Franz, *Psychology from an Empirical Standpoint* (New York: Routledge, 2014).

Davidson, Donald, "Agency," in *Essays on Actions and Events* (Oxford: Clarendon Press, 2002), pp. 43–62.

Descartes, René, *The Geometry of René Descartes*, trans. David Eugene Smith and Marcia L. Latham (New York: Dover, 1954).

Descartes, René, *Meditations on First Philosophy*, in: *Discourse on the Method and Meditations on First Philosophy*, ed. David Weissman (New Haven: Yale University Press, 1996).

Descartes, René, *Passions of the Soul, The Philosophical Writings of Descartes, Volume 1*, trans. John Cottingham, Robert Stoothoff, and Dugald Murdoch (Cambridge: Cambridge University Press, 1985).

Dewey, John, "The Reflex Arc Concept in Psychology," *Psychological Review* 3 (1896), 357–70.

Dewey, John, *The Public and Its Problems* (Athens: Swallow Press, 1954).

Durkheim, Emile, *Emile Durkheim on Morality and Society* (Chicago: University of Chicago Press, 1973).

Edwards, Jonathan, *Resolutions: and Advice to Young Converts* (Philipsburg: P and R Publishing, 2001).

Fletcher, Joseph, *Situation Ethics: The New Morality* (Louisville: Westminster John Knox, 1966).

Freud, Sigmund, *The Ego and the Id*, trans. Joan Riviere (New York: Dover, 2018).

Habermas, Jürgen, *Theory of Communicative Action: Reason and the Rationalization of Society, Volume 1*, trans. Thomas McCarthy (Cambridge: Polity Press, 1984).

Hegel, G. W. F., *The Phenomenology of Mind*, trans. G. B. Baillie (New York: Harper, 1967).

Heidegger, Martin, *Being and Time*, trans. John Macquarrie and Edward Robinson (New York: Harper and Row, 1962).

Hobbes, Thomas, *Leviathan* (Cambridge: Cambridge University Press, 1996).

Hume, David, *A Treatise of Human Nature*, ed. L. A. Selby-Bigge (Oxford: Clarendon, 1978).

Izawa, Shuntaro, et al., "REM sleep–active MCH neurons are involved in forgetting hippocampus-dependent memories," *Science* 365:6459 (2019), 1308–13, https://www.doi.org/10.1126/science.aax9238

Jacobs, Jane, *The Death and Life of Great American Cities* (New York: Vintage, 1992).

James, William, *The Varieties of Religious Experience: A Study in Human Nature* (Penguin: New York, 1982).

James, William, "The will to believe," *The Writings of William James*, ed. John J. McDermott (New York: Modern Library, 1968), pp. 717–35.

Kane, Robert, *A Contemporary Introduction to Free Will* (New York: Oxford University Press, 2005).

Kant, Immanuel, *Critique of Pure Reason*, trans. Norman Kemp Smith (New York: St. Martin's, 1965).

Kant, Immanuel, *Critique of Judgment*, trans. Werner S. Pluhar (Indianapolis: Hackett Publishing, 1987).

Kant, Immanuel, *Groundwork of the Metaphysics of Morals*, trans. Mary Gregor (Cambridge: Cambridge University Press, 1997).

Koolhaas, Rem, *Delirious New York* (New York: Monacelli, 1997).

Laplace, Pierre Simon, *An Essay on Probabilities*, trans. F. W. Truscott and F. L. Emory (New York: Dover, 1951).

Laugier, Marc-Antoine, *Essay on Architecture* (London: HardPress, 2013).

Leibniz, G. W. V., *Monadology and Other Philosophical Essays*, trans. Paul Schrecker and Anne Martin Schrecker (Indianapolis: Bobbs-Merrill, 1965).

Lennon, John, McCartney, Paul, The Beatles, "With a little help from my friends," *Sgt. Pepper's Lonely Hearts Club Band*, Capitol Records, June, 1967, © Northern Songs Ltd, England.

List, Christian, *Why Free Will is Real* (Cambridge: Harvard University Press, 2019).

Locke, John, *An Essay Concerning Human Understanding, Volume Two* (New York: Dover, 1959).

Locke, John, *The First and Second Treatises of Government* (Cambridge: Cambridge University Press, 2018).

Marx, Karl, "Excerpts from James Mill's Elements of Political Economy," *Early Writings*, trans. Rodney Livingston and Gregor Benton (London: Penguin, 1975), pp. 259–78.

Marx, Karl, *Critique of the Gotha Program* (Rockville: Wildside Press, 2008).

Maudsley, Henry, *Body and Mind: An Inquiry Into Their Connection and Mutual Influence, Specially in Reference to Mental Disorders* (London: HardPress, 2018).

Mead, George Herbert, *Mind, Self, and Society*, ed. Charles Morris (Chicago: University of Chicago Press, 2015).

Mead, George Herbert, *George Herbert Mead: On Social Psychology—Selected Papers*, ed. Anselm Strauss (Chicago: University of Chicago Press, 1964).

Mill, John Stuart, *On Liberty* (Indianapolis: Hackett, 1978).

Mill, John Stuart, *A System of Logic, Volume 1* (London: HardPress, 2016).

Mill, John Stuart, *Utilitarianism* (Indianapolis: Hackett, 1979).

Nagel, Ernest, *The Structure of Science* (New York: Harcourt, Brace, and World, 1961).

Nietzsche, Friedrich, *Thus Spake Zarathustra*, trans. Walter Kaufman (New York: Viking, 1954).

Nietzsche, Friedrich, *On the Genealogy of Morals* and *Ecce Homo*, trans. Walter Kaufmann (New York: Random House, 1969).

Peirce, C. S., *Collected Papers of Charles Sanders Peirce, Volumes I–VI*, eds. Charles Hartshorne and Paul Weiss (Cambridge: Harvard University Press, 1934–35).

Plato, *Republic, Collected Dialogues*, eds. Edith Hamilton and Huntington Cairns(New York: Pantheon, 1961).

Quine, Willard Van Orman, *From a Logical Point of View* (Cambridge: Harvard University Press, 1980).

Rousseau, Jean-Jacques, *The Social Contract and Other Later Political Writings* (Cambridge: Cambridge University Press, 1997).

Ryle, Gilbert, *The Concept of Mind* (New York: Barnes & Noble, 1949).

Sartre, Jean-Paul, *Being and Nothingness*, trans. Hazel Barnes (New York: Citadel, 1956).

Schulkin, Jay, *Effort: A Behavioral Neuroscience Perspective on the Will* (Mahwah: Psychology Press, 2006).

Simmel, Georg, "The Metropolis and Mental Life," *Perspectives on Urban Society: Preindustrial to Postindustrial*, ed. Efren N. Padilla (Boston: Pearson, 2006), pp. 134–44.

Tonnies, Ferdinand, "On Gemeinschaft and Gesellschaft: Conclusions and Outlooks," *Perspectives on Urban Society: Preindustrial to Postindustrial*, ed. Efren N. Padilla (Boston: Pearson, 2006), pp. 92–99.

Van Inwagen, Peter, *An Essay on Free Will* (Oxford: Oxford University Press, 1983).

Weber, Max, *Economy and Society, Volume 2*, eds. Guenther Roth and Claus Wittich (Berkeley: University of California Press, 1978).

Wegner, Daniel M., *The Illusion of Conscious Will* (Cambridge: MIT Press, 2002).

Weissman, David, "Dispositions as Geometrical-Structural Properties," *Review of Metaphysics* 32:2 (1978), 275–97.

Weissman, David, *Hypothesis and the Spiral of Reflection* (Albany: State University Press, 1989).

Weissman, David, *A Social Ontology* (New Haven: Yale University Press, 2000).

Weissman, David, *Zone Morality* (Berlin: Walter De Gruyter, 2014).

Weissman, David, "Autonomy and Free Will," *Metaphilosophy* 49 (2018), 609–45.

Weissman, David, "Christian List, Why Free Will is Real," *Metaphilosophy* 50 (2019), 743–47.

Wirth, Louis, "Urbanism as a Way of Life," *Perspectives on Urban Society: Preindustrial to Postindustrial*, ed. Efren N. Padilla (Boston: Pearson, 2006), pp. 134–44.

Wittgenstein, Ludwig, *Philosophical Investigations*, trans. G. E. M. Anscombe (New York: Macmillan, 1953).

Wundt, Wilhelm, *Principles of Physiological Psychology, Volume 1* (Emeryville: Franklin Classics, 2018).

Index

absence 9, 83, 100, 130
Absolute 149, 150, 177
academy 114
accident 9, 54, 116, 138, 162
action 1, 3, 4, 5, 6, 8, 9, 10, 17, 20, 22, 23, 26, 28, 38, 41, 43, 52, 53, 64, 65, 66, 68, 71, 72, 73, 76, 79, 83, 89, 91, 92, 97, 111, 119, 120, 121, 124, 125, 127, 129, 131, 132, 135, 136, 148, 149, 150, 152, 153, 154, 155, 156, 157, 158, 159, 160, 161, 162, 163, 164, 177
adaptation 63, 64, 158
admiration 144
adversity 19
aesthetic 9, 29, 31, 35, 82, 91, 162
agency 1, 3, 9, 10, 11, 30, 31, 34, 36, 101, 111, 134, 141, 162, 174, 177
aim 19, 22, 31, 32, 33, 35, 36, 37, 42, 48, 64, 82, 87, 93, 96, 99, 106, 107, 108, 109, 115, 121, 132, 136, 139, 140, 142, 152, 154, 167, 169, 174
alienation 19, 112, 166
allegory 2, 55, 97
ambiguity 1, 50, 55, 56, 123, 130, 131, 135, 161, 169, 170
ambitious 49, 166, 171
ambivalence 38, 83
analogy 41, 91, 104, 117, 142, 147
analysis 22, 60, 83
anarchy 123, 130, 170
ancestry 54, 57, 60
anchor 66, 78, 139
anger 4, 112, 121, 131, 166
Anscombe, G.E.M 4, 22, 23
anxiety 24, 138, 151, 166
appetite 41, 141
approval 128, 143
Aquinas, Thomas 159
arc 2, 5, 39

architecture 76
argument 7, 15, 22, 41, 49, 57, 66, 75, 83, 85, 149, 164
Aristotle 1, 3, 6, 11, 14, 20, 25, 32, 33, 36, 37, 38, 45, 60, 90, 107, 167, 168
artist 26, 27, 28, 70, 87, 115, 122
artistry 25
ascent 137
aspiration 32, 97, 106, 123
assembly 45, 46, 48, 50, 60, 84, 86
assent 13, 147, 149
assertion 141, 173
association 28, 108, 109
atomism 95, 97
attachment 124
attention 25, 32, 68, 71, 78, 158, 168
attitude 140, 143
attunement 124
audience 26, 34
Augustine 141
authenticity 28
authority 18, 30, 32, 33, 42, 117, 126, 136, 157, 163, 173
autonomy 1, 4, 5, 6, 10, 11, 18, 28, 30, 31, 33, 38, 40, 41, 42, 43, 44, 45, 46, 47, 54, 65, 69, 74, 75, 83, 93, 95, 96, 97, 100, 101, 105, 107, 108, 109, 111, 112, 117, 120, 121, 122, 124, 125, 127, 128, 129, 139, 141, 142, 143, 144, 146, 147, 149, 150, 165, 166, 177
awareness 2, 12, 20, 28, 41, 51, 71, 133, 164, 167

Bachelard, Gaston 103
balance 9, 32, 96, 132, 139, 140, 160, 175
Bannister, Roger 37
Beethoven, Ludwig von 48, 87, 111
behavior 4, 6, 21, 22, 23, 42, 56, 58, 78, 82, 99, 107, 108, 110, 111, 125, 129,

134, 138, 139, 141, 143, 146, 154, 156, 159, 161, 162, 166, 169, 172
behaviorism 21, 23, 119
belief 6, 9, 38, 60, 82, 151, 153, 163, 171, 172, 174
Berkeley, George 2, 12, 149
biography 103
biology 7, 115, 123
birth 66, 140
blame 11, 77, 94, 121, 142, 157, 169
body 4, 6, 34, 43, 87, 91, 122, 129, 148
brain 4, 6, 41, 63, 66, 81, 82, 91, 132
Brentano, Franz 21
buffer 8, 63, 75
bureaucracy 112, 116, 156
bureaucrat 149

canopy 117
capacity 30, 44, 50, 62, 134, 152
career 37
Cartesian 1, 3, 11, 15, 21, 35, 124
Caruso, Enrico 101
cat 119, 120, 171
category 123
causa sui 45
cause 11, 13, 20, 22, 25, 29, 33, 47, 50, 51, 52, 58, 60, 65, 68, 70, 71, 73, 79, 83, 84, 85, 90, 93, 96, 121, 155, 157, 158, 160, 162, 165
challenge 17, 20, 29, 37, 88, 113, 120, 138, 156, 159, 168
chance 54, 57, 66, 119, 146
change 4, 6, 32, 37, 44, 45, 46, 54, 55, 56, 57, 58, 61, 65, 74, 84, 86, 88, 89, 90, 91, 92, 102, 118, 132, 140, 147, 161, 162, 169
character 1, 3, 7, 8, 11, 13, 15, 16, 34, 41, 48, 49, 52, 53, 55, 63, 67, 69, 75, 76, 95, 98, 102, 104, 106, 110, 135, 137, 140, 143, 154, 162, 163, 171, 172, 175
child 71, 116, 122, 135, 140, 157, 167, 168
chimera 128
choice 4, 5, 6, 7, 8, 11, 26, 38, 39, 40, 42, 43, 46, 48, 49, 53, 54, 58, 59, 62, 63, 64, 66, 68, 70, 71, 72, 73, 74, 76, 77, 78, 79, 80, 81, 82, 83, 88, 89, 91, 92, 93,
94, 96, 98, 99, 108, 117, 122, 123, 125, 126, 128, 131, 132, 136, 137, 141, 143, 148, 149, 152, 157, 159, 160, 161, 162
choreographer 101
cipher 98
citizenship 109
city 31, 58, 71, 105, 113, 114, 122, 140, 143, 164, 174
civility 108
classification 123
cleric 149
climate 90, 102, 126, 147, 155
clumsiness 32
cogency 83, 168, 172
cogito 2, 6, 13, 15, 177
coherence 15, 16, 17, 27, 35, 52, 65, 83, 92, 123, 125, 126, 127, 130, 131, 142, 149, 175
collaboration 36, 38, 56, 102, 105, 107, 109, 122, 144, 149, 151, 177
collision 34, 51, 59
comfort 77, 120, 123, 128, 147, 174
command 19, 29, 110, 114, 139
commitment 22, 27, 108, 123, 135, 140, 173
community 29, 98, 103, 112, 113, 135, 136, 145, 146, 162, 171, 172
competition 125, 135, 139
complexity 4, 6, 38, 46, 48, 49, 62, 63, 67, 73, 84, 111, 114, 120, 125, 126, 129, 132, 135, 136, 138, 139, 143, 158, 169, 170
computer 7
conceit 24, 39, 44, 86
condition 2, 6, 9, 12, 13, 26, 31, 32, 38, 44, 48, 49, 52, 56, 75, 82, 90, 101, 115, 120, 125, 127, 134, 135, 151, 153, 161, 164, 172
configuration 58, 61, 72, 84
conflict 38, 68, 72, 96, 100, 135, 136, 138, 143, 144, 145, 148, 157, 161, 170
conformity 35, 100, 134
confusion 90, 130, 135, 166, 170
conscious 6, 11, 25, 28, 40, 41, 54, 71, 76, 87, 97, 99, 133, 152, 177
consensus 123, 144

conservation 55, 57
consistency 16, 83, 135, 136, 137, 145, 148
constraint 105
content 11, 12, 13, 14, 15, 17, 20, 24, 25, 26, 45, 55, 60, 87, 88, 92, 98, 99, 100, 167
context 6, 15, 16, 27, 34, 37, 43, 52, 68, 80, 83, 86, 93, 107, 120, 130, 132, 133, 171, 173, 177
contradiction 13, 16, 94, 125, 148, 149, 170
contrariety 142
control 3, 4, 5, 6, 9, 11, 21, 32, 33, 34, 35, 37, 41, 42, 45, 46, 49, 57, 60, 64, 71, 73, 74, 76, 77, 82, 83, 87, 91, 92, 114, 115, 120, 121, 122, 126, 127, 136, 137, 138, 141, 144, 145, 146, 149, 150, 152, 153, 154, 156, 162, 163, 165, 166, 170, 177
convention 122, 126
convergent 51
cooperation 5, 36, 77, 94, 100, 107, 109, 111, 125, 136, 138, 150, 161, 173
copse 109, 126, 142
core 43, 120, 130, 133, 139, 140, 144, 147, 157, 164
correspondence 3, 17, 172, 174
cosmos 2, 52
cost 32, 38, 131, 136, 146, 151, 155, 161, 170, 175
coupling 40, 52, 72, 101, 131, 137
courage 67, 144
craftsman 103, 166
creature 3, 97, 129
credit 11, 41, 67, 94, 115, 129, 148, 157
crowding 96, 125
cruelty 125
cultivation 9, 24, 103, 104, 113, 116, 127, 134
culture 25, 30, 48, 68, 103, 105, 122, 137, 148, 157
cynicism 140

Dasein 1, 2
data 1, 4, 6, 13, 14, 15, 16, 24, 45, 60, 88, 89, 119, 177
Davidson, Donald 3

decision 67, 69, 72, 88, 91, 119, 171
defense 15, 24, 58, 102, 124, 155, 160
deliberation 8, 9, 32, 41, 43, 52, 62, 63, 64, 72, 73, 74, 79, 82, 83, 84, 92, 94, 131, 138, 141, 152
delight 17, 31, 136
democratic 18, 24, 170
density 48, 110, 113, 116
Descartes, René 2, 6, 9, 11, 12, 13, 15, 17, 18, 20, 27, 40, 41, 44, 60, 124, 133, 141, 147, 149, 150, 158, 168, 174, 177
desire 4, 13, 14, 18, 28, 34, 41, 43, 80, 89, 96, 97, 103, 117, 121, 130, 141, 150, 162, 166
despair 112
determinism 5, 6, 7, 8, 9, 39, 42, 44, 45, 46, 47, 48, 49, 50, 51, 52, 53, 54, 56, 57, 60, 61, 62, 65, 66, 67, 68, 72, 73, 75, 80, 86, 92, 93, 94, 132, 153, 158, 159
Dewey, John 4, 11, 32, 39, 107, 121, 124, 139
Diabelli, Anton 87
dialectic 53, 69, 98, 111, 166
difference 1, 6, 7, 18, 23, 25, 42, 45, 48, 52, 58, 67, 68, 79, 81, 91, 92, 97, 100, 102, 108, 109, 110, 113, 114, 128, 129, 135, 136, 142, 143, 147, 148, 157, 159, 160, 162, 163, 175
dignity 18, 146, 164
dilemma 29, 133, 136, 165
dimension 77, 107, 120
disagreement 123, 170
discipline 10, 19, 30, 32, 36, 43, 67, 76, 97, 102, 103, 114, 126, 139, 141, 146, 151, 152, 154, 159, 160, 166
discord 121, 125, 146
discovery 11, 29, 91, 96, 116, 127, 133
discretion 117, 140, 141, 162, 163
disequilibrium 115, 116
dishonesty 125
disorientation 21, 115
disposition 30
dissonance 110, 146
distinctness 11, 13
distress 82, 166
dogma 7, 117

doing 3, 11, 17, 28, 30, 33, 36, 43, 45, 73, 83, 95, 97, 100, 101, 102, 105, 108, 109, 111, 115, 116, 117, 125, 134, 138, 139, 142, 144, 152, 153, 154, 162, 166
domain 24, 25, 27, 35, 48, 73, 85, 95, 101, 150, 161
dopamine 41
dream 93, 96, 175
dresses 121
driver 31, 52, 53, 54, 71, 77, 122, 136, 157, 162
dualism 6, 21
Durkheim, Emile 147
duty 32, 34, 36, 43, 96, 108, 111, 130, 132, 138, 140, 158, 159, 167
duty-bound 130

education 19, 25, 29, 33, 101, 105, 113, 133, 134, 139, 151, 157, 163
Edwards, Albert 4, 141
efficacy 32, 37, 39, 46, 54, 59, 76, 107, 139, 145, 161
efficiency 46, 97, 113, 115, 119, 142, 153
ego 2, 6, 13, 150, 159, 166, 167, 177
emergence 8, 63, 73, 86
Emerson, Ralph Waldo 4, 139
emotion 9, 25, 132
empathy 147, 151, 164
end 55, 145, 157
energy 7, 32, 39, 42, 44, 46, 50, 54, 55, 56, 57, 58, 60, 62, 66, 72, 74, 76, 85, 102, 105, 114, 127, 177
engineer 6, 20, 25, 26, 73
Enlightenment 42, 117
ensemble 34, 63, 109, 110, 142
entanglement 51, 52, 53
enthusiasm 58, 123, 127
environment 142, 155, 160
equilibrium 56, 65, 115, 116, 141, 172
equity 151, 156
error 3, 12, 15, 17, 68, 76, 124, 150, 173
Escher, M. C. 13
ethics 149, 161
eudaemonia 167
event 7, 8, 22, 44, 46, 48, 49, 55, 57, 62, 72, 169

evidence 2, 4, 6, 7, 8, 12, 14, 17, 21, 26, 27, 38, 43, 48, 49, 53, 57, 62, 66, 71, 72, 76, 77, 81, 86, 89, 93, 99, 100, 102, 119, 131, 133, 134, 144, 146, 155, 163, 164, 165, 168, 172, 174, 177
evolution 8, 9, 37, 53, 56, 58, 60, 61, 67, 73, 74, 75, 84, 86, 87, 92, 164
existence 1, 2, 7, 8, 12, 21, 48, 49, 50, 53, 76, 172, 175
expectation 17, 32, 80
expectations 40, 66, 68, 110, 123, 140, 143, 145, 149, 169, 173
experience 2, 4, 13, 14, 15, 17, 23, 25, 39, 41, 52, 54, 57, 76, 79, 84, 94, 96, 99, 103, 105, 114, 115, 119, 133, 137, 152, 156, 161, 164, 177
experiment 8, 32, 47, 68, 73, 79, 87, 88, 114, 125, 138, 139, 161
explanation 6, 7, 20, 21, 40, 47, 49, 54, 60, 81, 82, 97, 158, 171
expression 5, 7, 18, 20, 25, 29, 32, 39, 77, 78, 83, 88, 101, 111, 116, 127, 128, 130, 131
extrapolation 89, 91

facility 25, 92
faculty 70, 74, 76, 91, 150
fad 42
fallible 12, 75, 83, 85
fantasy 16, 17, 100, 122, 123, 175
fault 123, 159, 165
fear 4, 25, 38, 69, 77, 82, 86, 107, 111, 113, 114, 126, 131, 132, 143
feedback 32, 33, 35, 42, 67, 76, 91, 141, 145, 152
feeling 25, 26, 27, 28, 69, 77, 95, 99, 103, 107, 110, 112, 122, 133, 136, 151, 159, 167, 168, 169, 173, 177
filter 41
finitude 29, 150
Fletcher, Joseph 161
force 8, 14, 19, 20, 38, 46, 65, 67, 75, 76, 90, 94, 102, 104, 106, 111, 112, 120, 121, 129, 138, 150, 163
Ford, Henry 87
foresight 79, 126, 138, 154, 155, 156
forest 34, 70, 105, 117

Forms 23, 55, 60, 63, 72, 73, 84, 87, 107, 116, 127, 161
fox 20
framework 135, 157, 170
freedom 5, 6, 7, 10, 30, 40, 42, 43, 44, 47, 54, 61, 68, 74, 79, 81, 95, 105, 109, 111, 117, 119, 122, 124, 125, 126, 127, 128, 131, 136, 147, 148, 149, 150, 170, 171, 175
Freud, Sigmund 3, 165, 166
frustration 3, 4, 26, 29, 37, 68, 73, 84, 102, 116, 134, 151
function 16, 53, 63, 110, 129, 130, 131, 159, 168, 172
future 7, 20, 23, 35, 41, 46, 51, 60, 61, 85, 156, 158, 166, 177

gamble 49, 79
gap 4, 12, 17, 28, 68, 115, 134, 149
gemeinschaft 112
gender 123, 131
general will 18, 106, 138, 151, 154
generational 67, 110
gesellschaft 112
gestalt 52, 65, 66, 69, 73, 92
ghost 21
god 2, 9, 12, 20, 29, 106, 131, 135, 140, 147, 150, 158, 159, 164, 172
God 48, 49, 52, 54, 58, 59, 62, 64, 84, 85, 86, 89, 92, 93
good 18, 35, 43, 77, 92, 105, 106, 127, 132, 135, 136, 138, 151, 156, 165, 167, 169, 171, 172
government 116, 117, 139, 145, 156
grammar 4
grammarian 122
gratification 116
grid 79
grief 169
grievance 131, 134, 141
groundskeeper 159
guilt 132, 146, 168, 169

habit 17, 25, 31, 59, 79, 89, 90, 94, 97, 119, 132
happiness 141, 167, 168

hard determinism 5, 7, 8, 9, 42, 46, 47, 51, 52, 53, 56, 65, 66, 68, 73, 86, 93, 153, 158
harm 30, 95, 96, 125, 131, 146, 149, 154, 155, 156, 162
harmony 35, 53, 158, 165
health 9, 36, 84, 90, 113, 115, 144, 155, 169, 172
heaven 128
Hegel, G. W. F 1, 98, 110, 137, 147, 149, 150, 177
Heidegger, Martin 1
herding 121, 163
"herd morality" 36
heuristic 28, 91, 152
history 5, 6, 7, 8, 24, 40, 42, 47, 48, 49, 51, 52, 53, 54, 56, 57, 58, 59, 64, 68, 69, 70, 72, 74, 75, 76, 77, 78, 79, 80, 81, 85, 86, 88, 89, 90, 91, 92, 93, 94, 97, 103, 111, 117, 120, 132, 135, 137, 140, 143, 147, 148, 152, 157, 158, 165, 173, 174
Hobbes, Thomas 111
holism 46, 53, 93, 97
home 19, 53, 80, 101, 103, 125, 143
homogeneity 100
homogenization 114
hostility 110, 123, 160
house 70, 103, 119
Hume, David 38, 45, 46, 60, 132, 147
hypothesis 7, 14, 26, 27, 65, 89

Id 165, 166
idea 2, 15, 19, 21, 23, 27, 28, 42, 43, 45, 49, 50, 51, 52, 56, 57, 60, 63, 72, 87, 88, 93, 97, 99, 105, 107, 111, 122, 123, 129, 134, 139, 143, 147, 158, 166, 174, 177
ideal 9, 18, 115, 137, 167
identity 6, 10, 15, 16, 27, 34, 42, 55, 74, 77, 78, 94, 95, 97, 98, 109, 112, 122, 123, 129, 130, 131, 135, 136, 137, 138, 140, 143, 152, 154, 164, 165, 166, 168, 169, 170, 171, 172, 174
idiosyncrasy 97, 100, 135
imagination 13, 14, 15, 17, 20, 27, 28, 36, 42, 47, 57, 64, 67, 69, 70, 74, 87, 88, 89, 90, 91, 98, 99, 106, 134, 153, 158, 175

immigrant 24
impatience 24, 104
imperative 29, 98, 107, 132, 135, 148, 149, 157
impression 53, 120, 137, 165
improvisation 102
impulse 17, 52, 82, 86, 97, 121, 141, 163, 164
inclination 6, 23, 25, 72, 109, 130, 131, 154, 159, 162
independence 52, 56, 57, 69, 72, 122, 165
indifference 27, 39, 114
individual 16, 36, 78, 86, 95, 96, 104, 110, 111, 112, 136, 137, 141, 142, 147, 149, 151, 152, 155, 160, 173
individuality 98, 139, 147
inference 13, 14, 41, 46, 50, 61, 70, 88, 89, 90
inflation 51
information 4, 14, 15, 27, 33, 35, 41, 48, 49, 57, 59, 61, 63, 65, 66, 67, 68, 71, 75, 79, 80, 88, 89, 90, 91, 92, 93, 100, 102, 110, 124, 135, 148, 150, 152, 158, 160, 171, 174
ingenuity 47, 67, 69, 80
inhibition 10, 11, 39, 46, 62, 73, 83, 84, 94, 125, 126, 138, 152, 160, 168
initiative 68, 73, 87
innovation 70
inquiry 1, 40, 68, 89, 106, 173, 175
inspection 3, 4, 7, 21, 41, 59, 71, 148
instability 67
instinct 37, 141
integrity 76, 79, 92
intellect 9, 18, 26, 30, 60, 61, 131, 135, 136, 143
intelligence 120
intention 4, 11, 19, 20, 21, 22, 23, 38, 81, 90, 121, 148, 154, 156, 157, 162, 172, 177
interdependency 30, 123, 138, 171
interest 31, 46, 81, 88, 89, 91, 106, 107, 108, 117, 130, 131, 137, 147, 150, 151, 153, 163, 165, 169, 172
interiority 9, 11, 23, 25, 99, 102, 103, 104, 112, 113, 139, 141

interpretation 16, 27, 52, 65, 68, 171
intrapsychic 20, 21, 22, 23, 66, 88, 99
introspection 25, 41, 164
intrusion 40
intuition 2, 20, 153
invention 73, 86, 87, 91, 94, 114, 173
inventory 4, 44, 88, 122, 152
irrelevance 78
isolation 124, 127
isomorphism 41

Jacobs, Jane 113
James, William 4, 153, 173
job 30, 97, 115, 122, 137, 159, 163, 168
Jordan, Michael 101
judgment 6, 7, 8, 9, 11, 18, 22, 28, 43, 63, 69, 70, 71, 72, 73, 74, 76, 83, 92, 104, 132, 135, 141, 152, 156, 159, 160, 161, 171
justice 115, 150, 151
justification 153, 168

Kane, Robert 44
Kant, Immanuel 2, 6, 10, 13, 14, 15, 16, 17, 20, 64, 72, 87, 98, 99, 107, 121, 125, 129, 135, 136, 137, 147, 148, 149, 150, 151, 152, 157, 159, 163, 164, 170, 177
keel 19, 65, 121
kingdom 10, 95, 98
knowable 11
Koolhaas, Rem 114

language 21, 23, 98, 100, 101, 123, 127, 137, 158
Laplace, Pierre 7, 39, 50, 51, 54, 60, 61, 67, 75, 83
Laugier, Marc-Antoine 70
law 40, 43, 46, 60, 61, 67, 77, 91, 128, 136, 139, 141, 149, 150, 157, 162, 170, 174
learning 19, 45, 67, 90, 98, 102, 104, 106, 152, 159, 162
legible 130
Lennon, John 133
liberation 117
life-force 8
limit 25, 43, 60, 68, 90, 104, 132, 137, 145, 148, 154, 156, 160

lineage 5, 6, 8, 38, 46, 49, 53, 54, 55, 57, 59, 64, 82, 85, 86, 90, 92, 94, 153
litigation 125
Locke, John 20, 111, 121, 125
loyalty 16, 17, 27, 122, 139, 147, 151, 173, 174
lying 2, 135, 148

machine 21, 25, 26, 36, 41, 91
majority 29
making 11, 15, 33, 40, 54, 71, 77, 80, 86, 87, 88
management 34
marketer 18
Marx, Karl 96, 115, 151, 166
matter 20, 28, 30, 33, 36, 69, 71, 72, 73, 76, 89
Maudsley, Henry 21
maxim 125, 148, 149
McCartney, Paul 133
Mead, George Herbert 97, 98
meaning 15, 17, 19, 23, 27, 29, 45, 70, 83
mechanism 61, 165
membership 109
membrane 92
memory 14, 42, 47, 57, 59, 66, 71, 87
Mengele, Josef 138
method 68
methodologist 24
Mill, John Stewart 30, 68
Minerva 119
minority 17
modular 69, 76
monad 2, 13, 63, 64, 75, 83
morality 36
motion 24, 30, 39, 45, 46, 48, 50, 58, 60
movement 22, 57
muscle 33, 57
myself 36, 78, 88
myth 16, 60

Nagel, Ernest 45
narrative 27, 67
nation 171
naturalist 20

nature 17, 25, 38, 39, 40, 42, 44, 45, 46, 48, 50, 51, 52, 53, 55, 56, 58, 60, 61, 67, 73, 74, 75, 83, 86, 93
necessity 12, 16, 74
neighbor 24, 50, 65
network 34
niche 36
Nietzsche, Friedrich 19, 20, 36, 87
node 34
normativity 45, 60
norms 36
number 52, 62

objective 26, 37
observable 21
observation 22, 73, 88
obstacle 65
official 156
omniscience 49, 54, 59, 85, 86
ontology 14, 45
opinion 12, 44
opportunity 29, 42, 77, 81
order 12, 13, 25, 45, 62, 76, 81, 82, 90
organization 16, 49, 70, 74, 84
origin 56, 90
originality 18, 68
Ouija 7, 172
outlaw 139
over-ride 25
overseer 126
oversight 36, 76

pain 23, 24, 25
participant 34
participation 18, 25, 36
particularity 1, 98, 137, 166
partner 40
passenger 24, 31, 78
passion 17, 27, 43, 67, 76, 80
passivity 29
pathology 107
patriotism 15
peace 96, 139, 170
Peirce, C. S. 3, 4, 11, 14, 32, 45, 153, 172
perception 13, 14, 15, 26, 36, 52, 57, 66, 69, 71, 84

performance 23
permeable 8
persistence 37
personality 65
perspective 34, 35, 41, 51, 68, 76, 77
phenomenology 1, 2
philosophy 60
physiology 72
piano 24, 25, 68, 91
Picasso, Pablo 87
planning 31, 32, 67, 76
plans 14, 15, 26, 37, 38, 43, 76, 83
plasma 52
Plato 28, 37, 55, 70, 89
pleasure 17, 20, 23, 24, 25, 28, 81
plenum 51, 53
policy 121, 126, 139, 151, 156
pollution 155
pool 55, 56
popular 24
Porter, Cole 87
posit 15, 22, 23
possibility 12, 30, 45, 49, 57, 73, 75, 85, 94
posture 34, 35, 77
power 13, 20, 24, 27, 32, 38, 39, 41, 42, 43, 44, 49, 63, 64, 68, 73, 80, 81, 82, 91, 94
practice 19, 25, 30, 32, 33, 35, 37, 76, 90
pragmatism 9
pragmatist 11
praise 152, 157, 162
predictability 35, 39, 40, 44, 48, 61, 72, 75, 84, 85, 86, 88
prediction 47, 48, 49
pressure 16, 20, 35, 49, 50
priesthood 109
principle 32, 48, 61, 70, 75, 85, 86
priority 16, 56, 57, 76, 77
privacy 25
productivity 35, 46, 68, 87, 91
project 51
promotion 83
prudence 32, 37
purge 23, 66
purpose 11, 19, 20, 21, 23, 26, 27, 30, 32, 36, 41, 72, 81

pursuit 19, 42
Pythagorean 17
question 16, 23, 26, 37, 48, 49, 53, 54, 68, 80, 82
Quine, Willard Van Orman 16
rationale 149
rationality 23
realism 31
reality-testing 64
realm 23
reason 17, 36, 38, 43, 60, 71, 75, 77, 82, 86, 87, 88
reciprocity 31, 67
reckless 125, 141, 143, 154, 155
rectitude 170
recurrence 87
reflection 41, 83, 89
regime 111, 121, 163
region 95, 124
regularity 60
regulation 34, 40, 42, 54, 76
relation 47, 48, 50, 51, 52, 55, 78, 86
relationship 40, 52, 55, 90
religion 16
repetition 37
resilience 19
resistance 16, 17, 19, 86
resonance 23, 25, 27, 65
responsibility 31, 38, 41, 77, 94
restraint 43
reverence 174
revision 14
rhythm 35, 84
right 42, 83
rigor 16
role 47, 66, 70, 77, 81
root 5, 34, 142
Rousseau, Jean Jacques 18
routine 77, 94
rule 19, 48, 60, 70, 77
Ryle, Gilbert 21, 22, 46
sabotage 38, 43, 106, 125, 136, 137, 170, 173

safety 32, 37, 41, 61, 77, 103, 107, 108, 114, 120, 126, 127, 132, 139, 140, 141, 142, 145, 147, 160, 161, 169, 173
Sartre, Jean-Paul 44, 133
schema 2, 6, 16, 99
schism 3, 171
Schoenberg, Arnold 94
school 19, 105, 110, 111, 113, 114, 122, 144, 146, 151, 157, 171
Schulkin, Jay 41
scruple 18, 33, 78, 105, 131, 137, 158, 168
sediment 78
self-appraisal 11, 36
self-awareness 12, 41, 71, 133, 167
self-control 5, 33, 41, 42, 73, 74, 76, 77, 82, 83, 122, 127, 136, 138, 141, 150, 152
self-correction 35, 156
self-direction 54
self-esteem 29, 36, 144
self-expression 18, 29, 116, 130
self-identification 122–123
self-inspection 4, 7, 71
self-interest 130, 131, 151, 155, 169
self-knowledge 41, 170
self-love 141, 150
self-maintenance 93
self-perceiving 13, 122, 123, 129, 165, 174
self-regulation 4, 6, 34, 40, 42, 54, 76, 122, 124, 126, 152, 165
semantics 11, 16, 120
sensibility 9, 11, 18, 23, 24, 25, 26, 28, 29, 30, 65, 66, 67, 82, 94, 102, 103, 107, 112, 120, 121, 126, 127, 129, 131, 133, 135, 136, 137, 141, 143, 149, 165, 169
sentiment 34, 65, 87, 95, 146, 164, 173
shadow 55, 97, 98
sign 40, 83, 108, 119, 128, 140
significance 16, 17, 27, 29, 84, 115, 140, 157, 171, 172, 175
Simmel, Georg 113
singularity 28, 102
situation 5, 7, 8, 9, 25, 27, 32, 37, 40, 47, 49, 51, 52, 53, 56, 57, 58, 59, 61, 65, 66, 67, 68, 69, 70, 71, 73, 74, 76, 78, 79, 80, 82, 83, 84, 86, 88, 90, 92, 93, 94, 99, 114, 115, 120, 129, 132, 135, 136, 148, 152, 154, 158, 160, 161, 166, 170, 171
skepticism 2, 3, 7, 36, 54, 163
skills 8, 9, 18, 19, 24, 27, 28, 30, 31, 32, 33, 37, 42, 43, 69, 96, 97, 100, 101, 103, 104, 106, 110, 113, 114, 115, 116, 122, 124, 126, 127, 129, 134, 136, 152, 158, 167, 172
sobriety 17, 148, 174
sociality 25, 93, 98, 100, 107, 108, 109, 110, 122, 147
socialization 4, 10, 18, 19, 29, 30, 31, 36, 91, 96, 97, 99, 100, 102, 112, 113, 114, 121, 124, 144, 150
society 4, 5, 10, 29, 32, 40, 65, 96, 98, 100, 104, 107, 110, 115, 116, 122, 125, 126, 130, 135, 136, 137, 138, 151, 156, 165, 170, 174
Soft determinism 7, 46, 47, 48, 72, 132
solution 8, 53, 68, 86, 125, 152, 157, 170, 171
soul 2, 72, 147, 159, 172
sovereignty 34, 109, 117
space 9, 18, 24, 29, 33, 34, 43, 48, 60, 61, 63, 64, 68, 72, 73, 74, 75, 78, 87, 94, 95, 96, 97, 98, 102, 103, 104, 105, 106, 109, 111, 113, 115, 121, 125, 126, 134, 139, 142, 146, 148, 150, 160, 161, 162, 175
spacetime 45, 48, 58, 63, 93
specialist 111
specialization 139
speech 5, 22, 24, 31, 33, 56, 173
sphere 139, 142
Spinoza, Baruch 141
spontaneity 43, 72, 113, 126, 153
sport 24, 25, 56, 62, 105, 114, 115, 136
stability 14, 15, 16, 32, 37, 55, 56, 59, 62, 65, 73, 79, 91, 96, 116, 123, 127, 136, 137, 145, 146, 161
standard 7, 15, 16, 24, 34, 35, 36, 77, 82, 91, 93, 96, 101, 103, 107, 108, 114, 115, 135, 136, 137, 142, 146, 147, 159, 161, 166
stasis 100, 102
station 24, 114, 148, 152
stitch 57, 62

story 27, 51, 55, 59, 67, 98, 129, 131, 165, 166, 171, 173
strand 52, 56, 57, 62, 66, 67, 69, 95
strategy 63, 64, 68, 72, 74, 75, 79, 134, 141, 160
stream 47, 64, 72
street 15, 22, 76, 79, 105, 106, 113, 122, 140, 143, 177
structure 2, 40, 63, 65, 82, 92, 103, 107, 124, 129, 134, 145
style 15, 22, 48, 65, 70, 87, 103, 109, 112, 114, 121, 140
subject 3, 12, 21, 61, 82, 87, 95, 103, 129
submission 103, 165
subway 24, 77, 112, 114, 159, 166
success 36, 37, 49, 106, 111, 120, 125, 152
summary 73, 165
Superego 165
system 4, 6, 7, 10, 16, 24, 43, 44, 51, 62, 63, 69, 76, 81, 91, 92, 102, 105, 111, 112, 141, 144, 145, 146, 147, 156, 163

task 7, 18, 19, 24, 25, 27, 29, 30, 31, 35, 36, 38, 71, 76, 78, 87, 96, 97, 100, 101, 103, 107, 108, 109, 110, 111, 114, 126, 127, 130, 135, 137, 138, 139, 140, 144, 152, 160, 161, 162, 171, 173
taste 9, 10, 17, 24, 26, 28, 30, 35, 65, 74, 81, 82, 95, 99, 100, 104, 107, 108, 111, 114, 120, 127, 131, 136, 139, 140, 142
teacher 34, 102, 103, 107, 108, 109, 113, 114, 133, 134, 137, 144, 145, 175
technology 24, 91, 99, 112, 113, 126, 162
temperament 103
temperance 33, 76
tenacity 153
tension 29, 36, 105, 116, 153, 165, 175
theology 45, 95, 149, 158
theory 3, 16, 46, 73, 177
therapeutic 116
thinkable 2, 11
thought 1, 7, 13, 14, 15, 18, 22, 24, 26, 29, 30, 34, 40, 47, 48, 56, 57, 66, 67, 76, 79, 83, 88, 90, 91, 92, 94, 95, 99, 100, 103, 107, 112, 121, 123, 125, 137, 141, 158, 162, 167, 168, 169, 172, 177

thoughtlessness 78
tide 5, 8, 38, 39, 40, 44, 47, 54, 56, 63, 64, 65, 69, 72, 74, 93, 147, 152, 159
time 5, 7, 18, 20, 24, 25, 27, 32, 37, 38, 39, 43, 45, 46, 48, 49, 50, 51, 54, 55, 57, 59, 60, 72, 73, 75, 85, 93, 94, 100, 112, 127, 130, 133, 150, 158, 160, 162, 164, 174
tolerance 34, 36, 45, 65, 102, 107, 110, 117, 145, 147, 150, 155, 169, 173
tone 63, 94, 151, 167
training 25, 29, 30, 113, 114, 134, 163, 166
trajectory 2, 5, 7, 49, 50, 62, 64, 77, 80, 84, 98, 143
transcendence 29
transcendental 2, 6, 13, 106, 150, 159, 177
tree 34, 61, 69, 105, 109, 117, 142
trial 124
trigger 68, 165
truth 3, 13, 15, 16, 17, 26, 27, 29, 30, 36, 46, 57, 64, 106, 123, 133, 157, 161, 168, 170, 171, 172, 173, 174, 175

uncertainty 5, 23, 28, 42, 48, 61, 67, 73, 81, 84, 148, 157, 160, 161, 166
unconscious 13, 71, 164, 165, 166
understanding 3, 4, 9, 10, 21, 34, 48, 68, 69, 89, 90, 106, 110, 131, 150, 165, 177
universal 1, 39, 42, 45, 50, 51, 61, 136, 141, 150
universality 98, 137
universe 60, 61, 74, 86, 94
utility 78

value 2, 7, 9, 15, 16, 17, 19, 27, 31, 34, 35, 36, 37, 38, 43, 46, 49, 59, 64, 65, 67, 72, 76, 77, 78, 80, 84, 86, 87, 88, 89, 90, 91, 92, 93, 94, 96, 102, 103, 105, 106, 111, 115, 123, 124, 126, 127, 129, 130, 131, 135, 136, 140, 142, 148, 150, 152, 155, 157, 158, 159, 160, 161, 162, 163, 166, 169, 171
Van Inwagen, Peter 46, 47, 54
variability 16, 48, 104, 110, 135, 136, 143, 150, 161
variable 26, 41, 47, 63, 110, 135, 162, 168
vector 106, 122, 140
vehemence 141, 153

vehicle 6, 27, 140, 177
verifiability 17, 66
verification 4, 20, 24, 99, 133
violence 107, 125, 135, 141, 163
virtue 10, 17, 36, 41, 95, 98, 144, 154, 169, 170
vocabulary 25
vocation 18, 33, 34, 36, 95, 101, 108, 109, 112, 113, 115, 117, 133, 137, 138, 139
volition 39, 41, 46, 48, 52, 54, 73, 94
voluntary 23, 41, 71, 76, 77, 81, 82, 96, 159
vulnerability 130, 131, 138, 147

Watson, John 21
weakness 38, 169
weave 51, 52, 56, 57, 65
Weber, Max 149
Wegner, Daniel 164
weight 115, 129, 138, 169
Weissman, David 2, 13, 31, 40, 44, 132, 144, 145, 149
well-being 18, 66, 75, 107, 108, 116, 137, 138, 142, 154, 160, 162, 166, 167

whole 19, 45, 50, 51, 52, 60, 70, 93, 110, 137, 142, 147, 151
will 13, 17, 18, 20, 38
Wirth, Louis 113
wit 70, 100, 139
Wittgenstein, Ludwig 4, 21, 22, 23
wood 34, 109, 142
work 18, 20, 27, 28, 31, 35, 36, 37, 40, 41, 70, 77, 96, 105, 109, 110, 111, 112, 113, 114, 115, 116, 117, 120, 122, 124, 126, 127, 131, 140, 143, 144, 145, 146, 148, 159, 163, 164, 173, 174
worker 29, 34, 96, 109, 112, 113, 116, 126
world 1, 2, 3, 4, 6, 9, 11, 12, 14, 15, 17, 27, 32, 45, 46, 47, 52, 55, 56, 58, 65, 66, 86, 111, 112, 125, 129, 139, 140, 141, 150, 158, 172, 173, 175
worth 33, 87, 103, 112, 134, 140, 144, 152
Wundt, Wilhelm 21

zone 140, 141, 144, 146, 157, 169, 170

CPSIA information can be obtained
at www.ICGtesting.com
Printed in the USA
LVHW061339251020
669765LV00034B/1560

9 781013 295263